PALESTINIAN AND ISRAELI PUBLIC OPINION

INDIANA SERIES IN MIDDLE EAST STUDIES

Mark Tessler, general editor

Palestinian and Israeli Public Opinion

*The Public Imperative
in the Second Intifada*

JACOB SHAMIR AND KHALIL SHIKAKI

INDIANA UNIVERSITY PRESS
Bloomington and Indianapolis

This book is a publication of

Indiana University Press
601 North Morton Street
Bloomington, Indiana 47404-3797 USA

www.iupress.indiana.edu

Telephone orders   800-842-6796
Fax orders   812-855-7931
Orders by e-mail   iuporder@indiana.edu

♾The paper used in this publication meets the minimum requirements of the
American National Standard for Information Sciences—Permanence of Paper for
Printed Library Materials, ANSI Z39.48-1992.

Manufactured in the United States of America

LIBRARY OF CONGRESS CATALOGING-IN-PUBLICATION DATA

Shamir, Jacob.
  Palestinian and Israeli public opinion : the public imperative in the second intifada
/ Jacob Shamir and Khalil Shikaki.
      p. cm. — (Indiana series in Middle East studies)
  Includes bibliographical references and index.
    ISBN 978-0-253-35437-2 (cloth : alk. paper) — ISBN 978-0-253-22172-8 (pbk. : alk. pa-
per) 1. Public opinion—Palestine. 2. Public opinion—Israel. 3. Elections—West Bank.
4. Elections—Gaza Strip. 5. Al-Aqsa Intifada, 2000– I. Shiqaqi, Khalil. II. Title.
  HM1236.S513 2010
  303.3'8095694090511—dc22   2009032069

          1 2 3 4 5 15 14 13 12 11 10

To Michal, Gil, and Avital

To Wafa, Muna, Ibrahim, and Leila

CONTENTS

PREFACE

This book is the product of a joint Israeli-Palestinian endeavor spanning from the Camp David summit in July 2000 and the eruption of the second Palestinian Intifada to the 2006 election turnabouts in Israel and the Palestinian Authority. This project, the Joint Israeli-Palestinian Poll (JIPP), is intended to analyze as well as influence the domestic and international environment surrounding the Palestinian-Israeli conflict. As such, it represents a rare case where public opinion of two sides to an intractable conflict is studied in depth in a coordinated and joint manner over time.

There are other works about the Palestinian-Israeli conflict and about this time period. This book, however, focuses primarily on the role of public opinion in the conflict and the attempts to resolve it. This focus and the use of a theoretical framework based on the two-level game metaphor and a multifaceted conceptualization of public opinion give it its unique perspective. The book relies on the JIPP data and draws attention to public opinion as a central imperative in the Israeli-Palestinian conflict. Our theoretical integration between the two-level game conceptual framework and our conception of public opinion as a multifaceted phenomenon highlights new ways in which public opinion constitutes a meaningful player in the two-level game. We explore, then, how Israeli and Palestinian public opinion evaluations, expectations, mutual perceptions and misperceptions, and overt political action feed into the domestic policy formation and international negotiation process during the second Intifada. Along the way, our book provides a wealth of systematic data on trends in Palestinian and Israeli public opinion during this period.

The book is structured simultaneously around our theoretical themes about public opinion as an actor in two-level conflict resolution games and chronologically along critical events in the second Intifada. We analyze the failure of the 2000 Camp David summit and the role of public opinion in this failure—as a powerful constraint in two-level games. We continue into the outbreak of violence, focusing on the frames that were used by Israelis and Palestinians to account for their failure at Camp David and the role of violence and use of force in two-level games. We further focus on Ariel Sharon's unilateral disengagement from Gaza to illustrate the role of public opinion not only as a constraining factor on leaders' international games but also as providing them with policy opportunities. And we end our excursion with the electoral connection in the dramatic 2006 elections in both societies, to reaffirm it as the ultimate sanction of public opinion over leaders' performance. These elections brought to power Kadima in Israel and the Hamas in the Palestinian Authority.

The JIPP reflects the acknowledgment of the importance of public opinion in the conflict by the Palestinian Center for Policy and Survey Research (PSR) in Ramallah and the Truman Institute for the Advancement of Peace at the Hebrew University of Jerusalem. This has not been a simple task. Beyond the usual hurdles of a joint project, such as different schedules and academic differences, we also had to reconcile rivaling national identities and conflicting national narratives. Optimism paid off, and the JIPP project runs into its ninth anniversary these days. We wish to thank the Truman Institute directors since the initiation of the project for their support: Professors Moshe Maoz, Amnon Cohen, and Eyal Ben Ari; and Idit Avidan, the project coordinator at the Truman Institute during the period covered in the book. Similarly we wish to thank PSR's board of trustees and its ethics committee for the unlimited support they gave to the project.

The JIPP project has been supported over the years by grants from the Cairo office of the Ford Foundation and the Ramallah and Jerusalem offices of the Adenauer Stiftung. We gratefully acknowledge this generous financial assistance. We would also like to thank the United States Institute of Peace (USIP): under its auspices and with its support we presented and published some of the analyses further developed here, and the book began to take shape. Jacob Shamir acknowledges the highly productive year he spent at USIP as a Senior Fellow in the Jennings Randolph (JR) Program for International Peace in 2004–2005.

Earlier versions of some of the analyses appeared in articles we published jointly and separately in *Political Psychology,* the *Journal of Peace Research,* the *International Political Science Review,* and the *Journal of Democracy.*

Khalil Shikaki wishes to acknowledge the valuable assistance of colleagues Walid Ladadweh, Alaa Lahluh, and Olfat Hammad. They led the teams that collected the Palestinian data during extremely challenging conditions of violence and military closures. Jacob Shamir wishes to acknowledge the especially able and involved research assistance provided by Shira Dvir, Gitit Poran, Liran Harsagor, and Rotem Nagar throughout the different stages of this project. Many thanks to Mina Zemach, director of the Dahaf Research Institute, for her good advice and accurate and prompt data collection of the Israeli polls' data. The book builds upon the rich and comprehensive JIPP data we collected jointly since July 2000. Throughout the book we complemented the analysis with survey data collected by other research organizations, and we thank them as well, in particular Asher Arian and the Public Opinion and National Security project of the Jaffee Center for Strategic Studies at Tel Aviv University, the Tami Steinmetz Center for Peace Research at Tel Aviv University, the Jerusalem Media & Communication Centre, and the Center for Palestine Research and Studies. We would also like to thank Rachel Wiesen who did the primary editorial work; the Indiana University Press reviewers and editor; and Mark Tessler of the University of Michigan, who showed great interest in the project since its inception and encouraged us along the way.

J. S.
K. S.

PALESTINIAN AND ISRAELI PUBLIC OPINION

CHAPTER ONE

Introduction

The circumstances surrounding the collapse of the Camp David summit between U.S. president Bill Clinton, Israeli prime minister Ehud Barak, and Palestinian Authority (PA) chairman Yasser Arafat in July 2000 are still hotly debated by scholars and experts on the Israeli-Palestinian conflict. Among the many accounts of what led to the breakdown, some point the finger at flaws in the leaders' personalities and their perceived differences in negotiation styles; others stress the lack of sufficient preparation for the summit and the initial unbridgeable differences between the parties attending the summit. Most experts agree, however, that domestic considerations played a major role in the summit's progression and eventual breakdown. In fact, the Camp David drama can be easily cast as a two-level game[1] wherein Barak and Arafat played one game at the international table while simultaneously playing a second game with influential domestic opponents, each at his own domestic table.[2]

One of the most detailed accounts of the Camp David summit, that of Israel's foreign minister at the time, Shlomo Ben-Ami, appears in his book *A Front without a Rearguard* (2004). This title resonates well with the familiar Israeli conception of peacemaking as a battle to be fought and won. It was chosen, however, mainly to express the difficult domestic political environment surrounding the Camp David summit:

> The name of the book—a front without a rearguard—touches upon the environment within which we acted. . . . [I]n part these were structural imperatives which turned this journey into a struggle of a vanguard unit operating in a complex front while deprived of a stable and supportive

rearguard . . . the political system has disintegrated as negotiations went along abandoning those doing the job without political, parliamentary and popular support. . . . Yasser Arafat and his people too faced a reality of a front without supportive rearguard in the Arab world, while in the territories the expectations of his domestic rearguard were skyrocketing to unattainable heights. (Ben-Ami 2004, p. 16)

The earliest Palestinian account of the Camp David summit written by Akram Hanieh, Arafat's political adviser and confidant during the talks, made a similar point: Arafat repeatedly reminded his hosts, "you are forgetting the Palestinian people." He went on to remind them that the Palestinian people had their institutions, that there was a government, a council of ministers, a legislative council, national and central councils, an active and determined opposition. Above all, he said, there was unanimous agreement on all the major principles, and while the people had "agreed to make sacrifices for the sake of peace, they were not prepared to make further concessions." He reminded them that Israel did not have a monopoly on accountability and concerns about the opposition (Hanieh 2001, p. 85).

This description highlights the critical function of domestic imperatives, and particularly public opinion, in the formation of foreign policy. The Camp David failure was an outcome of severe public opinion constraints on both sides with which the leaders failed to cope while also miscalculating each other's red lines. This example stresses the disabling role of a lack of popular support on the one hand, and the constraining impact of unrealistic popular expectations on the other. Indeed, the first poll in the joint Palestinian-Israeli public opinion research project,[3] conducted shortly after the summit in July 2000, beautifully illustrates the observations made by Ben-Ami and Hanieh. Among Israelis, 57 percent believed that Israel compromised too much, 13 percent thought Israel could compromise more, and only 25 percent suggested that the position Barak offered was correct. Among Palestinians, however, only 15 percent believed that Arafat's position at Camp David offered too much of a compromise, 6 percent thought it was not enough, and fully two-thirds of the public (68%) believed his position to be correct. Thus the Palestinian public's expectations from the summit, in tandem with their delegation, were much higher than what Israel was willing to offer at the time.

A close examination of the evolution of the Israeli-Palestinian conflict and the major attempts to resolve it reveals the central role of public opinion as a principal domestic imperative that determines much in the leaders' policy decisions. Although the public imperative is elusive, it cannot be evaded or avoided: it demands attention, as it has the power to direct, restrain, and command those in power. Closely tied to legitimacy, it is primarily normative in nature; however, it is embodied in various manifestations including public opinion polls, Internet talk backs, mass demonstrations, media talk shows, and election and referendum results.[4]

The drama of the second Intifada highlights the public imperative and elaborates upon the various ways in which leaders consider both their own side's public opinion and the public opinion of the other side, or fail to do so. Such examples abound, and in the following chapters we outline in detail several of these modalities: situations where public opinion severely constrains leaders' bargaining (chapter 5); occasions when public opinion avails leaders of new opportunities (chapter 7); times when the leader of one side exploits the other side's public opinion to exert political pressure on his counterpart (chapter 7); and situations when public opinion sees the use of violence in the game as an instrument to pressure the other side's public to change its leader's policy (chapter 6).

From Camp David to Disengagement, Kadima, and Hamas—A Brief Overview

This book examines the Palestinian-Israeli conflict from the July 2000 Camp David summit through the electoral turnabouts in both societies in 2006. The failed Camp David summit provides a clear example of the constraining role of public opinion in conflict resolution. Public opinion, however, can also provide leaders with new opportunities, and this is indeed what we found on both sides in later stages of the conflict.

Following the collapse of the Camp David summit, violence broke out in what came to be known as the Al-Aqsa (or the second) Intifada, giving the final kiss of death to the Oslo peace process. The 1993 Oslo Accord between Israel and the Palestinian Liberation Organization (PLO), as the representative of the Palestinian people, had been the most significant breakthrough in the century-long Israeli-Palestinian conflict. It yielded mutual recognition of Israel and the PLO, and the establishment of a Palestinian National Authority (PNA or PA) in the West Bank and Gaza, which Israel had occupied since 1967.

The political peace process disintegrated gradually, long before the eruption of the Intifada. Both sides reneged on their Oslo commitments, and the Oslo process lost support in both public constituencies over time. Following the assassination of Prime Minister Rabin in 1995, subsequent Israeli governments regarded the Oslo process as an opportunity to consolidate their grip on the occupied territories by accelerating the expansion of the settlement project. The Palestinian side did not relinquish violence, and its leadership viewed the Oslo peace process as a springboard toward fulfilling its political ambitions rather than as an opportunity for serious state building. The Palestinian Authority that was established in the occupied territories was a far cry from the entity Palestinians yearned for as the embodiment of their national aspirations, and their resentment and frustration grew.

With the clouds of violence gathering, and the target date for reaching a final status agreement looming on the horizon, Israel's prime minister Barak proposed a summit meeting that would bring together Palestinian, Israeli, and American leaders in an attempt to reach a framework agreement for a final status settlement of the Israeli-Palestinian conflict. The summit was convened at Camp David on July 11, 2000, at the invitation of U.S. president Clinton to Barak, and a reluctant Arafat, wary that the U.S. and Israel were setting a trap for him. The summit ended on July 25 with no agreement reached.

About two months later, on September 28, violent clashes broke out between Palestinians and Israeli security forces following a provocative visit of the then opposition leader Ariel Sharon at Jerusalem's mosque compound of the Temple Mount (*Har HaBayit* in Hebrew, *Al-Haram Al-Sharif* in Arabic). The breakdown of the Camp David summit is widely seen as the primary catalyst for the eruption of violence that had been boiling just under the surface for quite some time. Young Palestinian nationalists, sorely disappointed with the twin failure of the PLO old guard to end occupation through diplomacy and to build a democratic political system that was not corrupt, resorted to violence to assert themselves not only against Israel but domestically as well (Shikaki 2002).

Despite the failure of the Camp David summit, scattered talks between the parties continued throughout October and November 2000 in an attempt to salvage the peace process against the backdrop of intensifying violence, the disintegration of Barak's government, and the near termination of the Clinton presidency. Negotiations continued first in the region and then, from December 19 to December 23, 2000, in Washington, D.C., under the auspices of President Bill Clinton. On December 23 President Clinton presented bridging proposals to the two sides for a final status settlement known as the "Clinton Parameters." These were presented to the parties not as an official American proposal but as ideas that could facilitate an agreement. These ideas have become the baseline for ensuing negotiations, as well as the point of reference of influential second-track peace initiatives such as the Geneva Initiative. Clinton's parameters provided an extremely useful compilation of the most creative and promising ideas developed during the prolonged period of negotiations between the parties; they were designed to grapple with the most fundamental issues of contention in the conflict, including the matters of territory, sovereignty, security, Jerusalem, refugees, and the end of the conflict.[5]

Talks between the sides resumed in Taba, an Egyptian resort in the Sinai Peninsula, between January 21 and January 27, 2001. The Taba talks also did not yield an agreement, although some progress was reported to have been made in narrowing the gaps in the positions of the two sides. Nevertheless, these negotiations remained controversial both in terms of their actual content as well as Barak's motivation to exploit them to salvage his deteriorating political prospects in the early elections he had declared. The elections took place on February 6, and Ariel Sharon won the office of prime minister by a landslide.

The Intifada intensified, with numerous Palestinian suicide bombings of Israeli civilians and Israel's sealing off the Gaza Strip and its reoccupation of the West Bank. The continuing violence claimed the lives of more than one thousand Israelis and more than four thousand Palestinians, with many more injured.[6]

Throughout this period several additional efforts to end the violent confrontation and renew the peace process were attempted, all to no avail. One such attempt was a Saudi plan adopted by the Arab League at its summit in Beirut in March 2002, calling for peace with Israel in return for a full Israeli withdrawal from all territories occupied in 1967 and the return of Palestinian refugees.[7] The most politically significant plan was the "Quartet's Roadmap," sponsored by the United States, the European Union, the United Nations, and Russia. The principles of the plan were first outlined by U.S. president George W. Bush in a speech on June 24, 2002, when he called for an independent Palestinian state living in peace with Israel. The official Roadmap plan was released in April 2003 following the appointment of Abu Mazin as prime minister of the PA, in a move meant to limit the political power of PA president Arafat. The Roadmap plan, as its name suggests, focused on the process rather than the details of the end state, and in that, it differed from the Clinton parameters. It has been described by its sponsors as a performance-based, goal-driven plan. It was comprised of several phases, each as a precondition for the next, with the end of the conflict and the establishment of a Palestinian state as the ultimate goal. The first stage called for Palestinian democratic political reform and a cessation of violence and terrorist attacks, as well as Israeli withdrawal and a freeze on settlement expansion. Thereafter, an independent Palestinian state with provisional borders was to be established with further negotiations leading to the end of the conflict.[8] Both sides endorsed the plan but with considerable reservations. It was never implemented beyond some partial steps specified in its first phase.

Toward the end of 2003 a group of Israeli and Palestinian doves launched the Geneva Initiative—a proposal for a full-blown final status agreement, largely modeled on the Clinton parameters.[9] This initiative provides a superb example of the role that nongovernmental organizations (NGOs) can assume in conflict resolution processes by modifying public discourse, shattering inhibiting norms, and preparing public opinion for compromise, when domestic leaders are apparently unwilling or unable to do so. It was meant to demonstrate that substantial common ground existed between Israelis and Palestinians on a comprehensive solution to the conflict. It was further intended to break the belligerent climate of opinion that engulfed the Israeli and Palestinian communities since the beginning of the Intifada in late 2000. While receiving lukewarm support at the time, it succeeded in reviving hopes for a long-lost political option after the collapse of the Camp David summit in July 2000. In two-level game terms, it was a bold move on the part of domestic players to interfere with the leaders' game, and, as such, both Sharon and Arafat saw it as a threat.

The Geneva Initiative turned out to be a major trigger for Sharon's Gaza Disengagement Plan, although many factors were behind this plan. Among these were other expressions of public opinion as well as political considerations such as Sharon's attempt to thwart international pressure or divert attention from corruption scandals he and his sons were embroiled in. Sharon first announced his plan in December 2003, approximately two months after the Geneva Initiative was placed on the public agenda. Overcoming a multitude of domestic and international hurdles, he was able to carry it through in August 2005. All Israeli settlements in the Gaza Strip and four more in the Northern West Bank were dismantled, and both the Israeli civilian and military presence in the Gaza Strip ended.

The disengagement case demonstrates that public opinion should not be viewed solely in terms of a constraint on policy but rather as a force that can also open important opportunities to leaders involved in two-level games. Thus it provides a powerful demonstration of the dynamic relationship between public opinion and leaders. Since the end of 2001 a majority of Israelis have already supported the dismantling of most settlements for peace. This provided an opportunity and an impetus for Sharon's dramatic policy turnabout. This step, however, was still not perceived as normative.

Sharon's declaration of his plan legitimized the dismantling of settlements in the eyes of the Israeli public.

The disengagement, it turned out, was one of the most formative events in the course of the conflict since the second Intifada began. It embodied a totally new approach to the conflict and implied a completely different game. It built on, but also perpetuated, the dominant discourse in Israeli society since the 2000 Camp David failure that there is no partner on the Palestinian side. The disengagement set in motion the political turnabout in Israel and facilitated the rise of Hamas to power in the PA. On both sides, of course, public opinion through the electoral connection was the major player. In Israel the combination of the successful implementation of the Gaza Disengagement Plan, the internal strife within the ruling Likud Party, and the electorate's policy preferences brought about Sharon's call for early elections and the establishment of the Kadima Party in November 2005. In the March 2006 Knesset election—without Sharon and with Olmert at its head—Kadima won and formed the new coalition government. Olmert continued Sharon's unilateral logic, suggesting a similar approach on the West Bank that he now labeled "Convergence."

The impact of the disengagement and, more broadly, of Sharon's unilateral approach on the Palestinian Authority domestic game was more complex, and it provides a fascinating and rare example of a game in which a leader of one side of a conflict exploits public opinion on the other side to exert political pressure on his counterpart. This was the logic of Sharon's game, and, without question, it strongly influenced the standing of Abu Mazin and contributed to the victory of Hamas in the parliamentary elections held in January 2006.

Hamas's electoral victory complicated the search for peace. Domestic and international focus shifted to finding ways to moderate the views of the Islamist group. Financial sanctions and a diplomatic boycott were imposed on the Hamas government. Fatah refused to join a coalition with Hamas. A grassroots initiative of senior Fatah and Hamas leaders in Israeli prisons succeeded in forging an agreement on a document, known as the Prisoners' Document, requiring Hamas to introduce significant moderation in its views regarding the peace process. Initially Hamas refused to endorse the document, but under tremendous popular pressure and the threat of a possible referendum on the document, Hamas agreed in May 2006 to a revised version dealing with some of its reservations.[10]

These developments bolstered the importance of public opinion to the point where leaders on both sides relegated to it the capacity to arbitrate foreign-policy decisions. Two such instances in 2006 were Abu Mazin's threat to submit the Prisoners' Document to a referendum, and Olmert's attempt to secure a mandate for his Convergence Plan by presenting it to the voters just before the elections. Moreover, leaders on both sides have committed themselves to a public referendum if they reach an agreement, effectively granting their publics direct ratification power.

By early 2006, and despite Sharon's disappearance from the political scene, unilateralism seemed to have restructured the rules of the Israeli-Palestinian two-level game—but not for long. Palestinians viewed the unilateral disengagement as a victory and also an indication that violence paid off. Following the disengagement, shelling of civilian communities from Gaza intensified. The second war in Lebanon during the summer of 2006 associated, for Israelis, the threat from Hezbollah with the dangers of turning over more territory into Hamas's hands without due political returns. As a result, only a year after the Gaza disengagement, the concept of unilateralism suffered a severe blow and Olmert's Unilateral Convergence Plan had to be put aside.

Outline of the Book

The book sets out to achieve three major goals. First, it seeks to make a theoretical contribution to the conflict resolution literature regarding the role of public opinion in two-level games; second, it provides a unique account of Israeli and Palestinian public opinion on core issues surrounding the conflict since the beginning of the Al-Aqsa Intifada; and, third, it outlines the major contours of the "win-set" of both publics during the period in question—the set of all possible agreements that might gain domestic majority support.

Chapter 2 offers a historical and methodological overview of the Joint Israeli-Palestinian Poll (JIPP). It discusses the origins of this joint survey research project and its major goals, and provides information on the frequency of polls, sampling, and interviewing methods we employed. In this chapter we also discuss the advantages and potential pitfalls of the use of survey research in a comparative study of an intractable conflict. We exemplify this discussion by a fascinating study of Palestinians' and Israelis' perceptions of terrorism.

Chapter 3 provides the theoretical foundation of the book. It outlines the currently dominant paradigm in international relations that acknowledges the role of domestic imperatives on foreign policy, and attempts to more accurately specify the dynamics at work in these situations. We draw heavily on Putnam's (1988) seminal metaphor and the extensive body of research on two-level games that it generated. In this chapter we stress the unique characteristics of public opinion as a domestic imperative that have until recently been largely neglected. We further provide a broader and more complex conceptualization of public opinion as a multidimensional entity that goes beyond the traditional approach, viewing it as the distribution of opinions in public opinion polls.

Chapter 4 provides the necessary background for understanding the origins of the Palestinian and Israeli publics' foreign policy preferences and perceptions when influencing and being influenced by policy makers.

The next four chapters are structured simultaneously around our theoretical themes about public opinion as an actor in two-level conflict resolution games and chronologically along critical events in the second Intifada. Chapters 5, 6, and 7 provide several detailed examples of the role public opinion played during critical moments of the conflict and the efforts to resolve it. Chapter 5 attempts to fill a lacuna in the numerous accounts of the 2000 Camp David summit failure. These accounts largely neglect the role of public opinion and the publics' preferences in constraining the bargaining game that took place in the summit. The analysis in this chapter focuses on two concepts: first, that of negotiators' claims of "tied hands" because of constraints by domestic veto players that might provide a bargaining advantage; and, second, that of the "closed lips syndrome" where leaders refrain from attempting to shift public opinion in a more conciliatory direction for fear of weakening their bargaining position. We believe that the role of public opinion was critical in the course of the summit and its outcome, and that understanding the two-level game dynamics in these terms provides valuable insights for the future.

Chapter 6 analyzes public opinion in the period after the collapse of the Camp David summit and the eruption of violence. The collapse of the summit has given rise to two competing frames that attempted to account for the summit's failure. These contradicting interpretations were promoted by the leaders on each side, and, resonating with deeply held values and conceptions of each public, had a lasting and debilitating impact on the efforts to resolve the conflict. We establish in both publics solid support of the use of violence and expand on their role in the management of the conflict in terms of the extent to which violent or diplomatic means should be used. The chapter exposes, furthermore, the simultaneous support for violence and compromise, surprisingly similar in the two societies. We discuss these puzzling trends from the perspectives of political psychology and two-level game rationality, explain this seemingly contradictory pattern by the ability of public opinion to distinguish between violence as a means and conflict resolution as a goal, and apply different cost-benefit calculations to each within the context of the two-level game.

Chapter 7 demonstrates that public opinion should not be cast solely as a constraint on leaders but can also open new policy opportunities for them. It provides a unique account of Israeli and Palestinian public opinion on the core issues surrounding the conflict and outlines the major contours of the current win-set of the two publics. It focuses on the interplay between the public and leaders surrounding the Geneva Initiative from October 2003; Sharon's Gaza Disengagement Plan, announced two months later and carried out in August 2005; and the subsequent political turnabouts in Israel and the PA in the parliamentary elections in both societies in early 2006. These events are intimately related; they are, in different ways, a function of public opinion but at the same time have shaped Palestinian and Israeli public opinion and the Israeli-Palestinian two-level game.

Chapter 8 provides another angle on the public opinion–policy nexus by focusing on the electoral connection. In two-level games terminology, elections provide the public indirect power to ratify an international agreement. We demonstrate the wide-ranging role of elections in Israel in producing dynamic representation on both means and end goals over the period since the first Intifada. We focus on the March 2006 elections, which realigned the party system and in which Olmert unequivocally acted to obtain a mandate from the public for his Convergence Plan. In its analysis of the Palestinian Authority, the chapter briefly examines the history of elections in the PA and provides a detailed analysis of the January 2006 parliamentary elections in the PA that brought Hamas to power.

The concluding chapter brings together the theoretical insights from our study of public opinion as a domestic imperative in the Palestinian-Israeli conflict, and outlines policy implications and recommendations regarding conflict resolution and conflict management when the former seems out of reach.

CHAPTER TWO

The Joint Israeli-Palestinian Poll
Context and Methodology

The Joint Israeli-Palestinian Poll (JIPP)

The research project on which the book is based is a joint initiative of the Truman Institute for the Advancement of Peace at the Hebrew University of Jerusalem and the Palestinian Center for Policy and Survey Research (PSR) in Ramallah.[1] It was initiated in July 2000, in the wake of the Camp David summit, at a crucial turning point in Israeli-Palestinian relationships.

This joint Palestinian-Israeli survey research project is unique in several respects. First, in terms of its academic significance, it is the only joint project that systematically tracks both the Israeli and Palestinian public since the beginning of the Al-Aqsa Intifada. Moreover, as far as we know, it is the only project that simultaneously tracks two sides of an intractable conflict in a coordinated and joint manner over a prolonged period. Furthermore, this research is largely theory-driven.[2] As detailed in the next chapter, it builds upon a broad conception of public opinion as a multifaceted phenomenon (Shamir and Shamir 2000) and studies it within Putnam's (1988) two-level game framework, highlighting the distinct characteristics of public opinion as a crucial domestic imperative in two-level games. This theoretical rationale dictated our research design in terms of the timing of our surveys and the questions we present. It led us to explore public opinion evaluations, expectations, mutual perceptions and misperceptions, and overt political action, and how they interact with the policy formation and negotiation process.

The JIPP is not only an academic research project but also aspires to contribute to conflict resolution efforts between Israelis and Palestinians.

Within the context of Palestinian-Israeli relations, it is one of the few joint projects that survived the violent turnabout in Israeli-Palestinian relations with the breakdown of the Oslo peace process, and throughout the bloodiest periods of the Intifada. On the most basic level it constitutes an extremely successful model of productive scientific cooperation between Israeli and Palestinian scholars, based on close professional and personal relations between the two principal investigators, guaranteeing its continuity for many years to come.

In terms of policy, the project contains several objectives that we hope will promote a ripening process in the leadership and public of both groups, leading toward a final status settlement. In publicizing the JIPP results, we seek to expose and remedy pluralistic ignorance and mutual misperceptions currently standing in the way of ripening. For negotiators on both sides, the JIPP data provide a better grasp of the constraints and degrees of freedom they face from both public constituencies in their attempt to reach a final status settlement. Second, the research attempts to detect and promote post-settlement reconciliation orientations for which we have set a baseline in our past surveys. Perhaps most important, we seek to identify a realistic "win-set" that could be ratified—a set of international agreements that would "win" support among both domestic constituents.

The joint polls, and the media exposure they have received in Israel, the Palestinian Authority, and the international community, thus assume an active role in promoting a ripening toward a political settlement in the conflict by turning *private* opinions on the conflict, peace, and reconciliation into *public* opinion. In effect, the JIPP helps to involve both the Palestinian and Israeli publics as active players in the peacemaking "game," in the hope that this will increase its chances for success.

Our first survey in July 2000 was meant to assess both publics' support for their delegations' positions in the failed summit. Since then, we have conducted seventeen more surveys covering the period 2000–2006. The first surveys were conducted irregularly because of uncertainty as to available resources; since December 2004 the surveys were conducted approximately every three months.

In terms of research design, stemming from our theoretical focus, each of the surveys was administered in close proximity to an important juncture in the Al-Aqsa Intifada, such as the release of the Roadmap plan, the war in Iraq, Abu-Mazin's first attempt at reaching a cease-fire (Hudna), the Geneva Initiative, Sharon's Disengagement Plan, the death of Arafat, the political turnabouts in Israel and the Palestinian Authority (PA), and the second war in Lebanon.

In each of these surveys we trace both publics' attitudes on the core issues related to the conflict, their perceptions of majority support in their own and their enemy's society, as well as their expectations of future developments. We have also constructed a reconciliation scale (Shamir and Shikaki 2002a), repeated periodically to track long-term prospects for reconciliation between the two societies. In addition to standard socio-demographic items, we regularly include media use questions and political sophistication measures of the Israeli public. In each of the surveys we also devote a significant portion of the questionnaire to issues high on the conflict's agenda at the time, such as unilateralism, the political reversals in both societies, and the second war in Lebanon. Each survey, therefore, includes questions we jointly ask Israelis and Palestinians and questions specific to each public. Most important, we periodically examine in detail Israelis' and Palestinians' positions on the most essential components of a final status settlement based on President Clinton's parameters as a potential win-set. These include the end of the conflict, a demilitarized Palestinian state, sovereignty, security and border issues, Jerusalem, and refugees. JIPP survey results we refer to in the book can be found at http://www.pcpsr.org/survey/index.html and http://truman.huji.ac.il/polls.asp.[3]

The range of Palestinian samples is around 1,270 adults interviewed face-to-face in the West Bank, East Jerusalem, and the Gaza Strip in 127 randomly selected locations. Since January 2006, when the last parliamentary elections took place, the Palestinian sample has been weighted by vote reflecting the outcome of those elections. The Israeli surveys are based on telephone interviews with a representative sample of approximately 600 adult Israelis interviewed by phone in Hebrew, Arabic, or Russian. Four of the Israeli surveys also included expanded samples of the Arab citizens of Israel.[4] These samples were properly weighted according to the proportion of the respective Jewish and Arab sectors in the population to produce the overall Israeli estimates. The Israeli samples are also weighted by vote in the last election which took place before the survey.

Comparative Research of an Intractable Conflict

Few opportunities arise where public opinion on two sides of an intractable conflict can be studied in depth in a joint, coordinated manner. The comparative nature of such research opens a range of possibilities for public opinion scholars to study the in-depth projective and reflexive processes inherent in public opinion dynamics. It allows, for example, for the possibility of detecting mutual misperceptions critical to conflict resolution efforts, and clarifying the parallel self-serving orientations that feed hatred and violence. Our study of self-serving perceptions of terrorism among Palestinians and Israelis (Shamir and Shikaki 2002b) is a fascinating example of this type of research.

Since the events of 9/11 in the United States, and the American declaration of war against terrorism, the question of how terrorism should be defined has been pronounced. Clearly no universally accepted definition exists, and most definitions offered in the international arena are tainted by self-serving motivations. These self-serving views presumably stem from the stigmatic connotations and illegitimacy of the term "terrorism." Thus, although there is no consensus of what constitutes "terrorism," most people believe that it is bad and should be eradicated. It is not too risky, then, to predict that nations in conflict tend to perceive their own acts of political violence as legitimate while condemning the other side's violence as terrorism. More interesting is the extent to which these self-serving tendencies extend to perceptions of the existing international norms on terrorism. In other words, do people project their own definitions of terrorism onto the international community, or do they perceive an international norm as different from their own?

A vast body of literature in social psychology suggests that projective processes are extremely common in social thinking. People tend to assume that their behavior and opinions are typical, and that comparable others think and behave as they do, particularly when such projections provide self-serving conclusions. Various aspects of this phenomenon have been studied under different terms.[5] Traditionally both motivational and information processing explanations have been offered to account for social projection, and both probably have some validity depending on the situation (Fiske and Taylor 1991; Krueger 1998; Marks and Miller 1987).

Given this robust body of research, and the assertion that social projection is a major mechanism by which people maintain that their own opinions are correct (Fiske and Taylor 1991), it is tempting to speculate that groups in conflict will tend to project their own definitions of terrorism onto the international community. However, the sweeping condemnation of the global media toward acts of terror could perhaps offset self-serving perceptions of what constitutes legitimate or illegitimate political violence. Furthermore, the international community may not necessarily represent close or comparable others to which sheer projection makes sense but, instead, may signify an external third party.

In this case we might expect another self-serving attribution. Group members may acknowledge divergent world definitions of terrorism but discredit them as biased against their in-group. Similar attributions have been documented in the context of media coverage of groups in conflict and have been labeled "the hostile media phenomenon" (e.g., Giner-Sorolla and Chaiken 1994; Matheson and Dursun 2001; Price 1989; Vallone, Ross, and Lepper 1985). The hostile media phenomenon is seen as a group-based response pattern, whereby partisan individuals tend to perceive a hostile bias against their in-group, and in favor of the out-group, in media coverage of the conflict between the groups.[6] In line with social identity theory (Hogg and Abrams 1988; Tajfel and Turner 1979; Turner 1982), it was suggested that this group-mediated bias works to support the need of group members to derive positive and distinct in-group identity while maintaining group status and integrity (Duck, Terry, and Hogg 1998; Gunther 1992; Matheson and Dursun 2001). Indeed, identification and involvement with a group have been found to account for the strength of hostile media perceptions.

The comparative context of the Palestinian-Israeli survey project provided an ideal research design to examine these issues of social perception. Specifically we were interested in comparing Israelis' and Palestinians' perceptions of terrorism in terms of their own actions and those of the other side, as well as in reference to the international norm. In addition, within Israel, the Arab minority is especially noteworthy in our exploration of the legitimization of political violence. Comprising a national minority, torn between their Israeli citizenship and Arab-Palestinian nationality and kinship, their delicate social and political position is obvious. We wished to explore the extent to which they could legitimize or condemn as terrorism political violence carried out by Israel compared to acts of violence committed by Palestinians. We also looked at these groups' perceptions of political violence outside the region, particularly the events of 9/11.

The study was based on the December 2001 surveys of the JIPP.[7] All respondents (Israeli Jews, Israeli Arabs, and Palestinians) were administered a battery of eleven questions, each referring to a violent incident. All could easily be labeled as acts of terror by Israelis, Palestinians, or both, and in fact have been referred to as such in the Israeli and Arab media. The list included four incidents in which Israelis were the victims, four incidents where Palestinians or Israeli Arabs were the victims, and three international incidents including the 9/11 attack. In describing each event to respondents, we made a great effort to avoid loaded words and concepts. We did not use the term "terrorism," and we also refrained from using words such as "murder," "suicide bombing," and other similar terms. The questions submitted to the different samples were identical, with minor adaptations called for by the different context and the use of Arabic and Hebrew in the respective surveys.

Respondents were asked to rate, on a standard 4-point Likert scale, the extent to which they agreed or disagreed that each of the eleven incidents could be defined as a terrorist act. They were then asked to assess, regardless of their personal opinion, whether each incident is or is not considered an act of terrorism by the international community. The list included the following incidents in this order:

1. "The killing of 29 Palestinians in Hebron by Baruch Goldstein at the Tomb of the Patriarchs (for Jews)/Al Ibrahimi Mosque (for Palestinians) in 1994."
2. "The distribution of Anthrax envelopes in the U.S."
3. "The assassination of Minister Rechavam Zeevi by Palestinians."
4. "The destruction of the Twin Towers in New York City by people suspected to be members of Bin Laden's organization."[8]
5. "The killing of 21 Israeli youths by a Palestinian who detonated himself at the Dolphinarium night club in Tel Aviv."
6. "The explosion of a Pan-Am jet over Lockerbie in Scotland by suspected Libyan agents and the killing of 270 people."
7. "The assassination of Abu Ali Mustafa, head of the PFLP [Popular Front for the Liberation of Palestine] by Israel."
8. "Shooting on Gilo[9] by the Palestinians."
9. "The killing of 13 Israeli Arab demonstrators by the Israeli police during the early days of the al Aqsa Intifada."
10. "Invasion of Israeli military forces to designated A territories[10] and the shooting of Palestinian civilians."
11. "The killing of three Israeli civilians in the Naharia railway station by an Israeli Arab who detonated himself."

The "Israeli" and "Palestinian" incidents were chosen to be equivalent as much as possible relative to the consequences of the violence. The three international stimuli were included for their salience and timeliness but mainly as controls. The results that this comparative design yielded are revelatory.

Table 2.1 presents the judgments of Israeli Jews, Palestinians, and Israeli Arabs as to whether the eleven acts of violence are acts of terrorism and their perceptions of world opinion. Comparing the judgments of Israeli Jews (column 2) to those of Palestinians (column 4) shows a diametrically

TABLE 2.1. Own Views and Perceptions of Worldview of Acts of Violence as Terror (%)

	(1)	Israeli Jews		Palestinians		Israeli Arabs	
		(2) Own View**	(3) World-view***	(4) Own View	(5) World-view	(6) Own View	(7) World-view
Goldstein Incident	(IS)*	74**	86***	98	42	86	74
Abu Ali Mustafa Assassination	(IS)	19	53	92	28	76	69
Shooting on Civilians in "A" Areas	(IS)	17	51	94	30	72	67
Arab Demonstrators' Incident	(IS)	19	48	90	31	75	68
Dolphinarium Incident	(PAL)	100	95	15	91	70	88
Rechavam Zeevi Assassination	(PAL)	96	84	11	89	64	85
Shooting on "Gilo" Neighborhood	(PAL)	90	61	13	87	58	77
"Naharia" Incident	(IA)	99	90	16	88	71	87
Pan-Am Lockerbie Incident	(F)	96	92	46	88	75	87
9/11 Incident	(F)	100	99	41	94	74	87
Anthrax Incidents	(U)	95	97	63	93	79	89

* Perpetrator's identity: IS-Israel, Pal-Palestinians, IA-Israeli Arab, F-Foreign, U-Unknown.
** All differences in own judgment among groups significant at p<.000.
*** Differences in perceptions of worldview among groups significant at p<.05 or higher except for the "Naharia" incident, the Dolphinarium incident (Israeli Jews vs. Palestinians and Palestinians vs. Israeli Arabs), the Zeevi incident (Israeli Jews vs. Israeli Arabs), the Pan-Am Lockerbie incident (Palestinians vs. Israeli Arabs), and the Anthrax incident (Israeli Jews vs. Palestinians).

opposite pattern with respect to the "local" incidents. With the exception of the Goldstein case, Israeli Jews greatly underrate acts of violence committed by Israel as terrorism,[11] whereas all acts of violence committed by Palestinians are overwhelmingly judged as terrorism. Similarly Palestinians consistently rate violent acts committed by Israelis as terrorism but largely exclude from the definition acts committed by their own side.

In examining the perceptions of the international incidents (the three bottom rows in the table), it becomes evident that significantly fewer Palestinians view them as acts of terrorism compared to the number of Israeli Jews who do so. Israeli Jews regard these incidents as terrorism to a similar degree that they define the acts perpetrated against them in the "local" conflict. Palestinians' rating of these incidents as terrorism falls midway between their definitions of the incidents perpetrated by them and against them.

Clearly, then, the definition of terrorism by both Israeli Jews and Palestinians is self-serving. This applies not only to incidents where Israelis and Palestinians were directly involved but evidently also to the international incidents whose perpetrators were identified as Muslim. Only with the Anthrax incident, where no perpetrator has yet been identified, does a majority of Palestinians (63%) define it as terrorism.

Turning to the Israeli Arabs' responses (column 6), a completely different pattern emerges. Here a significant majority of Israeli Arabs defines all acts of violence, irrespective of their perpetrator or victims, as acts of terrorism. This is their solution to their difficult position in terms of social identity, torn between their Israeli citizenship and Palestinian kinship. These data provide a striking attitudinal demonstration of the same political approach taken by the Israeli Arab leadership when asked to comment on violent Palestinian acts in the media. The standard response is: "We are against violence from any side." Obviously the ratings of incidents also vary. All acts committed by Palestinians receive lower ratings as terrorism compared to those committed by Israelis. Finally, much higher percentages of Israeli Arabs define the international incidents as terrorism compared to Palestinians, but still less than Israeli Jews. Among the three international incidents Israeli Arabs rate the Anthrax case, in which no Muslim perpetrators are implicated, as highest. This pattern is similar to that characterizing the Palestinian sample, but it is much less pronounced. The major finding with respect to Israeli Arabs' judgments is their similar and high rating of all acts of violence as terrorism.

We turn now to the respondents' perceptions of the international community's definition of the violent incidents as such, as well as relative to their own judgments. These perceptions are presented in columns 3, 5, and 7, for Israeli Jews, Palestinians, and Israeli Arabs, respectively.

First, it is evident that all three groups exhibit, on average, higher perceived world ratings of terrorism for the international incidents than for the local incidents. Second, the differences between the three groups in their perceptions of the world's position on terrorism are usually smaller than the differences between the judgments within each group.

Examining the differences between the groups' own judgments and world perceptions reveals a systematic and noteworthy pattern. In all acts of violence perpetrated by Israel (first four rows), Israeli Jews systematically overestimate the international community's definition of terrorism compared to their own ratings. Clearly this pattern does not support a projection bias interpretation; it suggests, instead, that Israelis understand that the world judges their violent acts more severely than they themselves do. The next four incidents, however, which are all violent incidents committed by Palestinians against Israelis, offer another perspective. In all these incidents, Israeli Jews perceive the world's ratings of terrorism to be lower than their own. Thus, consistent with the hostile media phenomenon, Israeli Jews seem to perceive a hostile world that is less stringent toward Palestinian acts of violence and harsher toward Israeli acts of violence than they are. As with the hostile media bias, these hostile world perceptions are self-serving in the sense that they may help to discredit the world's critical outlook on acts of violence committed by the respondent's community by denoting it as biased.

The hostile world interpretation receives even stronger support when we turn to the Palestinian perceptions of the worldview (column 5). Here we receive virtually a mirror image when comparing Palestinians' own and world assessments in the four incidents committed by Israeli Jews to the next four incidents carried out by Palestinians. Without exception, in all four incidents perpetrated by Israelis, Palestinians greatly underrate the world's definition of terrorism compared to their own. Even greater differences between their own and the perceived worldview are found in the next four incidents where Palestinians were the perpetrators. Similar but smaller gaps exist for the international incidents, which are the last three in the table.

Columns 6 and 7 present Israeli Arabs' own judgments and perceptions of the worldview of the eleven incidents as terrorism. Here we find relatively high percentages of respondents who define all acts as terrorism, and also attribute this view to the international community.

Given the robust support of our data in the hostile world notion, we wondered whether this phenomenon, too, is influenced by the level of in-group identification and involvement, just as previous research on the hostile media phenomenon has demonstrated. Indeed, we found that indicators of stronger in-group orientations, such as right-wing political orientations and religiosity, are related to the strength of the hostile world perceptions among both Israeli Jews and Palestinians.

This study provides a striking illustration of the advantages of a joint project such as ours in tapping simultaneously competing perspectives of reality, held by two sides, to an intractable conflict. It illustrates the old adage that "one man's 'terrorist' is another man's 'freedom fighter.'" The virtual mirror image of Palestinian and Israeli perceptions of terrorism apparently suggests precisely that. Israeli Arab responses, falling in-between the two, are another example of the strong self-serving component of the views on terrorism. They indicate that even apparently impartial views on terrorism may not be devoid of self-interest or social position.

Our analysis illuminates additional aspects of this old, seldom examined cliché. First, it is striking to witness the magnitude of in-group legitimacy and consensus that a range of political violence acts can acquire in times of conflict. Both Israeli and Palestinian sides overwhelmingly justify violent means by their ends. This tendency appears to be stronger among Palestinians who constitute the weaker side in the conflict compared to Israelis, and we return to this issue in our discussion of public opinion on the use of violence in chapter 6. Even more remarkable is that both Israelis and Palestinians insist on their self-serving definitions of terrorism at the same time that they perceive an international norm that largely diverges from their own point of view. Moreover, each side tends to inflate world judgment of its own acts of violence as terrorism and to underestimate world judgment when the other side's violence is considered. These "hostile world" perceptions are consistent with the "hostile media" phenomenon and have been documented previously as a group-mediated bias.

Issues in Comparative Research of Publics Engaged in Violent Conflict

Our joint project has obvious advantages of research design, but it highlights a host of other issues critical to proper evaluation and interpretation of the study of publics engaged in violent conflict, and comparative research in general. Most often referred to in the context of comparative research are issues of equivalence (Sekaran 1983), those concerned with the validity of cross-cultural comparisons and most often with the functional equivalence of the data (attitudes, behaviors, etc.) elicited by the research. Attitudes or behaviors are said to be functionally equivalent when they fulfill similar functions, have similar antecedents, and similar correlates and consequences in different cultural settings (Peng, Peterson, and Shyi 1991; Crockett et al. 2005). An important prerequisite for the existence of functional equivalence is the need for the behaviors or attitudes in question to preexist as naturally occurring phenomena in the different cultures, for example, in response to similar problems shared by the groups under study (Berry 1979; Sekaran 1983). In this regard, the study of two publics engaged and involved in the same violent conflict easily fulfills this prerequisite. However, numerous other issues of equivalence have been raised in the vast body of comparative research, and here we address only some of the most important ones.

The question of instrumentation is frequently raised in this context. It refers to the extent to which the instruments employed in the research can be seen as equivalent and as eliciting functionally equivalent responses. In survey research this issue boils down mainly to the degree of equivalence of the questions posed to the target publics and the quality of translation among the different languages. This raises the issues of vocabulary equivalence, idiomatic equivalence, grammatical and syntactical equivalence, and experiential or pragmatic equivalence, which has to do with the inferences respondents draw from the questions they are asked (Sekaran 1983). The standard practice scholars employ to enhance cross-cultural survey questions equivalence is "back translation," where the questions translated from the source language to the target language are translated back independently from the target to the source. The translation is considered adequate if the back translation succeeds in grasping the meaning of the source language without further adaptations.[12] In our research we apply back translation between Hebrew and Arabic and between Hebrew and Russian, given the sizable Russian minority in the Israeli population.

Our study of two publics entangled in a century-long conflict gives rise, however, to dilemmas that stem from its specific context. Inter-communal and international conflicts are contexts of high emotions, and they tend to sensitize societal beliefs, value systems, collective memories, and identity perceptions, all of which shape public opinion and public discourse. They are further characterized by contradicting narratives, diverging daily realities, and the self-serving discourses of the two sides. What might be understood as a legitimate or normative expression in one public is often then perceived as malicious or derogatory by the public with which it is engaged in violent conflict. For example, as we saw in the previous section, Israelis usually refer to Palestinian acts of violence as acts of terror, whereas Palestinians view them as resistance operations, and vice versa. Clearly "terrorism" and "resistance" are not direct semantic antonyms and do not necessarily convey opposite meanings. Nevertheless, we use these terms in our questionnaires, as we believe that adapting survey questions to the prevailing discourse, and the widest shared meaning in each society, is the best solution available under the circumstances. Consistent with this approach, methodologists concerned with cross-national research, such as Sekaran (1983) and Sechrest, Fay, and Zaidi (1972), warn against an obsession with equivalence that might obscure important cultural differences and preclude the cultural uniqueness from surfacing. Similarly Harkness (2003) stresses the importance of the pragmatic equivalence of questions, claiming that pragmatic meaning is context sensitive and contextual considerations are cultural considerations.

Sometimes, however, normative pressures might altogether preclude the ability to tap certain attitude domains exhaustively, particularly when attempting to measure extreme positions of these domains. For example, in our measurement of reconciliation among Israelis and Palestinians (Shamir and Shikaki 2002a), we decided to relinquish some theoretically important items in the Palestinian reconciliation scale, given their non-normative ring to Palestinian ears. The reconciliation scale we devised is based on a series of steps often mentioned in the reconciliation literature as prerequisites for successful reconciliation following protracted conflicts. The steps ranged in order of difficulty and commitment from normalization measures, such as open borders and economic cooperation, through steps toward political alliance, to transformative steps intended to change the national ethos such as fundamental modifications in school curricula. There were two additional ethos transforming items in the scale: "teach your side's role in the outbreak and the continuation of the conflict in schools" and "officially recognize your side's violent acts against the other side throughout the conflict." Although transformative approaches to reconciliation contend that reconciling issues of responsibility and guilt is mandatory, the requirement is often not symmetrical when inter-communal conflicts are concerned. This demand places much greater emotional burden on those who see themselves as victims in a conflict than on those who feel they emerged as winners. Although these items posed no problem with Israelis, they seemed to fall out of the normative range of Palestinians and were dropped from the Palestinian scale. Overall we should remember that in this project we compare an Israeli public that has fulfilled its national aspirations and seeks to secure them to a Palestinian public still struggling to fulfill its own national dreams.

Another equivalence issue is the use of different data collection methods in our joint project. Given the low level of telephone penetration in the Palestinian Authority (42%),[13] Palestinian surveys employ face-to-face interviews. Israeli polls, however, use telephone interviews, which are advantageous in Israel as they allow us easily to implement multilingual interviews (in Hebrew, Arabic, and Russian when the need arises) from a central location. A central location also facilitates quality control and enhances the quality of the data obtained. However, the inability to see conversational partners may impair the feeling of legitimacy and the natural flow of the interview but increase the sense of anonymity (Miller and Cannell 1982) when sensitive questions are presented. Further, the faster pace of telephone interviews results in shorter responses to open-ended questions, and scattered indications in the literature are that cognitive processing in these interviews is more superficial with closed-ended questions (Groves 1990). Studies on interview mode effect generally suggest that interviewing by telephone may be advantageous in some ways and disadvantageous in others. Regarding differences in distributions in survey answers, the findings are mixed. A considerable body of research demonstrates that the distributions of survey answers, when collected face-to-face and over the telephone, are quite similar (e.g., Aneshensel et al. 1982a, 1982b; Groves and Khan 1979; Klecka and Tuchfarber 1978).

In Israel we are aware of two studies that examined this issue systematically. The first was conducted in 1995 by Asher Arian and Michal Shamir. As part of the data collection of the yearly survey of the Jaffee Center for Strategic Studies' National Security and Public Opinion Project, under the direction of Arian, a national sample of 1,220 Israeli Jews was randomly divided so that half the participants were interviewed face-to-face and the other half by telephone. A comparison of the distribution of survey answers and of intercorrelations did not result in meaningful differences.[14] Another (unpublished) study was conducted by Sammy Smooha, as part of his survey of the Arab-Jewish Relations Index 2003. In his 2004 Index, Smooha reports having found marked differences between the two kinds of surveys among Israeli Arabs, and therefore his 2004 Index relied on face-to-face interviews with Arab respondents and telephone interviews with Jewish respondents (2005, nn. 8 and 9). There is no consensus among Israeli pollsters regarding the preferred mode of interview among Israeli Arabs, but because Arabs comprise only a small minority of the Israeli population, most surveys of the general Israeli population rely on telephone interviews for both Jews and Arabs. We followed this practice.

In conclusion, the simultaneous inquiry of two societies in violent conflict with each other provides a rare setting, allowing a systematic examination of projective and reflexive processes inherent in public opinion dynamics. These processes pose important theoretical questions, and the hostile world phenomenon is but one example. Numerous other examples are embedded in the following chapters. To those interested in conflict resolution and substantive policy issues, in-depth examination of the perspectives and sentiments of publics in violent conflict with each other is indispensable to the formation of rational policy recommendations and conflict resolution programs. For these readers our book provides a rich array of data spanning the six years of the Al-Aqsa Intifada. As this chapter suggests, however, scholars should approach this wealth of data with sensitivity to the context as well as an awareness of equivalence issues. Despite the efforts of the best survey researchers to functionally standardize instrumentation and data collection procedures, these may reflect differences in collective memories, contradicting narratives, diverging daily realities, and self-serving discourses by the two sides.

CHAPTER THREE

The Public Imperative
Public Opinion in Two-Level Games

A Useful Metaphor and Some Theoretical Concepts

One need not be an expert on the Palestinian-Israeli conflict to realize the extent to which powerful domestic interests and deeply rooted values are vested in the conflict and in the attempts to resolve it. Over the years this bitter intractable conflict has structured both societies' economies, politics, and value systems (e.g., Arian 1995; Bar-Tal 2007; Khalidi 1997; Kimmerling and Migdal 2003; Shafir and Peled 2002; Said 2000; Sayigh 2000; Tessler 1994). Thus any attempt to resolve the conflict necessarily creates domestic distributive problems that are reduced, eventually, to the question of who will gain and who will lose from such a process. It is not surprising, then, that, consistent with Putnam's (1988) two-level game metaphor, powerful bureaucracies, political institutions, and key interests have become eager players in both sides' domestic game, pressuring their leaders directly or through public opinion to embrace the policies they favor. At the international table, in turn, the leaders of each side have sought to maximize their degrees of freedom to satisfy these domestic pressures while trying to contain the harmful impact of foreign developments.

Putnam's two-level game model provides a useful mode of thinking on the dynamics of many international negotiations, and the Israeli-Palestinian game is no exception. In his model, two heads of government negotiate an agreement that must be ratified by their constituencies. A simultaneous bargaining process is conducted among each leader's constituents, and between them and the leader, concerning the proposed agreement and its ratification. All players obviously have distinctive preferences regarding the potential negotiation outcomes they attempt to promote.

Ratification may be any domestic decision-making process required for the implementation of the agreement. Referendums, popular elections, parliamentary legislation, or votes of confidence are all familiar modes of ratification. However, approval does not necessarily need to be formal or even democratic, and offensive agreements risk being spoiled by uncooperative bureaucracies or dissenting, belligerent political factions. Those agreements, however, that would gain the necessary support at home belong to what Putnam labels the "win-set," the set of all international agreements that would "win" support among domestic constituents.

By definition, domestic win-sets must overlap for the international negotiators to reach a successful agreement. Larger win-sets therefore have a greater chance of overlapping to produce agreements. The relative size of the domestic win-sets and the contours of their intersection define the joint gains from the international bargain. Larger win-sets may project greater flexibility, inviting pressure to concede. Smaller win-sets, in turn, allow negotiators to claim tied hands but necessarily afford leaders less domestic slack. The two-level game scenario obviously does not guarantee agreement, and the possibility of defection hovers over the negotiation tables. Defection could either be voluntary owing to egotistic motives or involuntary as a result of ratification failure. Both games are played iteratively, linked to each other by a complex array of expectations, moves, and countermoves.

Putnam's seminal paper produced a slew of theoretical and empirical work that examined the central aspects of international two-level games (e.g., Evans, Jacobson, and Putnam 1993; Moravcsik 1993). In the rich body of formal models that emerged, special attention was given to Schelling's (1960) idea, further developed by Putnam, that domestic constraints allow negotiators to extract concessions from the other side. Here the characteristics of the constraining actors, the severity and credibility of constraints, and the informational base of the negotiators all received additional formal treatment (e.g., Mo 1994, 1995; Pahre 1997; Milner and Rosendorff 1997a; Bailer and Schneider 2006; Fearon 1997; Hug and König 2002; Lida 1993). Other issues explored in this paradigm focus on heterogeneity in the domestic players' preferences and the implications of side payments (e.g., Mayer 1992; Milner 1997; Milner and Rosendorff 1997a, 1997b), issues of ratification institutions, coalitions, and divided governments (e.g., Pahre 1997, 2006). We rely on this literature, in our subsequent analysis, as it pertains to the role of public opinion in the Israeli-Palestinian game. We turn now to draw a fuller picture of the two domestic tables, their major players and the web of interests surrounding them. We then discuss the nature of public opinion as a special kind of domestic imperative on foreign policy.

The Israeli and Palestinian Domestic Tables

Although two-level games may vary in their duration, those played in the context of intractable conflicts may last for many years. In these cases the game is often disrupted for prolonged periods, players come and go, and the underlying rules can change dramatically. This is indeed the nature of the painfully enduring Israeli-Palestinian game. A full-blown, two-level analysis of this generation-long conflict is an enormous task, beyond the scope of this book. The period we study is the second Intifada between 2000 and 2006, fluctuating between phases of high- and low-intensity violent clashes. In this period we focus on several critical phases that highlight the role of public opinion as a player in the two-level game, provide theoretical insights, and allow for policy recommendations.

Sitting at the Israeli domestic table during this period are, first and foremost, the Jewish settlers in the occupied territories and the political forces supporting them. The settlers have been the most influential factor in shaping Israel's policy on peace and the territories over the last three decades. The formative years of the settlers' movement were the mid-1970s and early 1980s, and its ideological and political engine was "Gush Emunim" (Hebrew for Bloc of the Faithful). It consisted of a small but extremely dedicated group of national religious activists devoted to resettling the ancient Jewish homeland as a divine tenet and a means of redemption for all the people of Israel (Zertal and Eldar 2004; Susskind et al. 2005; Sprinzak 1991).

Over the years the movement became routinized and diversified. In addition to younger generations born into a bitter conflict with the Palestinians, it also attracted many Israelis who moved into the territories to improve their quality of life. Thus, in time, it came to represent strong economic interests as well as ideology. Nevertheless it would be a mistake to portray the still significant segment of the ideological settlers as mere colonizers. The settlement project was motivated from the outset by ideological and political aspirations reaching far beyond the territorial dimension, targeting the very identity and value system of Israeli society as a whole (Sheleg 2004). The settlers viewed themselves as fulfilling a national mission of historic magnitude, and as the genuine followers of the Zionist founders of Israel. They aspired to transform Israel's national identity by strengthening its Jewish religious dimensions over the more secular universalistic values of the Israeli Left. Thus the dismantling of settlements and the return of land to Arabs constitutes the breakdown of a national religious ethos and a moral defeat of the settlers' movement by the Israeli Left.

Alongside the settlers, and with their own considerable impact, sits the Israeli military and security establishment. It includes, in addition to the IDF (Israel Defense Forces) high command, the heads of Israel's other security services such as the Shabak and the Mossad. As is often the case in societies in conflict, the Israeli military and security establishment plays a major role in most of the important decisions with regard to the conflict with the Palestinians (Peri 2006). These include not only purely military decisions such as the policy of targeted assassinations but also decisions with important strategic implications such as deeming Arafat irrelevant as a negotiation partner, charting the contours of the separation barrier, and planning the details of the Gaza Disengagement Plan. No less important, the international Israeli-Palestinian game has been heavily influenced by a fierce power struggle within the Likud Party between Sharon and Benjamin Netanyahu, which set the stage for the establishment of the Kadima Party by Sharon in late 2005 and the political turnabout in Israel in March 2006. Finally, powerful economic interest groups have long been pushing the Israeli political leadership toward more accommodating positions in the conflict, given its detrimental impact on the Israeli economy and its standing in the international markets (Shafir and Peled 2000).

The Palestinian domestic table during this period is similarly crowded and even more complex, given the acute fragmentation of the Palestinian political scene as a result of its separation of power between the president and prime minister, the generational conflict within the Fatah Party, the competition between the various wings of Hamas, and the dispersion of millions of Palestinian refugees, many of whom still live in dozens of refugee camps in the West Bank and the Gaza Strip, as well as several Arab host countries.

Hamas's role as the major opposition force to the Fatah leadership was turned around overnight when it won the 2006 parliamentary elections and became the primary bearer of responsibility for policy making, both domestically and with regard to the conflict with Israel. The political competition between its various wings further complicates the game. Here we can find the leadership residing in the Palestinian Authority (Hamas "inside") and the one in exile ("Hamas outside"). There is also the division between the political and military wings of Hamas, which relieves its officials from responsibility for illegitimate acts of violence. Following Hamas's rise to power in the January 2006 elections, the impression was that a clear division of labor exists between its separate factions, with the inside arm assuming responsibility for domestic affairs and the outside branch handling foreign affairs. Indeed, most diplomatic missions to Turkey, Russia, and the Gulf states following the elections were conducted by leading members of Hamas's political bureau in Syria. The outside leadership's control of the financial resources appeared to give it the upper hand in shaping policy. However, the conflicting interests of the two wings quickly surfaced with the first crises that challenged the Hamas regime in the PA. The Prisoners' Document, Abu Mazin's threat to call a referendum over its adoption, and the calls for a national unity government exposed the intricate relationship between the domestic and international games and the resulting futility of what appeared to be a clear-cut division of labor between Hamas "inside" and "outside."

As to politics within the Fatah Party, the generational conflict did not subside following its electoral loss. At the base is a clash between the "old guard" and the "young guard" within the Fatah Party (Shikaki 2004). The actual state of affairs is more complex, however, involving more generations and a dynamic network of coalitions and alliances. The old guard, against whom the new forces have allied, consists of the founders of the Palestinian national movement, leaders of various guerilla organizations, and the PLO bureaucracy, who owe their positions mainly to Arafat's patronage. Following Arafat's death, these figures lost much of their political influence. The so-called young guard is composed mostly of Fatah activists who gained their prominence and rank within the Fatah movement during the first Intifada but whom Arafat largely excluded from the circles of power. Prominent among the young guard is Marwan Barghouti, the head of Fatah's militia, or Tanzim, in the West Bank, and Mohammad Dahlan, the founder of the Fatah's youth movement, or Shabibah, and later one of the top heads of the PA security forces. In the second Intifada Barghouti led the more militant and armed group, the "Al-Aqsa Martyrs." Young guards have become disillusioned with the corrupt PA bureaucracy and its official security forces, and have felt even more deprived of political power. But the young guards are not homogeneous; they represent diverse interests and are capable of forming potentially powerful coalitions and alliances that could influence policy considerably. These alliances are formed not only among Fatah factions and competitors but also among some of the Fatah grassroots groups and militant elements in Hamas.

Finally, more than half the Palestinians are refugees who lost their homes and property following the 1948 war and the establishment of the State of Israel. In the West Bank and the Gaza Strip, approximately 45 percent of the Palestinian residents are refugees, and about half of those residents still live in refugee camps. Although many of the refugees have been integrated into their economic and sociopolitical environment, their refugee status can be a lethal threat to any Palestinian-Israeli settlement that does not address their rights, grievances, and needs. Dozens of organizations representing the interests of refugees in the Palestinian territories and host countries have consistently insisted that any agreement with Israel to end the conflict must insure the full right of return to their constituency. Israelis view the demand for the right of return as an existential threat to the Jewish nature of the state.

The Nature of Public Opinion as a Domestic Imperative

Though all the players described in the previous chapter are central to the Israeli and Palestinian domestic games, we focus on public opinion as a unique type of player in the two-level game. Public opinion experts, political scientists, and scholars of international relations nowadays agree that public opinion affects foreign policy (e.g., Hinckley 1992; Holsti 2004; Russett 1990; Sobel 2001; Wittcopf 1990). This premise has largely replaced the post–World War II "Almond-Lippmann" consensus, which maintained that public opinion lacked coherence, was volatile, and provided inadequate foundations for stable and effective foreign policies, and indeed had little if any impact on foreign policy (Holsti 1992). Current research has gradually uncovered the complex nature of the relationship between public opinion and foreign policy, and the multitude of methods and modalities whereby public opinion can impact decision making (e.g., Foyle 1997; Risse-Kappen 1991). These may range from rather vague constraints on policy making (Key 1961; Sobel 2001; Stimson 1991) to the electoral connection and indirect ratification power of international agreements (Aldrich et al. 2006; Pahre 2006; Trumbore 1998) to actual and institutionalized veto power granted to it by negotiators.

The concept of public opinion has been acknowledged as an important domestic imperative, and yet it remains largely unexplored in the two-level game paradigm; in fact, case studies hardly refer to it at all (e.g., Lehman and McCoy 1992; Schoppa 1993). Of those scholars who demonstrated a particular interest in public opinion, most did not highlight its distinct characteristics as a policy-relevant imperative. Indeed, as Powlick (1995) observed, most studies of the public opinion and foreign policy interface used poll data and have left the phrase "public opinion" undefined. Typically these studies adopted the hegemonic view of public opinion simply as the aggregation of opinions expressed in opinion surveys (e.g., Jentleson 1992; Page and Shapiro 1992). However, public opinion as a player in the domestic game raises intriguing questions about its meaning and the signals it sends to leaders. These cannot be reduced to attitudes and vote intentions data, as they also involve behavioral expressions, as well as more tacit normative cues and expectations of future events and developments.

Another unexplored territory is the difference between public opinion and the many other actors representing key interests at the domestic table. First, it is not always clear who—if anyone—is the genuine representative of public opinion around the table, although many surely compete for this title. Second, unlike most other domestic political actors, leaders' wheeling and dealing with public opinion is a matter of public record and cannot be concealed—a fact that complicates their international game. Also, the incentive system that leaders can use to gratify public opinion is often less structured, and not as well articulated and understood, compared to the demands of other actors whose interests are far more homogeneous and clear.

Third, the leverage of public opinion in shaping foreign policy has usually been discussed in terms of direct or indirect ratification. But public opinion also appears to be influential in non-democratic systems, or when ratification is not on the foreseeable agenda. Public opinion, moreover, was usually cast as a constraint on policy, and only a few studies realized its potential as opening important opportunities to leaders involved in two-level games (e.g., Knopf 1998a, 1998b; Risse-Kappen 1991; Trumbore 1998).

In recent years formal models of two-level games began to bear more closely on public opinion. Of particular importance to a theory of public opinion as a domestic imperative in democracies are two underlying assumptions of this paradigm: first, that leaders are office seekers (Bueno de Mesquita and Siverson 1995; Schultz 1998; Stimson, MacKuen, and Erikson 1995); and, second, that they might accrue audience costs (Fearon 1997).

The common rational choice logic for the leverage that public opinion holds over leaders is their fundamental drive to seek office and their desire to maximize their chances for reelection. Constituencies' evaluations of their policy achievements can critically affect these chances. The idea of audience costs goes beyond sheer policy outcomes and is concerned with the leaders' degree of commitment to actually implement publicly stated policies (Fearon 1994, 1997; Leventoglu and Tarar 2005).[1] According to this research, leaders might suffer audience costs and be punished electorally if they back down or back away from a publicly stated policy. Several explanations have been proposed for this response on the part of constituencies. First, the domestic public might feel that the leader violated the "national honor" (Fearon 1994). Second, the leader who violates his public commitment might be perceived by his constituency as incompetent. Third, such a leader might lose his international credibility and accrue future losses for his nation's welfare because of ineffective foreign policy. Finally, the imposition of audience costs is in the interest of the domestic audience. Audience costs allow leaders to credibly communicate their resolve by attaching an actual price tag to retraction from their stated commitments. This might produce bargaining benefits that audiences share with their leaders (Leventoglu and Tarar 2005). In this body of research, leaders' public statements have been framed primarily in the context of attempts to narrow down the size of their domestic win-set to gain bargaining benefits.

Missing in these models is the awareness of the reverberations of these statements on the other side's public. Obviously leaders' public statements designed to restrict their domestic win-set as part of their negotiation tactics also affect the public on the other side. As such, those may restructure the demands of the other side's public from their own leaders as well, and alter the prospects for concluding an agreement.

Audience costs may also apply to cases of public statements designed to expand rather than limit domestic win-sets. In these cases conciliatory public statements or confidence-building steps may be used to increase the credibility of concession offers, but they may end up with significant audience costs when they do not bear fruit. Such instances are probably rare in negotiations, unless they significantly increase the odds of reaching a bargain and achieving greater payoffs for the leader contemplating this kind of public statement. One may view Anwar Sadat's visit to Jerusalem in 1977 in these terms as a visit intended to convince the Israeli public of his commitment to peace. Here Sadat's bold move greatly increased the chances of an Israeli-Egyptian deal. Fearing audience costs, he framed his visit in religious terms as a pilgrimage to Jerusalem. But when an autocratic regime is involved, as here, the cost may not be electoral defeat but rather the leader's head. Another example is the vision of "A New Middle East" publicly perpetuated by the Israeli Left, particularly by Shimon Peres during the Oslo years. This became a regional joke for which Peres paid dearly in his public standing and political career.

These ideas have become all the more relevant to the Israeli-Palestinian arena in recent years, with the introduction of elections in the Palestinian Authority and Hamas's rise to power in the 2006 parliamentary elections. First, electoral accountability has entered Palestinian politics. Second, Palestinian split government has brought about a fierce struggle for legitimacy involving potentially costly public statements by Fatah, and particularly by

Hamas leaders. Since their rise to power in the 2006 elections, Hamas ers have persistently and publicly emphasized their demand of reft right of return to Israel proper and of control over all of East Jerus These statements are designed to narrow Palestinians' win-set and tie any negotiators' hands. They might prove costly to leaders attempting to retract from these statements, but even more so in terms of risking any potential future bargain.

Another important characteristic of public opinion is its greater susceptibility to framing efforts compared to other domestic players such as interest groups, trade unions, economic organizations, and political institutions and parties. The general public is also far more dependent than are other domestic actors on the media and on experts for information about the negotiation intricacies as well as the actual meaning and implications of international agreements. Publics also seem to be highly sensitive to symbolic gestures and gains, such as acknowledgments of historical responsibility, repudiations of collective blame, gestures of identity recognition, and so on. Thus, when disputes possess an acute symbolic dimension, negotiators may have an incentive to converge on "constructive ambiguity" formulations in the hope of facilitating public approval.

Finally, most research relies on a narrow perspective of public opinion as the aggregation of opinions expressed in opinion surveys. However, a broader and more complex conceptualization of public opinion is needed to allow us to address these and other concerns related to the role of public opinion as a domestic imperative. A more sophisticated conceptualization of public opinion must acknowledge the element of publicity in public opinion: "public" opinion as distinguished from "private" opinion. Indeed, public opinion is a shared aggregate phenomenon. It is a collective social entity, and publicity is necessary for its formation. One must also understand the multidimensional nature of public opinion and its essential role in society. Public opinion mediates and accommodates social integration and social change. As a normative force it nurtures integration and stability. As a mechanism of aggregate foresight it paves the way for social and political change. Public opinion therefore involves not only the majority opinion but also the normative opinion—the opinion perceived to be the majority opinion—with the omnipotent presence of a social force that functions to achieve cohesion and value consensus in society (Noelle-Neumann 1993). Similarly important are people's expectations regarding future events and developments, as well as overt verbal, symbolic, and behavioral expressions of opinion.

This conceptualization (Shamir and Shamir 2000) illuminates important characteristics of public opinion as an influential factor in two-level games. It carries major advantages for negotiators by better informing them of their options, and for scholars, by allowing clearer interpretations of the sources of success and failure of these processes. For example, win-sets in two-level games, as defined by Putnam, are often constrained by perceptions of the public's policy preferences rather than by their actual preferences (Foyle 1997). However, sometimes crucial gaps appear between these perceived sentiments that index the prevailing norm and the public's actual preferences. Such discrepancies, labeled "pluralistic ignorance" (e.g., Allport 1924; Katz and Allport 1931; O'Gorman 1988; Shamir and Shamir 1997), raise critical questions as to what public opinion is, and may give negotiators more complete information on the actual width of their win-set. Adding to this complexity, publics may err not only in their percep-tion of what their own majority thinks but also in their understanding of their enemy's public sentiment. This, of course, is also extremely relevant to negotiators who often attempt to influence not only their own publics but also the other side's constituency, using what Putnam calls reverbera-tion strategies.

This conceptualization of public opinion can also help us better under-stand the role of public opinion in non-democratic regimes by acknowl-edging the normative influence of public opinion in explaining autocratic leaders' behavior. Public opinion confers legitimacy—people's willingness to submit voluntarily to authority. Legitimacy by its nature has a strong normative component and is intimately related to the normative facet of public opinion. This point is central to understanding the channels through which public opinion exerts its influence in the domestic Israeli and Pales-tinian games.

CHAPTER FOUR

The Israeli and Palestinian Publics
Differences and Similarities

The concept of public opinion, as outlined in the previous chapter, is also useful for placing our comparative research in its proper context. It directs us to differences, but also similarities, between Israeli and Palestinian public opinion along its most fundamental dimensions: information and knowledge, norms and values, expectations, and political participation. These are most significant to understanding their two-level game.

Information and Knowledge

The extent to which both publics are informed on daily affairs and political developments is crucial to their performance as players in the domestic political game. Indirect indicators commonly used in this context are literacy rates and educational level. Although literacy rates in both societies are quite similar, 95 percent in Israel and 90 percent in the Palestinian Authority,[1] Israelis tend to achieve higher educational levels compared to Palestinians. According to UNESCO's "Global Education Digest 2005," the gross enrollment ratio of Israelis in tertiary education programs for the year 2002–2003 was 57 percent compared to 35 percent of Palestinians.[2] Similarly our poll data showed 45 percent of Israelis as having partial or full academic education compared to 24 percent of Palestinians.[3]

A more direct assessment is provided by news media exposure patterns of Israelis and Palestinians. A PSR survey conducted in May 2006 demonstrated that 54 percent of Palestinians consider themselves interested or very interested in politics, and only 22 percent indicated that they were uninterested. Moreover, 79 percent responded that they follow the news often or very often. Israelis similarly report a high interest in politics. In the 2007 Israel Democracy Index, 82 percent reported that they follow politics in the mass media every day or several times a week (Arian, Atmor, and Hadar 2007, p. 92). In our December 2006 poll, 54 percent of Israelis and 30 percent of Palestinians reported to have watched the news almost every day on Israeli or Palestinian television, respectively. Further, 69 percent of Palestinians and 8 percent of Israelis also reported watching the news almost every day on satellite channels such as Al-Jazeera; a relatively small percentage of Israelis (13%) also watch CNN or the BBC almost daily. Israelis are avid radio news consumers, with 74 percent listening to the news twice or more every day. No comparable radio news consumption data are available for Palestinians. As for newspapers, 48 percent of Israelis report reading a newspaper almost daily compared to 13 percent of Palestinians. Only 15 percent of Israelis reported almost never reading a daily newspaper compared to 52 percent of Palestinians. PSR's May 2006 poll showed that 78 percent of Palestinians consider television as the most trustworthy media, followed by radio (12%) and newspapers (3%). A majority of 53 percent of Palestinians indicated that the Al Jazeera television news broadcast was their most trusted media source. Regarding Internet usage, 9 percent of Palestinians indicated that they use the Internet daily or almost daily. The corresponding figure among Israelis is estimated at 33 percent, according to an April 2006 survey of the Netvision Institute for Internet Studies at Tel Aviv University.[4] Thus both publics seem to be highly tuned to the news. Palestinians appear to obtain their current affairs information mainly from television. Israelis are also greatly exposed to television but to radio news as well, and they read significantly more print news than Palestinians, engendering more exposure to in-depth analysis by political experts and commentators.

To grasp the Israeli and Palestinian media environment, it is necessary to refer to the differences in the level of media control and journalists' professional standards in these two societies.

Neither Israel nor the Palestinian Authority receives particularly high scores in the "Freedom of the Press" survey conducted by Freedom House, a nonprofit nonpartisan organization. This survey examines the extent to which freedom of the press exists in each country, focusing on legal, political, and economic parameters. In the 2006 survey, Israel ranked 61 with a score of 28, barely managing to be included in the "free" category. The category "Israeli-occupied territories" refers to the performance of both Israel and the Palestinian Authority and obtained a "not free" score of 84, ranking it close to the bottom of the list (182 out of 194).[5] It should be emphasized that these figures did not yet reflect the performance of the new Hamas government. Nevertheless the legal tools created to control the media during Arafat's presidency, and his treatment of media professionals, seem to have set adverse norms in this domain. Actual control of the press was carried out extra-legally by means of threats. Journalists have been harassed, detained, and arrested. Editors received clear instructions on what can and cannot be printed. Radio stations were closed and some publications were forced out of business, all with no acknowledgment of any legal jurisdiction (Brown 2003a). In addition to these restrictions and the pervasive chilling effect they created, Palestinian journalists have also been accused of resorting to self-censorship, driven by a nationalistic outlook and cultural motivations.[6] Under Mahmoud Abbas, the Palestinian political system became more open and inclusive. According to the *Palestine Democracy Index* (Miqias al Dimokratiyya fi filisteen), an annual report of the status of Palestinian democracy issued by the Palestinian Center for Policy and Survey Research, freedom of the press and of expression, a sub-index based on nine empirically measured indicators, received 739 points out of a maximum of 1,000 points. This 2006 report showed a drop of about 10 percent to 662 points under the Hamas government.[7]

The Palestinian media environment is quite varied, with a multitude of local television and radio stations, and is therefore difficult to fully control. Further, the material that the Palestinian media could not broadcast was often broadcast by the Arab satellite networks, which, as mentioned above, nearly two-thirds of Palestinians watched almost daily.

Although Israeli media is not completely free of legal restrictions and censorship, it has rarely been subjected to this level of control and arbitrariness. Self-censorship and the national motivations guiding professional values were not foreign to Israeli journalists in earlier times, too, particularly during the years of state building. But with the proliferation of media channels in the early 1990s, and the increased competition between them, these tendencies have witnessed a significant decline.

Media news is probably the major source of information on public affairs and conflict-related developments, but it is only part of the public's information environment. Other important factors are at play such as individuals' daily firsthand experiences and interpersonal sources. This "popular wisdom" and "experiential knowledge" (Gamson 1992) help people to sense which direction the wind is blowing and form accurate expectations regarding the course of the conflict.

A sensitive daily barometer for the Palestinians on the state of the conflict has been the conduct of Israeli soldiers at the military roadblocks dispersed throughout the occupied territories. Other decisions such as whether and

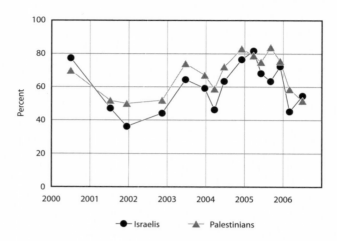

Figure 4.1. Percent Expecting Negotiations to Resume, 2000–2006

—●— Israelis   —▲— Palestinians

how many Palestinian workers can cross into Israel, or whether a closure is imposed or not, impacted directly on the daily life of all Palestinians. Similarly, Israelis were exposed firsthand to daily events and developments. They often heard about recent suicide bombings and ongoing military operations in the territories from relatives and friends over their cell phones before the news was even broadcast on the radio. Thus, in terms of being well informed on current affairs and key events, both publics appear to be similarly knowledgeable. Attesting to this are the realistic expectations they form as to how the conflict might evolve. In our surveys we regularly ask both publics to assess the likelihood for an end to the violence and the resumption of a political process. Respondents can choose one of three options: that "negotiations will resume soon enough and armed confrontations will stop," that "negotiations will resume but some armed attacks will continue," or that "armed confrontations will not stop and the two sides will not return to negotiations." When we combine responses to the first two options that refer to the resumption of negotiations, with or without violence, we achieve the noteworthy pattern presented in Figure 4.1.

As evident from the fluctuations in the figure, the expectations of both publics are very sensitive to political developments, and they read the political reality correctly. Expectations that negotiations will resume, irrespective of violence, drop sharply a year after the beginning of the Intifada and the persistence of violence. They reach their lowest point in our December 2001 poll. Expectations begin to rise after the announcement of the Quartet's Roadmap in September 2002, and more sharply after Abu Mazin's nomination for prime minister in April 2003 and the Aqaba summit with Sharon in May 2003. They drop somewhat in our December 2003 poll following Abu Mazin's resignation in September amid a power struggle with Arafat and an upsurge of violence. Expectations reach their peak after Arafat's death in November 2004. Following the victory of Hamas in January 2006, these expectations sink again. Particularly striking is that the expectations of both publics over time are virtually identical and move in tandem, even though each is exposed to different media and have divergent daily experiences.

Our polls indicate that both publics are involved and seek political information, but Israelis seem to be more versed in specific details of issues on the agenda;[8] Israelis also tend to entertain more coherent and consistent attitudes (Shamir and Shikaki 2002a). These differences stem from their living conditions, educational levels, and media environment; above all, however, they emerge because of Israel's well-established and long-standing political and party system, which provides ideological cues and identification with a particular party to help people become oriented to politics. Nevertheless, our data indicate that both publics are sufficiently knowledgeable regarding the conduct of the conflict to allow them to develop realistic expectations as to the prospects for the end of violence and the resumption of a political process. They are capable of realistically judging the impact of events and policies, an essential prerequisite for the publics' ability to sanction or reward leaders for their decisions. Moreover, this "aggregate wisdom," and the expectations it entails on the part of the public, are a major source of learning and attitudinal change, at times opening policy opportunities for their leaders' international game. We discuss such examples in detail in the following chapters.

Normative Characteristics

The normative grip of fundamental societal values is an essential characteristic of every society and expresses itself in the normative climate of opinion. It has however, special force when societies face external conflict and when they are in state-building stages. Periods of conflict intensify individuals' security needs and enhance their identification and attachment with the collective. On the group level, social collectives develop cultures of conflict that allow them to endure the strife. These cultures nurture beliefs of in-group love and out-group hate, breed discourses of group unity and cohesion, and sanction oppositional voices (Coser 1956). Just as external conflict brings to the fore communal attachment and collective concerns and priorities, so does the process of state building, particularly in its early years. These years are usually characterized by a scarcity of resources and strongly conflicting interests that threaten the entire nationalist project. These become times of intensified social mobilization wherein collectivist values largely dominate individualistic orientations, and collectivist social norms exercise extra power. The pre-state Jewish community (the Yishuv) and Israel in the 1950s and early 1960s is a good example, in contrast to Israeli society later on (Eisenstadt 1967; Horowitz and Lissak 1989). The Palestinian Authority is now at this stage, and this is well exemplified in school texts and curriculum (Brown 2003a). The normative grip of fundamental social values should therefore be meaningful in both societies, but more significant in the Palestinian than in the Israeli domestic game. Indeed, central societal values play a major role in shaping public opinion, public discourse, and the leaders' conduct in the Palestinian-Israeli game.

In the Israeli domestic game, the debate over the future of the territories captured in 1967 and the relations with the Palestinians is entrenched within a "security culture" embedded in the Holocaust and the nation-building experiences (Arian 1995; Bar-Tal 2007). This debate has encapsulated a value conflict between four fundamental values that can be traced to Israel's Declaration of Independence and comprise the basic tenets of Israeli political culture and its Zionist roots: Israel as a Jewish state and the homeland for the Jewish people, the principle of democracy, the yearning for peace and security, and territorial aspirations for a "Greater Israel" (Shamir and Shamir 2000).

The right of the Jewish people to its homeland embodies the Zionist justification for the establishment of the State of Israel. Concurrent with this value of Israel as a Jewish state, the second major semi-constitutional principle is that of democracy. The Declaration of Independence states that Israel will ensure complete equality of social and political rights to all its inhabitants, and the courts have further reinforced these rights over the years. These two values of Israel as both Jewish and democratic have been reiterated since the 1990s in legislation as the underlying foundation of the state. Further, the Declaration of Independence opens by referring to "Eretz Israel [Land of Israel]," binding the notion of the homeland closely to the land, another deeply ingrained value in the Zionist ethos of national revival. The Declaration also expresses aspirations for peace.

Much of Israeli politics revolves around the Arab-Israeli conflict, with the issue of the territories as the major source of contention, guided by different value priorities and value trade-offs. If Israel decides to opt for a democratic state with a Jewish majority, then the notion of keeping the territories becomes less realistic. If the country seeks Greater Israel, it must face a heightened probability of war, the possibility of a country without a Jewish majority, and either a bi-national state or trading off the democratic principles of equal political rights, and some even suggest a population transfer. Peace is attainable, according to the Israeli Left, only by returning the territories and ending the occupation. Those on the right of the political spectrum believe that the territories are strategically important, that only a strong Israel will eventually guarantee peace, and that the demographic problem can be offset by massive Jewish immigration. These are the value trade-offs that dominate Israeli politics and policy since the Six Day War.

The 1990s Oslo process signaled the primacy of the Jewish and democratic tenets and the aspirations for peace over Greater Israel. Sharon's Disengagement Plan and Olmert's Convergence Plan similarly indicated the predominance of the demographic factor and a willingness to trade territory to keep the Jewish state Jewish, and, albeit of lesser importance, also democratic, even if the prospects for achieving peace are not high. For example, in his December 18, 2003, Herzliyah speech, in which he announced his Disengagement Plan, Sharon began by emphasizing his "duty of shaping the face of the Jewish and democratic state of Israel."[9] Similarly, in his post-election speech on March 30, 2006, Olmert declared that "in the near future we will seek to shape the permanent borders of the state of Israel as a Jewish state with a permanent Jewish majority and as a democratic state."[10]

Palestinian society faces no less complex value trade-offs, and its political scene is similarly divided along five basic value dimensions and dilemmas, reflecting efforts over, and debates about, conflict, peacemaking, and state building. The hierarchy of priorities allocated to these values has changed over the years, reflecting the shifting political-security conditions. These values can be traced to three important documents: the Palestinian National Charter of 1968, the Palestinian Declaration of Independence of 1988, and the Draft Constitution of 2003. The Charter represented one phase of Palestinian political life, focusing on the conflict with Israel. In this phase the "liberation" of historic Palestine and the destruction of the State of Israel by means of armed struggle represented the most fundamental value underlying the creation of the Palestine Liberation Organization.[11] Although the Charter has been officially amended by the PLO in 1998 to remove references to liberation and the destruction of Israel, some factions, most prominently Hamas and Islamic Jihad, continue to this day to demand the return of historic Palestine to the Palestinians. The Charter of Hamas, published in 1988, argues that Palestinians can never abandon any part of historic Palestine since the land is considered an "Islamic Waqf," or religious trust, that can never be conceded to non-Muslims.[12]

The second fundamental value is the establishment of an independent and sovereign Palestinian state in the West Bank and the Gaza Strip, with East Jerusalem as its capital. Since the mid-1970s, the goal of independence and state building has become the basic tenet of the Palestinian national movement, and has been enshrined in the 1988 Declaration of Independence. Though decrying "the historical injustice done to the Palestinian Arab people" in 1948, the Declaration accepts the 1947 UN Partition Resolution 181 which, in its words, "partitioned Palestine into an Arab and a Jewish State." In fact, the Declaration opens by affirming that Palestine is "the land of three monotheistic faiths."[13] The Declaration asserts that the State of Palestine will adopt "a parliamentary democratic system of governance" and will be "based on freedom of expression and the freedom to form parties." Similarly the third draft of the Palestinian constitution, a document developed by the PLO in 2003 to be adopted once a state is established, asserts the Palestinian right to independence. The first article of the Draft Constitution reflects the yearning for a homeland by a dispersed people deprived of self-determination and normal citizenship status. Politically, however, it constitutes a purposeful statement by the Palestinian leadership that the nationalist project of state building is paramount to all other concerns.[14]

The third tenet might be labeled justice, and is embodied in the three pillars of the Palestinian position for a final status solution: the right of return, pre-1967 borders, and Jerusalem as the capital. Justice has, over the years, become the key idiom in Palestinian public discourse and in official statements to express Palestinian grievances and pleas to the international community. A 2003 PSR poll found that although the overwhelming majority of Palestinian refugees would seek to live in a Palestinian state or in the host country rather than in Israel, almost all refugees nevertheless insist that a permanent settlement with Israel will only be acceptable if Israel grants them the right of return to homes and properties inside Israel.[15] The right of return has gained the status of a sacred value, reflecting a discourse that centers on morality rights and entitlement rather than on utility gains and benefits. Justice also resonates powerfully with Arab and Muslim political culture, where it is a deeply rooted notion of good governance and the proper conduct of enlightened sovereigns (Sabet 1998).

The fourth fundamental value is Arab Islamic identity and unity as stated in the second article of the Draft Constitution: "The Palestinian people are part of the Arab and Islamic nations. Arab unity is a goal. The Palestinian people work on behalf of its realization" (Brown 2003b, p. 7). Similarly the Declaration of Independence states: "The State of Palestine is an Arab state, an integral and indivisible part of the Arab nation, at one with that nation in heritage and civilization." The relevance of this tenet in understanding the policy preferences of Palestinian leadership is vital.[16]

Although the unity clause refers broadly to all-Arab unity, it is the more specific Palestinian national unity that has gradually turned into a salient yet fragile value in the Palestinian political culture.[17] The quest for Palestinian national unity did not receive sufficient attention, perhaps because of the recurring failures to achieve it. However, it has shaped up to become a significant driving force in the Palestinian leadership's crucial policy decisions in recent decades. Modern Palestinian history has been marked by the substantial fragmentation of Palestinian society and deep divisions among its leading elites. These were often exploited by external forces such as the British and the Zionists during the mandate years, to undermine Palestinian national aspirations. The inability to organize their society to withstand these forces became a source of deep frustration and despair for Palestinians (Khalidi 1997). Palestinian society was further acutely fragmented following the 1948 war, which created the refugees' problem. Palestinians were dispersed among neighboring countries, primarily Jordan, Syria, and Lebanon, as well as other parts of the world. Those remaining in the West Bank, the Gaza Strip, and Israel became largely isolated from one another because of the political circumstances. Arafat and the PLO leadership understood from the outset that if they were to succeed, national unity had to be embedded into Palestinian political culture. Not only was it essential in rebuilding the shattered Palestinian national identity (Khalidi 1997), but it was also indispensable as a "harmonizing" instrument to control dissenting opposition forces (Brumberg 2003, 2004).[18] A political discourse stressing national unity is self-serving for societies involved in conflict and characterizes Israeli political culture as well.

Arafat and the PLO leadership, however, went beyond the use of national unity as just a rhetorical means. Over the years they made substantial efforts to integrate most Palestinian factions into the PLO.[19] Abu Mazin, who changed course on many of Arafat's policies, remained faithful to this legacy. Despite immense Israeli pressure to confront the Palestinian militant factions with force and "dismantle the terrorist infrastructure," he remained firm in his decision to co-opt them by integrating them into the Palestinian political game. This policy resulted in the April 2005 Cairo talks, where Hamas and the Islamic Jihad agreed to join the Palestinian national institutions and participate in the coming parliamentary elections.[20] The fragility of the Palestinian national unity value was exposed by the Hamas victory in January 2006, threatening powerful vested interests in the PA and their monopoly of the means of coercion.

For approximately a year after the elections, the Palestinians were still careful not to slip into internal strife. But occasional violence then took place, including dispersed fighting between PA security forces and Hamas militias. In an attempt to curb the explosive situation, the leadership of the prisoners from the various Palestinian parties jailed in Israel drafted, in May 2006, a National Conciliation Document that emphasized the need for national unity and listed eighteen points that would help reach this goal. The document obtained overwhelming support among Palestinians (in our June 2006 survey 74% supported it, and only 23% opposed it). Following Abu Mazin's threat to submit the document to a referendum, it was eventually endorsed by Hamas, and for a short time seemed to establish the basis for a new political status quo in the PA. Since then, however, the situation has further deteriorated into severe armed clashes in Gaza between Fatah and Hamas forces. This has been accelerated by Hamas's deployment of its own security force in defiance of Abbas's objections, and by a series of mutual assassinations and assassination attempts of senior security officials on both sides. During this entire period, efforts to form a national unity government failed, despite mediation attempts by Egypt, Jordan, Saudi Arabia, and others. On June 10, 2007, Hamas assumed a large-scale campaign designed to take over the Gaza Strip by force. This goal came to a full completion four days later when Hamas achieved full control over Gaza and established a separate government there. Once again Palestinian national unity was put in jeopardy.

The fifth fundamental value is peace and is asserted in the Declaration of Independence, which states that Palestine "announces itself to be a peace-loving state. . . . The State of Palestine herewith declares that it believes in the settlement of regional and international disputes by peaceful means, in accordance with the U.N. Charter and resolutions." The third article of the Draft Constitution states that "Palestine is a peace loving state that condemns terror, occupation, and aggression. It calls for the resolution of international and regional problems by peaceful means. It abides by the Charter of the United Nations." Just like Israelis, Palestinians perceive themselves as cherishing peace and involved in violence only for purposes of self-defense and reclaiming their rights.

These values require difficult trade-offs and balancing, similar to what Israelis face. Justice, especially when fueled by extremely high expectations, is difficult to achieve. An uncompromising position on the actual refugees' right of return may call for the surrender of peace or independence. With the route for independence and state building a major source of contention among Palestinian factions, unity, too, has been put to the test.

These values are powerful social forces in both societies, and the value trade-offs they entail present real and agonizing dilemmas for Palestinians and Israelis. For their leaders they signify both personal value conflicts and the political costs that any choice, but particularly wrong choices, may incur. Their actual decisions are thus influenced both by their personal attachment to these values and the likelihood and nature of costs they might pay in domestic politics as a result of powerful interests and general public opinion.

Behavioral Participatory Characteristics

Thus far we have compared the Israeli and Palestinian publics along the informational and normative dimensions. However, one cannot acknowledge public opinion and its impact in two-level games without considering its active, behavioral manifestations and its public and publicity aspects. These manifestations are at the heart of public opinion influence. They are the ones that often result in headlines and exert pressure on politicians, pressure that generates the motivation to consider the public's sentiment. Public opinion as public expression can range from symbolic and verbal expressions of opinion by individuals in different forums, through organized group activity and protest, to public referenda and election outcomes. What are the similarities and differences between Palestinians and Israelis within this dimension?

The most important difference between the Israeli and Palestinian publics relates to Israel as an independent state and a well-established democracy with regular elections, whereas the Palestinian Authority is not independent and is still in search of its constitutional makeup.

Israel is rated "free" by Freedom House, and receives a rank of 1 in political rights and 2 in civil liberties.[21] The rating Freedom House assigns to the Palestinian Authority/Israeli Administered Territories is combined. Under Arafat it was consistently rated as "not free," obtaining a score of 5 in political rights and 6 in civil liberties.[22] Following Arafat's death the 2006 civil liberties rating for 2005 improved from 6 to 5, and its status went from "not free" to "partly free," "due to an improved civil liberties environment that followed the death of Yasser Arafat and facilitated the success of relatively competitive and honest elections, along with the enhanced freedom of movement that followed Israel's abandonment of settlements in the Gaza Strip."[23] According to the Palestine Democracy Index, the status of democracy in 2005, under the presidency of Mahmoud Abbas and the Fatah parliamentary majority, has been assessed as receiving 509 points out of a maximum of 1,000 points. In 2006, under the control of Abbas and Hamas, the Index gave Palestinian democracy 481 points, a decrease of 28 points.[24] Despite this lower rating, however, far-reaching democratization reforms in the PA actually took place under the Abbas presidency, including free presidential and local elections in 2005 and the parliamentary elections in 2006 that resulted in a smooth transition of power. Before then, Palestinian residents of the West Bank and Gaza cast their ballot in general elections only once, in 1996, following the Oslo Accord and the establishment of the Palestinian Authority. However, when given the opportunity to participate in elections, Palestinians have done so at impressive levels. Palestinian turnout in the 2005 presidential elections is estimated to have been between 66 percent and 73 percent, depending on how it is calculated,[25] and in the 2006 parliamentary elections the turnout reached 75 percent.[26]

Not only are free general elections a relatively novel experience for Palestinians, but their parties and party system are less developed and less routinized compared to the Israeli system. Israeli occupation is at the root of this state of affairs, but analysts also emphasize the long-standing preference of Palestinian parties to invest in organization and direct action rather than in electoral competition. Palestinian parties have often shown a lack of interest in electoral politics, preferring dialogue and negotiation instead (e.g., Brown 2003a). This has characterized the PLO political life and Palestinian political culture in general for many years. Palestinian parties preferred to build their power base among labor unions and civil society organizations. As a result, Palestinians' political participation has been channeled into more informal modes of political participation, mobilized largely from above. Those include frequent support rallies, political advertisements, and letters of support published often in Palestinian newspapers. PSR's May 2006 survey found that 23 percent of the Palestinians identified themselves as members of nongovernmental organizations (NGOs), political parties, or labor and trade unions. About one-third indicated that they participated in meetings or other election-related activities.

We should also note the striking scope and diversity of Palestinian civil society, to a large extent the response of a society living under occupation and forced to organize itself for many years in the absence of a state providing essential public goods. This is not meant to indicate a complete detachment from authority or government. Rather, over the years, many governments have been involved in regulating and controlling these activities, including those of Lebanon, Jordan, and, of course, Israel. Moreover, Palestinian civil society organizations developed symbiotic relations with the PLO since its inception in 1964 and were considered an essential part of its state-building agenda. In time, and particularly since the establishment of the Palestinian Authority, the level of dependency of grassroots organizations and NGOs on the state further increased, given the PA's substantial efforts to regulate and control their activities.

In comparison with Palestinians, Israelis are accustomed to elections, election campaigns, and political parties as major political actors. Through 2006 they have participated in eighteen national election races.[27] Turnout in Israeli Knesset elections have fluctuated over the years at around 80 percent, but a noticeable decrease was observed in the 2003 and 2006 elections, to 68.9 percent and 63.5 percent, respectively.[28] It seems that Israelis are becoming disenchanted with traditional electoral politics and political parties, and are moving to less conventional forms of political participation, through protest demonstrations and civil society action groups (Wolfsfeld 1988; Yishai 2003; Arian and Shamir 2005).

When overt political action is involved, perhaps the most noticeable mode in which Palestinian public opinion makes itself visible is in its expressions of active resistance to the Israeli occupation, by peaceful as well as violent means. These expressions epitomize the prevailing norm of defiance and objection to the Israeli occupation and further reinforce the dominant nationalist climate of opinion surrounding the Intifada. Not surprisingly this nationalist sentiment has often been exploited to suppress genuine antigovernment criticism and protest in the PA, on the grounds that it hurts the struggle for national liberation. This has been the case, for example, with major teachers' strikes in 1997 and 2000, in which the PA used its security services to intimidate and arrest some of the strike leaders (Brown 2003a). A more recent strike took place in 2006 and was part of the power struggle between Fatah and Hamas. Mass demonstrations and rallies have not been rare in the PA but were usually organized either by the ruling party or by the strong opposition groups, Fatah and Hamas. Occasionally spontaneous instances of dissent have taken place to protest corruption or the strong hand of the PA security services, as in the violent demonstrations that erupted, in March 2000, at the Dehaishe refugee camp following the visit of Pope John Paul II in Bethlehem (Rubinstein 2001).

As for Israel, political protest has largely been tolerated by the authorities over the years. Nevertheless, there have been instances in which excess force has been used to suppress dissent, particularly against Arab citizens of Israel, at times with grave consequences. In October 2000 thirteen Arab protestors were shot and killed by the Israeli police during violent demonstrations in support of the Al-Aqsa Intifada. Dispersed acts of police violence have also been carried out against Orthodox Jews protesting the desecration of the Sabbath in Jerusalem and, more recently, against left-wing demonstrators protesting the building of the separation barrier. The largest scale of political protest was manifested in Israel in the summer of 2005 by disengagement opponents, primarily settlers from the West Bank.

Public Opinion Channels of Influence in Israel and the PA

Legitimacy—the voluntary deference to authorities—is considered a basic condition of rule for any regime. Legitimacy has a strong normative component and is often understood as the essential belief that everyone else defers to those in power. In other words, legitimacy is established when those involved in power relations share the belief that they are legitimate (Weber 1968). Such beliefs, however, are not whimsical and are usually grounded in substantive reasons that justify them. Thus, beyond the shared belief in the legitimacy of a regime, it is legitimate because it is congruent with people's values, satisfies their interests, and fulfills their expectations (Beetham 1991).

Until the institutionalization of elections in the PA, the influence of public opinion on foreign policy there worked primarily by means of informal channels and leaders' fear of losing their legitimacy. Yasser Arafat drew his power primarily from the unsurpassed level of legitimacy he managed to attain in the eyes of the Palestinian people. This level of legitimacy drew on both substantive and normative sources. Substantively he fulfilled the Palestinians' expectations beyond anyone's imagination. He gained world recognition for their tragedy, provided them with a strong sense of national identity, and brought them to the brink of establishing an independent state. Normatively these achievements and his persona have often been raised to mythological dimensions, serving to establish his extremely broad legitimacy base. This allowed Arafat to further personalize his rule, using effective neo-patrimonial practices (Frisch 1998) such as granting loyalists prestigious posts and access to illicit rent.[29] Under Arafat, the Palestinian Authority could be characterized as a liberalized autocracy[30] (Brumberg 2003). Arafat did everything he could to obstruct the establishment of institutions that would limit his control, including periodic elections and the enactment of a constitution. Institutions that were already in place Arafat systematically weakened, circumvented, or ignored. All this might imply complete disregard for public opinion, but actually Arafat's concern that his people see him as legitimate produced a far more reciprocal relationship with his public than the institutional analysis might suggest: People's values, expectations, and broad contours of policy aspirations acted as constraints on his political moves, as the case of Camp David, analyzed in the next chapter, exemplifies.

All this changed sharply with Arafat's death and with the electoral reforms implemented in the PA. Abu Mazin has never enjoyed Arafat's level of revolutionary legitimacy, and the institutional legitimacy he gained with his election for president has been critically eroded by defiant opposition factions, on the one hand, and Sharon's unilateral disengagement policy, on the other. Chapter 7 elaborates on this point.

Following the electoral reform in the PA, the channels through which Israeli and Palestinian public opinion have been affecting foreign policy became much more similar. In both systems, the public can exert its influence through formal and informal channels, and through ratification procedures and legitimacy threats. A good example of the latter in Israeli politics, discussed further in chapter 7, is the political struggle over Sharon's Disengagement Plan, which clearly entailed a fight over legitimacy. His opponents were trying hard to de-legitimize him (personally), the democratic institutions, and the decision itself. The disengagement proponents in turn relied heavily on public opinion polls that indicated substantial support for the plan.

As to formal channels, elections in Israel may be seen as having functioned as a relatively efficient mechanism of translating public opinion preferences into actual representation in the political arena, even during the era of Labor dominance (Etzioni 1959). This is especially the case since the 1990s, when dynamic representation can be established, and the dynamic relationship between leaders and their constituencies can be well encapsulated by the common rational choice logic which assumes that political actors are office seekers and will attempt to maximize the probability of being elected. As we demonstrate in chapter 8, in five of the six elections held, Israelis threw the incumbents out of office and altered the makeup of government. These choices at the ballot box followed their preferences on whether to pursue a more conciliatory or more activist policy toward the Palestinians, and were then generally translated into policy.

The logic of rational anticipation, where the political actors who wish to stay in power must consider their publics in order to keep their office, applies now more than ever to the Palestinian scene as well. The sweeping legitimacy the Fatah party owned as the embodiment of Palestinian national aspirations, and its historic role as the dominant party in Palestinian politics, did not save it from its devastating defeat in the 2006 elections. When given the opportunity, the Palestinian public held it accountable for institutionalizing corruption, and for its failure to enforce law and order in the Palestinian Authority.

CHAPTER FIVE

Camp David 2000
Tied Hands and Closed Lips

The question of who can walk away from negotiations without a deal is perhaps a better predictor of results than all the other factors combined.
—MARTIN INDYK, "CAMP DAVID IN THE CONTEXT OF US MIDEAST PEACE STRATEGY"

It is obvious that serious attention and concerted efforts must always be devoted to continuous, comprehensive public diplomacy—that is, explaining to the public the thinking behind the political process. But this did not happen in 2000. —GILAD SHER, "LESSONS FROM THE CAMP DAVID EXPERIENCE"

One of the most critical and formative junctures among the crucial events scattered along the path of the Oslo peace process between Israel and the Palestinians was the Camp David summit of July 2000. Not only did it dramatically alter the course of the peace process and the nature of the conflict, but its fingerprints will most likely remain imprinted on any future permanent settlement.

From our theoretical point of view, Camp David is a particularly notable case that highlights the role of public opinion as a domestic imperative in actual bargaining. It provides an opportunity to observe an event in which public opinion heavily constrained both negotiating teams who then failed to adequately cope with these constraints and also miscalculated each other's reservation price.[1] Camp David also exemplifies two sides of a central supposition in the two-level game paradigm: the "tied hands conjecture," which assumes that domestic constraints that narrow down the win-set provide a bargaining advantage; and the "closed lips syndrome," which

suggests that a reluctance to expand a narrow win-set by preparing a constraining public risks bargaining failure.

Camp David was the first serious attempt to grapple with the most difficult
and fundamental issues underlying the Israeli-Palestinian conflict. Despite
its eventual failure, it shed light on several vital dimensions of the conflict
that had previously been neglected or taken for granted. The ideas it generated will undoubtedly be incorporated into any future final status settlement when the time comes. A slew of books, papers, lectures, and academic
seminars attempted to decipher the riddle of what exactly happened at the
summit and who, if anyone, should bear the primary responsibility for its
collapse. Among the numerous accounts of the summit's breakdown, the
vast majority focused on the various elements of the game played by Arafat,
Barak, and Clinton on the international table. Fewer turned their attention
to the crucial games that took place on the domestic tables of the summit participants. One exception is Ben-Ami (2004), who painstakingly
describes Barak's disintegrating coalition while trying to reach a deal of historic dimensions with the Palestinians. Nevertheless, neither this nor most
other accounts of the summit provide a systematic analysis of Israeli and
Palestinian public opinion as a critical imperative in the summit's drama.
This chapter attempts to close this gap by examining the role of public
opinion in the Palestinian-Israeli two-level game before, during, and after
Camp David. We believe that public opinion played an important role in the
course of the summit and its outcome, and it is our hope that this analysis
will provide valuable lessons for the future. We suggest that Barak and Arafat entered Camp David with declining public support and eroding legitimacy for the ethos-shattering deal they were supposed to strike. However,
both failed to prepare their own and the other side's publics for the colossal
tasks they faced at the summit. This should have been an early warning
to all parties involved that the chances for a breakthrough were slim and
that they were heading toward a guaranteed failure. Public opinion preparation, as well as the absence of this preparation, often signals the breadth
of negotiators' win-set on the international table. Conciliatory public statements meant to prepare one domestic public could provide a bargaining
advantage to the other side. In addition, such statements might expose leaders to domestic pressures from their publics and to audience costs if their
public commitments do not materialize (Leventoglu and Tarar 2005). Leaders must then carefully assess whether consolidation or relaxation of public opinion constraints might provide a bargaining advantage or, instead, a
bargaining liability. In the case of Camp David, and given both sides' shaky

standing in their publics, Barak and Arafat seemed to have preferred to endorse the closed lips syndrome and refrain from public statements that might have exposed them either to additional demands from their interlocutor or to additional costs from their publics. We further believe that both leaders might have miscalculated each other's reservation price, failing to correctly estimate the amount of concessions the other side was willing and able to make in order to reach an agreement. Barak seemed to have erred in assessing Arafat's domestic degrees of freedom. Arafat in turn might have miscalculated Barak's political despair, given his faltering coalition government and his difficulty in walking away without a deal.

We divide our analysis into three main themes: first, the degree of preparedness of Palestinian and Israeli public opinion for the summit's ambitious goals; second, the closed lips syndrome that characterizes the treatment of public opinion in many two-level games; and, third, the Schelling conjecture (Schelling 1960; Milner 1997), which suggests that domestic constraints are often a bargaining advantage but under certain conditions (characteristic of the Camp David summit) might result in declining payoffs.

Public Opinion Goes to Camp David

Of the many accounts of the events that took place during the Camp David summit, there is largely a consensus regarding the details of how it came about. All generally agree that the summit was Barak's idea, that it was not difficult to convince the Americans to convene the summit, and that it was largely imposed on the Palestinians (e.g., Ben-Ami 2004; Sher 2001; Ross 2004; Ginossar 2005; Hanieh 2001).

The Camp David summit was the culmination of Barak's relentless effort to break away from the logic of the Oslo peace process to an all new regional game, incorporating Syria and Lebanon in addition to the Palestinians. Barak's timeline for this new game was unrealistic from the outset (Ben-Ami 2004) and eventually resulted in a hasty and premature convening of the Camp David summit. The first secret meetings with the Palestinians over a framework agreement for a final status settlement took place at the end of March 2000, approximately six months before the September 13 target date set in the Sharm el-Sheikh agreement for reaching a permanent status deal. The third "further redeployment" (FRD) scheduled for June 23 was another significant deadline that loomed on the horizon, adding to the pressures on Barak.[2] Barak feared that progressing along the interim path of Oslo and its follow-up agreements would deplete his domestic political capital and public support, and bankrupt him of any added political assets at a time he might need them the most (Ross 2004, p. 627; Swisher 2004). His sense of urgency was further exacerbated by Palestinian threats to declare independence, backed up by the Europeans, and his assessment that the peace process itself was on a collision course leading to a violent outbreak between Israel and the Palestinians (Barak 2005). Seeking to preempt these developments, Barak began to push for a quick summit meeting that would finalize a framework agreement for a final status settlement before the target date for the third FRD. Barak believed that a summit meeting would also serve as a means to prod the slow-moving Arafat to make decisions, and would test his sincerity with regard to a final status framework.

Once Barak raised the idea of a summit meeting, it was not difficult to persuade President Clinton to adopt the notion and eventually convene the summit. Some of the American negotiators were initially reluctant to accept the idea of a summit following the still painful embarrassment resulting from the recent failure of the Clinton-Assad summit in Geneva. Others, like David Miller (2005), feared that a century-long conflict could not be resolved during one week of negotiations, however intensive and resourceful those negotiations might be. Nevertheless, a permanent status agreement promised to strengthen the legacy that Clinton's presidency could leave for history apart from the Monica Lewinski episode, and time was running out (Indyk 2005).

Palestinians were also locked into a final status deal, and, given their unsatisfactory experience with Israel's reneging on past interim commitments, refused to consider any possibility of further interim agreements. They had to be virtually dragged to the summit. The Palestinians' reluctance stemmed from three major concerns. First, they assumed that the closer to the critical target date a summit is convened, the more leverage they might have on the Israelis. Second, Arafat may have suspected that Barak was planning to structure the summit as a take-it-or-leave-it deal. This is suggested by Arafat's repeated requests for assurances from Clinton that he not be blamed in case of failure (Swisher 2004). Finally, and perhaps most important, Arafat was aware of the erosion of his legitimacy and the support for the Fatah party among Palestinians since the signing of the Oslo Accord with Israel. Furthermore, given the end of the election term for the Palestinian Legislative Council and the office of president, he feared that, without electoral legitimacy, other sources of legitimacy, such as Islamist or pre-Oslo PLO revolutionary legitimacies, might reassert themselves (Shikaki 2004).

By the time the Oslo peace process was nearing the possibility of a successful conclusion, it had been long eroded by both sides' reckless imple-

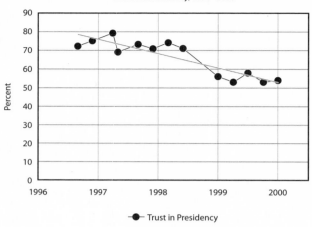

Figure 5.1. Percent of Palestinians Positively Evaluating the Performance of the PA Presidency, 1996–2000

mentation of its interim stages. Following Rabin's assassination, subsequent Israeli governments considered the Oslo process as an opportunity to consolidate their hold on the occupied territories by expanding the settlements there. The Palestinian leadership in turn viewed it as an opportunity to further its political aspirations rather than dedicate itself to the challenging task of state building. The Palestinian Authority established in the occupied territories was not the national entity to which Palestinians aspired. The neo-patrimonial system established by Arafat and the PLO old guard quickly developed into a protectionist system that nurtured corruption and suppressed civil rights (Brown 2003a; Frisch 1998; Shikaki 2004). Even more frustrating was the decline in the Palestinian economy and quality of life, a result of Israel's careless implementation of agreements and policies from which Palestinians would have benefited such as economic and water agreements that were never fully implemented (Dajani 2005; Swisher 2004). Finally, Israel's large-scale confiscation of land, along with its settlement policy, generated outrage and feelings of alienation from the PA, the official body held accountable for facilitating Israel's expansionist policy. Gradually the PA's standing began to diminish in the eyes of the Palestinians, and Arafat's legitimacy was severely crippled (Shikaki 2006b).

Figure 5.1 presents the percent of Palestinians positively evaluating the performance of the institution of the presidency from September 1996 to January 2000.[3] It is evident that Arafat's standing in the eyes of the Palestinians gradually declined over time. The figure also demonstrates that the most significant decline, from 71 percent to 56 percent, occurred in early

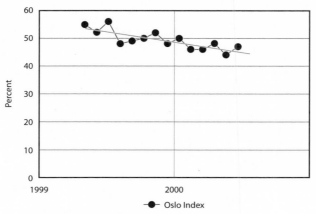

Figure 5.2. Oslo index during Barak's Tenure, 1999–2000

Source: *The Tami Steinmetz Center for Peace Research (www.tau.ac.il/peace/)*

1999 during Netanyahu's term in office as prime minister, and following the Wye River Plantation memorandum of October 1998.

Like the Palestinians, Israeli Jewish public opinion also demonstrated signs of disillusionment with the Oslo peace process before Camp David. This is evident in Figure 5.2, based on the Tami Steinmetz Center for Peace Research Oslo index that systematically tracks Israeli Jews' support for the peace process since the inception of the Oslo process.[4] Support for Oslo began to decline during Barak's tenure, immediately after he took office in May 1999 and more than a year before the Camp David summit was convened (Hermann and Yuchtman-Yaar 2002). Further decline occurred during 2000. The implementation of the second FRD and Palestinian demands to include three villages around Jerusalem in this redeployment were publicly debated during this period. Adding to these difficulties, violent Palestinian-Israeli clashes erupted on May 15, the Palestinian Nakba day, in which PA police and Israeli security forces exchanged gunfire in the worst fighting witnessed since September 1996. The last point in the figure (from June 2000) shows a slight recovery in the support for Oslo, probably reflecting a more general air of satisfaction with Barak's withdrawal from Lebanon in May of that year, or perhaps indicative of the climate surrounding the forthcoming summit. In any event, Barak's coalition began to disintegrate as the convening of the summit neared. Those who were among the first to disembark from Barak's Camp David bandwagon, for example, Nathan Sharansky, Barak's interior minister, and David Levi, his foreign minister, apparently accurately sensed the Israelis' disappointment with Oslo, along with the prevailing pessimism regarding the chances of reaching a settlement with the Palestinians.

Also noteworthy is that on the Palestinian side the decision to withdraw unilaterally and fully from Lebanon had serious unintended consequences on the Palestinian public, and on its expectations from its own leaders in their final status negotiations with Israel. In May 2000 young guard nationalists, led by Marwan Barghouti, were already openly challenging Arafat's control by orchestrating violent confrontations with the Israeli army to protest the lack of movement in the negotiations over the release of Palestinian prisoners from Israeli jails.

Closed Lips and Unprepared Publics

Not only did Barak and Arafat enter final status negotiations with less than the full backing of their publics, but most analysts agree that Israeli and Palestinian publics were not adequately prepared by their leadership for the colossal task that was an inherent assumption of the summit (e.g., Ben-Ami 2004; Ross 2004; Sayigh 2001).

For example, Yezid Sayigh, a noted professor of Middle East studies at King's College London and a former negotiator of the Oslo Accords, wrote that,

> [Arafat's] most serious leadership failing has arguably been the absence of any sustained effort to deliver a specific political message to the Israeli government, parliamentary parties and voting public. . . . The other side of the coin is the Palestinian leadership's failure to address its own constituency. . . . Indeed this is consistent with the PA leadership's reluctance throughout the negotiations (up to, and including the Camp David and Taba peace talks), to engage in debate, whether publicly or even internally, about the substance of what would constitute an acceptable deal. The close-lipped manner in which Arafat led the process . . . left the Palestinian public unprepared for necessary compromises and trade-offs, even when the balance of evidence suggested that the public correctly anticipated these and was willing to entertain them. (Sayigh 2001, pp. 53–54)

Sayigh goes on to accuse Israeli negotiators of the same error in judgment.

Our first joint survey, conducted a few days after the official announcement of the summit's collapse on July 26, documents the large gaps that existed then between the positions of Palestinians and Israelis regarding the core elements of the settlement negotiated by their leaders at the summit.

We asked our respondents to assess the positions of their respective delega-tions at the summit, based on reports that were already leaked to the media at the time of the survey.[5] Although these reports were incomplete, our sur-vey clearly showed that the ideas entertained at the summit as solutions to the core issues in dispute were way beyond both publics' "win-set," the set of agreements that would "win" support among domestic constituents.

For example, on the issue of an independent *Palestinian state and its borders,* only 41 percent of the Israelis supported the establishment of a Palestinian state on approximately 90 percent of the territories, including parts of the Jordan Valley and the annexation of major settlement blocks. Fifty-six percent of the Israelis felt that this was too much of a compro-mise. Among Palestinians, even fewer (43%) supported a much better deal: the establishment of a Palestinian state in 96 percent of the West Bank and the Gaza Strip, and receiving additional territory from inside Israel in exchange for the remaining 4 percent of settlement blocks that would be annexed to Israel. Fifty-one percent opposed it.

On the more difficult issues, the gaps were much greater. On the issue of *refugees,* 64 percent of the Israelis rejected as too compromising a solution in which Israel would acknowledge the suffering of the refugees, but with no moral or legal responsibility, and would annually absorb several thou-sands of refugees, with the rest of the refugee population resettled in the Palestinian Authority. The position that gained Palestinian majority sup-port (76%) was demonstrably entirely unacceptable to Israelis. It demanded Israeli admission of responsibility for the refugee problem, recognition of UN Resolution 194, and a willingness to absorb hundreds of thousands of refugees who wished to return to the Palestinian state. Even so, 20 percent of the Palestinians viewed this position as too great a compromise.

On *Jerusalem,* 36 percent of the Palestinians would accept, and 57 per-cent would reject, a solution in which Palestinians would maintain full sovereignty over the Arab neighborhoods and holy places in East Jerusa-lem, apart from the Jewish Quarter and the Western Wall, which would be under Israeli sovereignty, together with Ma'aleh Adumin, Givat Zeev, and Gush Etzion, and become part of West Jerusalem. Among Israelis, only 40 percent would accept, and 57 percent would reject, a solution that allowed full Palestinian sovereignty over some East Jerusalem neighborhoods and wide autonomy in others, together with a special arrangement in the Old City of Jerusalem, where Palestinians would become the guarantors of the Temple Mount under overall Israeli sovereignty.

Table 5.1 summarizes Palestinian and Israeli evaluations of their leaders' respective positions on the core elements of the settlement negotiations at

TABLE 5.1. Support for the Positions of Arafat and Barak at the 2000 Camp David Summit (%)

	Israelis (n=525)			Palestinians (n=1,259)		
	Too Much of a Compromise	Just Right	Not Enough of a Compromise	Too Much of a Compromise	Just Right	Not Enough of a Compromise
Arafat's/Barak's overall position at Camp David*	57	25	13	15	68	6
Arafat's/Barak's position on the issue of Jerusalem	57	24	16	57	27	9
Arafat's/Barak's position on the issue of refugees	64	22	11	20	68	8
Arafat's/Barak's position on the issue of the Palestinian state and borders	56	28	13	51	32	11
Arafat's/Barak's position on the issue of settlements	52	28	16	55	25	12
Arafat's/Barak's position on the issue of security arrangements	38	46	13	68	14	11
*Scale** mean		29.5			31.2	
s.d.		29.9			18.3	
reliability: Cronbach α		.91			.60	

* Figures represent raw percentages. DK/NA percentages are not presented.
** Scale scores were transformed so that they would range from 0 to 100 for comparability.

Camp David. It is apparent from the table that both publics felt there was no room for further compromise on the most critical issues of the conflict. In fact, the majority in both samples believed that their delegations offered too much of a compromise at the summit. Also evident is that, overall, Arafat received considerably greater support for his standpoint than Barak did. Sixty-eight percent of the Palestinian public thought at the time that the overall position taken by Arafat in the talks was correct compared to only 25 percent of the Israeli public who believed this with regard to Barak's position. Clearly, then, the leaders had exhausted their mileage for concessions in the eyes of their publics.

These vast discrepancies between Palestinian and Israeli public opinion were not obscure undercurrents but rather common knowledge. The substance of these core issues defined the essence of the Palestinian-Israeli conflict for generations and constituted the stuff of politics in both societies for many years. In fact, both Israelis and Palestinians were highly skeptical about the chances to resolve these discrepancies within a short period. For example, in April 2000 only 12 percent of the Palestinians trusted the intentions of the Israeli government headed by Barak toward reaching an Israeli-Palestinian peace settlement,[6] and in June 2000 only 18 percent of the Palestinians believed that a final status agreement between Israel and the PA could be reached by September 2000, the deadline specified in the Oslo Accord.[7] Similarly, a month before the summit, only 29 percent of Israeli Jews believed that the Israeli-Palestinian conflict could be resolved in the foreseeable future by the signing of peace agreements; 64 percent believed that "reaching peace is a lengthy process whose end is difficult to foresee."[8]

How can this failure to prepare public opinion be explained? It would be extremely difficult to attribute it to the notion that the leaders discounted the role of public opinion in policymaking. On the contrary, Barak's large appetite for public opinion polls throughout his period in office, and particularly during the Camp David summit, has been well documented (e.g., Hanieh 2001; Dajani 2005; Drucker 2002). Arafat, too, has been quoted often as expressing anxieties regarding his own public's reaction to sweeping compromises, including threats to his personal safety (e.g., Barak 2005, p. 119). The most plausible explanation for this low level of public opinion preparedness on both sides lies in the dynamics inherent in many two-level games of the kind Barak and Arafat played at Camp David. These dynamics often suggest a trade-off between the leaders' need to expand their own and the other side's win-set, and their desire to retain their bargaining edge. This dilemma is particularly relevant concerning public opinion constraints. Interactions between leaders and their publics are of necessity a matter of public record. Acts or statements designed to mold public opinion in more conciliatory directions might disclose information on the leader's reservation price. They are often taken to signal genuine policy preferences, given the leader's willingness to risk his political stakes by disclosing unpopular policy positions. This exposes leaders to further demands from the other side and can spoil the deal they were hoping to achieve at the outset. As a result, leaders tend to keep their lips closed, and, consequently, their hands remain tied by their unprepared constituency which again might undermine an agreement. We call this vicious circle the "closed-lips syndrome" and it is characteristic of many two-level games where public opinion is a decisive player on the domestic table.

Tied Hands—the Schelling Conjecture

Just as attempts to shift public opinion in a more conciliatory direction might weaken a negotiator's bargaining position, constraints by domestic veto players, such as an opposing legislator or a dissenting public, might provide a bargaining advantage. This is the well-known Schelling conjecture—the paradox of the power of the weak (Schelling 1960; Milner 1997). Putnam's (1988) seminal paper expanded on Schelling's argument and commented that a tied-hands strategy is often not perceived as credible. Indeed, Evans, Jacobson, and Putnam (1993) examined fourteen international bargaining case studies and concluded that a deliberate tied-hands strategy is infrequently used and usually ineffective. Putnam's original paper (1988) produced a host of research designed to specify the conditions under which the Schelling conjecture is supported (e.g., Mo 1994; Pahre 1997, 1999; Milner and Rosendorff 1997a, 1997b; Bailer and Schneider 2006; Fearon 1997; Hug and König 2002; König and Hug 2000; Lida 1993).

For example, Tarar (2001) modeled a case of international bargaining with two-sided domestic constraints and demonstrated that tied-hands claims are not necessarily a bargaining advantage when both sides are constrained. It depends rather on the relative level of their constraints, the game's turns, and the amount of information available—the leaders' respective beliefs regarding their own and the other side's constraints. Moreover, in cases where both sides are highly constrained, a delay in reaching an agreement may result in losses for both sides, where they receive discounted payoffs compared to what they would respectively be receiving if neither side were constrained.

Domestic Constraints and Information

In the case of Camp David both sides were clearly constrained by their publics, and the leaders devoted much attention to this understanding. It is also clear that Barak's assessments of his own degrees of freedom were better informed than Arafat's.

Most accounts of Barak's conduct at Camp David, and during his tenure in general, attest to the central role that public opinion–related considerations played in his policy decisions. One of the most detailed descriptions of Barak's affinity for public opinion polls is provided by Drucker (2002). Following his election for office, Barak established two separate and compartmentalized systems for public opinion research, which together conducted more than a hundred polls, not including numerous others conducted for him by several independent survey research organizations. During the period of the Camp David summit alone, Barak commissioned eight public opinion surveys, exploring, among other things, various configurations of potential final status packages with the Palestinians. The bottom line in these surveys, just as in our study, was that Israelis objected unequivocally to the division of sovereignty in Jerusalem that Barak eventually agreed to in Camp David (Drucker 2002, pp. 75–86, 206–234).

Arafat, too, was severely constrained by Palestinian public opinion, despite his tremendous prestige as the embodiment of the Palestinian nation and the Palestinian revolution (Shikaki 2004). Agha and Malley (2001) observed that, "unlike the situation during and after Oslo, there was no coalition of powerful Palestinian constituencies committed to the success of Camp David. Groups whose support was necessary to sell any agreement had become disbelievers, convinced that Israel would neither sign a fair agreement nor implement what it signed" (p. 71).

In addition, as indicated in Figure 5.1, Arafat's legitimacy gradually eroded over the years. By the time he arrived in Camp David he was left with a rather slim majority approval of the performance of his presidency. Contrary to what would intuitively be expected from an autocratic leader like Arafat, his sensitivity to public opinion was not less, and perhaps even more than, Barak's. Indeed, as we suggested in chapter 4, autocratic leaders paradoxically tend to highly value political legitimacy precisely because they cannot draw upon institutional legitimacy.

A systematic examination of the Palestinian press before and during the summit reveals three major themes that reflect much concern with public opinion: first, a need to assure the Palestinian public that Arafat stands firm on Palestinian interests, particularly on Jerusalem and the right of return, and will not "sell them away" by any means; second, an attempt to moderate expectations with regard to the chances for the summit's success; and, third, building a case for blaming a possible failure on Israel and the U.S. Indeed, as the summit approached, and during the negotiations themselves, Palestinian newspapers printed numerous petitions and ads, and Palestinian streets witnessed many rallies in support of Arafat's heroic efforts to withstand Israeli and American pressures. These and other public expressions, though far from being spontaneous, nevertheless might have left their impressions on Arafat, who often asked to see these reports and petitions in person. In contrast to Barak's account of public opinion, Arafat's was apparently much more impressionistic and self-serving. Omar Dajani quotes one of the PLO political advisers on this point: "The two sides have a different sense of public opinion. For Israelis it's connected to elections, etc. It's much more structured. Ours is very impressionistic. Of course when we're negotiating we mention public opinion. But we never came with a poll. We would come and say public opinion would screw us, but we never produced the tools. We tend to think about other power centers, instead" (Dajani 2005, p. 68).

Miscalculating the Game

We believe that the breakdown of the Camp David summit lies in informational deficits and leaders' miscalculations regarding the other side's reservation price. It appears that Barak failed to acknowledge Arafat's concerns regarding his domestic constraints, projecting his own beliefs onto Arafat. According to Ross (2004), Barak's estimates of his margin for concessions to the Palestinians was based on his belief that he would be able to convince Israelis to accept far-reaching concessions if he could only promise them the end of conflict with no more claims forthcoming from the Palestinians.[9] In a personal interview,[10] Barak explained these assessments, saying that an end-of-conflict clause would have amounted to a conceptual turnabout for Israelis and a complete change of reality. A conceptual change of this scale, he added, is difficult to simulate in public opinion polls using hypothetical questions. This is why he was not overly concerned at the time with the discouraging poll results. Moreover, he reasoned at the time that he would have to sway only half the opposing public, which was viewed as a realistic goal.

Consistent with these beliefs, Barak attributed much importance to the leader's abilities to rise above domestic constraints. In his interview with Barak, Morris (2002) says that despite the fact that intelligence assessments of the chances of success at Camp David was 50 percent, Barak's "own feeling at the time was that he 'hoped Arafat would rise to the occasion and display something of greatness, like Sadat and Hussein, at the moment of truth. They did not wait for a consensus [among their people], they decided to lead.'" Barak also tended to dismiss Arafat's anxieties regarding his personal safety if he ventured too far in concessions to Israel.

Given Barak's well-documented convictions regarding his own degrees of freedom, we suspect that Barak, projecting these beliefs onto Arafat, failed to assess Arafat's concerns realistically regarding his own domestic constraints.

As for Arafat, it seems that Barak's domestic constraints impressed him little and did not produce significant concessions. Indeed, Arafat viewed Barak's disintegrating coalition government as a bargaining vulnerability, signaling an acute need for a comprehensive agreement that would save his political future. Commenting on Barak's situation, Martin Indyk (2005, p. 29) stated that "[Barak] had already expended so much political capital on the [Camp David] process that his political future was hanging by a thread. He could survive politically only by concluding a deal." Arafat's miscalculations may have been reinforced by Barak's negotiation style, according to Ben-Ami (2004) and Malley (2005). Ben-Ami (2004) has criticized Barak's approach in negotiating the status of Jerusalem as inconsistent, maintaining that his red lines were quite flexible. "This approach, and not his initial generous proposals, entrenched Arafat in his positions, causing him to think that he could extort more and more from Barak" (p. 186). Similarly Agha and Malley commented on Arafat's refusal to accept the parameters that Clinton advanced to the two sides on December 23, five months after the Camp David talks ended. They wrote that "given the history of the negotiations, they [Palestinians] were unable to escape the conclusion that these were warmed-over Israeli positions and that a better proposal may still have been forthcoming."[11] These hopes were probably fueled by the Palestinian public's high expectations from the summit's result, as evident in Table 5.1, feeding back into the negotiation process.

CHAPTER SIX

The Eruption of the Intifada

The Role of Violence in Two-Level Games

It is of course well known that the only source of war is politics—the inter-course of governments and peoples. . . . We maintain . . . that war is simply a continuation of political intercourse, with the addition of other means.

—CARL VON CLAUSEWITZ, *On War*

The failure of the Camp David talks proved to be critical in the course of the Palestinian-Israeli conflict, and approximately two months later the Al Aqsa Intifada (the second Intifada) broke out. Pessimism and mutual mis-trust engulfed Israelis and Palestinians alike. We begin this chapter by dis-cussing how the two sides framed the failure of the negotiations, and then examine public opinion since the eruption of the Intifada and the role of violence and hope in the Israeli-Palestinian two-level game.

Framing the Failure of the Negotiations

The collapse of the Camp David summit sent strong shockwaves into both Palestinian and Israeli societies, resulting in mirror image frames but contrasting reactions to the leaders in the two publics. Whereas Barak's popularity sank further and he was eventually ousted from his post as prime minister, Arafat returned to the PA as a victor, having successfully held back a coordinated American-Israeli plot to defeat the Palestinians and deprive them of their national aspirations.

Arafat and the Palestinian leadership presented the Camp David failure as proof that Israel will never accept a historic compromise, one that would give it 78 percent of historic Palestine—the territories Israel acquired in the

1948 war—while offering the Palestinians the remaining 22 percent that Israel occupied in 1967 (Qurei 2007).[1] Arafat, repeatedly insisting that the Israelis were not ready for peace, concluded that they did not view the Palestinians as peace partners. He asserted that Israeli demands regarding holy places could lead to a spectacular religious war; that the Israelis wanted everything, including an end to the conflict and recognition, without paying the price; that they did not want to return all the land, did not want to concede full sovereignty to a Palestinian state, and did not want to pay any price for their role in the creation of the refugee problem. He asserted that he had no peace partner on the Israeli side, that the Americans did not play the role of an honest broker, and that the point of departure for U.S. policy was the protection of Israel's vital needs and the desire to save Barak's coalition. Arafat felt that American bridging proposals were, in fact, Israeli ideas (Haniyeh 2001). Ahmed Qurei (2007) (also known as Abu Ala), the top Oslo negotiator, placed the responsibility for the failure at Barak's and Clinton's doorstep.[2]

This has become the dominant frame to explain the Camp David failure in the Palestinian press and commentary. Akram Hanieh, who was the editor in chief of the Palestinian daily *Al-Ayyam* and a member of the Palestinian team at Camp David, promoted this frame, writing that "what was strange was that the Israelis thought they could, with American support, impose their peace on the Palestinians" (Hanieh 2001, p. 81). He further stressed that, "at Camp David, Yasser Arafat fought tooth and nail to defend Palestinian national rights, including in Jerusalem" (p. 85). Hanieh then went on to detail the three lines of defense Arafat used at Camp David that align this frame with the Palestinians' cherished values and narrative, outlined in chapter 4: first, faithfulness to the aspirations of the Palestinian people who unanimously refuse to give up their rights; second, Palestinian rights are historic rights and have acquired international legitimacy; and, third, any concession, particularly in Jerusalem, concerns the larger Arab world of which the Palestinians are an integral part, and, as such, they do not have the liberty to make these concessions on their own. The cultural values underlying this frame are accountability, justice and entitlement, and Arab unity.

The frame promoted by Barak resonated in turn with fundamental Israeli values and central themes in the Israeli narrative, as discussed in chapter 4 (see, too, Arian 1995; and Bar-Tal 2007). Barak's frame has been summarized succinctly in his interview with Benny Morris (2002, p. 42): "The true story of Camp David was that for the first time in the history of the conflict the American president put on the table a proposal, based on UN Security Council resolutions 242 and 338, very close to the Palestinian demands, and Arafat refused even to accept it as a basis for negotiations, walked out of the room, and deliberately turned to terrorism. That's the real story—all the rest is gossip." Barak went on to describe Arafat's plot to annihilate Israel gradually and in stages.[3] The "stages plan"[4] resonated with the deepest Israeli Holocaust fears and anxieties, and Barak's insinuation of these fears in his frame of the Camp David failure was clearly a strategic framing step on his part.

A third theme in Barak's frame was that the Palestinians did not come to Camp David to negotiate in good faith, and that for the time being Israel did not have a real partner for peace. Although he did not use these precise words, he presented a gloomy outlook of the chances for success of future negotiations, and consequently advocated unilateral steps on the part of Israel. The "no partner" claim was perpetuated later on by Sharon, Netanyahu, and Olmert, and it became the major justification for Sharon's unilateral steps in the following years.

Barak's strategic framing of the Camp David failure was effectively orchestrated (Bar-Tal and Halperin 2008; Rachamim 2005; Swisher 2004; Wolfsfeld 2004), and it proved to be extremely successful and damaging. It resonated well with basic Israeli cultural tenets, and actual developments in the course of the conflict granted it credibility among Israelis. First and foremost was the eruption of the second Intifada in September 2000, two months after the summit's collapse.

On September 28 Ariel Sharon, in his capacity as opposition leader, visited the Al-Aqsa mosque plaza of the Temple Mount (Haram Al-Sharif) in the Old City of Jerusalem, escorted by Likud party officials and a large force of Israeli riot police. The compound is the holiest site for Jews and the third holiest site for Muslims. Although they did not enter the Muslim mosques, Palestinians considered the visit a deliberate political move to assert Israelis' right to visit the Temple Mount, restricted until then by Israeli security authorities and forbidden by a rabbinical injunction against visiting the Temple Mount. Like many other events in the Israeli-Palestinian conflict, the actual circumstances of the visit are disputed, particularly the extent to which it was coordinated and approved in advance. The visit ended without any explicit violent incidents, despite Fatah leaders' calls for mass demonstrations (Enderlin 2003). On the following day, Friday, at the conclusion of prayers in the mosques, riots erupted in the Old City of Jerusalem. Four Palestinians were shot and killed, and 160 were wounded. Fourteen police officers were also wounded (Enderlin 2003). The Al-Aqsa Intifada had begun.

The eruption of the Intifada was viewed by Israelis as the most convincing evidence for the Palestinians' premeditated plan to impose their conditions on Israel. Arafat, who did not enjoy much international credibility, could not hope to convince Israelis that this was, in fact, a national uprising and that he could not control the conflagration. In addition, Clinton, who had significant leverage among Israelis, blamed Arafat for the failure, thereby adding further credibility to Barak's frame. But, above all, this frame resonated with Israelis' most deeply held beliefs, values, and narratives. Revisionist voices began to be heard only months later, but they were weak, and they would not succeed in cracking Barak's frame for a long time. Some of the counter-frames attempted to repudiate Barak's insinuation of the PLO's "stages plan," arguing that if Palestinians indeed contemplated such a plan, it would have been in their interest to accept Clinton's proposals at Camp David rather than reject them, since a Palestinian state would have been a useful springboard to the implementation of such a plan. Others raised reservations over Barak's portrayal of what he termed a generous Israeli offer (Dajani 2005; Agha and Malley 2001; Swisher 2004; Enderlin 2003: Rubinstein et al. 2003), and still others contradicted his claims that Palestinians made no concessions at all (Telhami 2001).

Barak's frame was quite damaging to subsequent efforts to resolve the conflict and, together with the spreading violence, generated pessimistic expectations and a hawkish climate of opinion in the Israeli public. If, in February 2000, 71 percent of Israeli Jews believed that peace would be enhanced over the next three years, this figure dropped to 35 percent in April 2001 (Arian 2001). Eventually Barak's narrative did not save his political career, and his defeat to the more hawkish and militant Ariel Sharon in the 2001 elections for prime minister was unprecedented. Paradoxically the "no partner" frame weakened following the rise of Hamas and the failure of the Gaza unilateral disengagement. Israelis have come to recognize gradations in the Palestinian leadership and overwhelmingly supported talks with Abu Mazin and the Fatah leadership (60% in our March 2006 survey and over 70% in June 2006, compared to only about half the public that supported talks with Hamas at that time).

On the Palestinian side, the failure of the Camp David summit and its framing rendered Arafat a victor who held firm against the Americans and Israelis. However, this left him and the nationalists' old guard with a failed peace process, allowing the more militant young guard nationalists and Islamists to seize the initiative, as we detail later in this chapter. Arafat, too, may have felt that without the pressure of violence Israel might not show more flexibility than it did at Camp David. He had already seen young nationalists threaten, in May 2000, to resort to violence because of Israel's refusal to release Palestinian prisoners. He complained to Labor Knesset member Dalia Itzik that the young guards, under the influence of the Hezbollah model, were pressing him to allow them to return to an armed struggle in the face of Israeli intransigence. The climate of opinion among Palestinians became cloudy, paralleling that among Israelis, and pessimism engulfed expectations on both sides. If, in the July 2000 poll, 23 percent thought that the peace process "is dead and there is no chance of reaching an agreement in the coming years," this figure doubled to 46 percent in July 2001; 59 percent expected violence and confrontations over the next five to ten years, almost double that of the previous year (31%).

In summation, in the aftermath of the failure at Camp David, the framing process utilized by the leaders on both sides focused on the delegitimation of the other, denying that there is a partner, and declaring the impossibility of reaching a settlement through diplomacy. Thus diplomacy was discredited and violence became the alternative.

The Role of Violence and Use of Force in Two-Level Games

Clausewitz's description of war as a "continuation of politics [*politik*, in German] by other means" is well known. However, the meaning of the German term he used is somewhat vague and has been taken to mean both policy and politics. Clausewitz understands policy as representing all the interests of a community; and hence war, as the implementation of foreign policy, is intimately related to domestic politics as well. Given the revolution in military affairs since Clausewitz's times (Esposito 1954), scholars have been debating the relevance of Clausewitz's ideas to modern violent conflicts, which are usually on a small scale and often take the shape of national liberation wars, terrorism,[5] and ethnic conflicts. However, since all these forms of political violence are motivated by political goals, we can confidently apply to them Clausewitz's conception of war as an instrument of policy, and as one affected by domestic politics. We argue here that public opinion, a central actor in the domestic political arena, played a major role in defining the leaderships' preferred policy options—violence versus diplomacy—and often determined the intensity of the violence.

Throughout the book public opinion is cast as an active and informed player in the Palestinian-Israeli two-level game. We suggest that public opinion contains a prospective informational component that is embodied in the aggregation of people's expectations. These serve as an aggregated foresight that functions as a collective and dynamic social force. In chapter 4 we demonstrated that both the Israeli and Palestinian publics are well informed and hold similar expectations as to the future course of the conflict. Throughout the book we document policy constraints and opportunities that Israeli and Palestinian public opinion put to their leaders. Here we suggest that the policy dimensions affected by public opinion are not restricted to negotiations at the international table but rather cover the full range of leaders' strategic decisions in a two-level game.

In this regard, the adoption of armed struggle as an instrument of policy has been well understood and overwhelmingly supported by the Palestinian public, as we discuss in detail in the next section. When asked, in December 2000, to select the best way to achieve Palestinians' national goals and end the occupation—the Intifada only, negotiations only, or both—52 percent of the Palestinians preferred the use of both instruments whereas the other options gained 28 percent and 12 percent, respectively.[6] Similar results were obtained throughout this period. These preferences highlight a classic dispute that has long characterized national liberation conflicts and attempts to resolve them: the weaker side seeks to maintain the use of force as a policy instrument by all possible means, whereas the stronger side seeks to deny its use as a legitimate instrument. The Palestinian-Israeli international game can be easily cast in these terms, too. Sharon's call for dismantling the terrorist infrastructure was meant, first and foremost, to delegitimize the use of violence by Palestinians. Similarly Israel's insistence on applying the Roadmap framework to any renewed political process with the Palestinians was part of this classic international game, as the Roadmap calls for the PA to conduct effective operations aimed at dismantling terrorist capabilities.

Our conception of public opinion as a central domestic imperative capable of forming aggregate rational considerations suggests that public opinion, like other collective domestic players, behaves in a rational manner in the domestic game in order to influence the international game of their home country. The literature on rational choice in international relations provides notable cases that establish this point. For example, Dorussen and Nanou (2006) demonstrate that political parties in the European Union member states respond to a decline in their states' bargaining power because of European integration policies by a decline in the range of policy alternatives, and converge to more common positions that more effectively tie the hands of the national government, thus increasing its negotiation power. Similarly we maintain that both Israeli and Palestinian publics understand the nature of the game in which mutual violence and diplomacy alternate with, and impact, each other throughout the course of the conflict. For example, in a 2005 poll, the majority of Israelis (54%) believed that if no progress was made in the negotiations with the Palestinians, a third Intifada was bound to erupt.[7] Given the changing circumstances, the weight the two publics put on these alternative means changed, and they conveyed their expectations to their leadership accordingly. Studies in political psychology have added the role of external and perceived threat to these dynamics in leading individuals to support aggressive violent reactions to the enemy, as well as more militant political forces in their own society. Such findings on the individual level abound, among Israelis, Palestinians, and in other societies as well (e.g., Arian 1989; Friedland and Merari 1985; Gordon and Arian 2001; Herrmann, Tetlock, and Visser 1999; Huddy et al. 2005; Huddy, Feldman, and Cassese 2007).

In chapter 8 we demonstrate how Israelis' preference for diplomacy versus military means has fluctuated over the years since the first Intifada began, in response to political developments, and how these preferences influence electoral outcomes.[8] With Palestinians, too, these preferences ebb and flow in relation to events and developments in the conflict, as we detail in the next section.

Growing Support for Violence
The 1990s—A Prelude to the Second Intifada

Palestinian PSR[9] survey data from the second half of the 1990s indicates that support for negotiations remained high throughout this period, reflecting public confidence in diplomacy. Between 1993 and 2001, with the sole exception of 1994, Palestinian support for the Oslo agreement never dropped below 60 percent. Throughout most of this period, a majority of Palestinians viewed negotiations as the most effective means of achieving vital Palestinian national goals. Subsequently, in most surveys, the number of respondents supporting violence was lower than the number opposing it. Nevertheless, a clear trend toward increased support for violence was evident from the period of Netanyahu's term in office. Figure 6.1 shows the overall trend and the ups and downs in Palestinians' support and opposition for "armed attacks against Israeli targets" leading to the second Intifada, in the period between September 1995 and July 2000.

In September 1995, when optimism about the success of the Taba/Oslo II negotiations was prevalent, 71 percent supported the continuation of negotiations and only 18 percent supported armed attacks against Israeli civilians inside Israel. In March 1996, in the aftermath of several suicide attacks against Israeli civilians inside Israel, public support for the "current peace process" reached 78 percent and only 21 percent supported armed attacks against Israelis. Indeed, three-quarters of the Palestinians believed

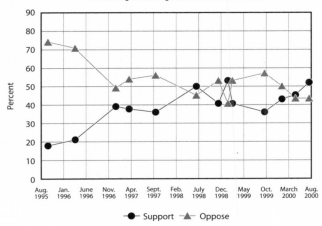

Figure 6.1. Support for and Opposition to Armed Attacks against Israeli Targets among Palestinians, 1995–2000

that armed attacks against Israelis would impede the peace process. Therefore only 32 percent opposed the crackdown on the Islamists who carried out the suicide attacks at that time, whereas 59 percent supported them. In other words, to most Palestinians, negotiations were seen as the best means of achieving Palestinian goals, and violence was viewed as counterproductive and consequently should be avoided.

The election of Netanyahu in 1996 affected Palestinian public support for violence but did not reduce support for the continuation of the peace process. Growing distrust in the intentions of the new Israeli leadership boosted the search for alternative means to end the occupation, and in December 1996, six months after Netanyahu's election, support for violence increased to 39 percent. But most Palestinians did not consider diplomacy useless, and 79 percent supported the peace process. Increased support for violence at this time reflected not only early doubts about the viability of diplomacy but also a greater perception of threat among Palestinians. This was a result of Israel's decision, in September 1996, to open a tunnel in an area adjacent to Muslim holy places in Jerusalem's Al-Haram Al-Sharif, resulting in violence and dozens of casualties on both sides.

The four surveys between June 1998 and February 1999 provide an exceptional demonstration of how public opinion is intrinsic to the Palestinian-Israeli two-level game by closely following and responding predictably and promptly to events and developments. In a period of less than a year, Palestinians' support for armed attacks against Israeli targets oscillated significantly in response to Israeli policy and domestic developments within Israel. In

June 1998, with the Netanyahu government ignoring the deadline for further redeployment from the West Bank, support for violence increased considerably, to 50 percent. In November 1998, two weeks after the signing of the Wye Memorandum in Washington, D.C., the support for negotiations increased to 75 percent and support for violence decreased significantly to 41 percent. Only two months later, in early January 1999, following the Israeli government's decision to suspend the implementation of the Wye agreement, support for armed attacks against Israelis jumped from 41 to 53 percent, and support for the peace process dropped to 66 percent. Public response to the stalemate in 1999 was to demand diplomacy and violence simultaneously. The pubic saw armed attacks as a tactic, and as a means of responding to perceived Israeli intransigence and violation of peace agreements, but when asked to choose between diplomatic and non-diplomatic options a majority (60%) still supported the diplomatic option and only 30 percent supported violent means. Once the government of Netanyahu fell and new elections in Israel were agreed upon in January 1999, Palestinian public opinion changed quickly again. By the end of January into early February 1999, support for the peace process had risen to 73 percent, and the level of support for armed attacks against Israeli targets dropped to 41 percent.

In September 1999, following the electoral victory of Labor and Ehud Barak, support for the peace process stood at 75 percent and support for violence dropped to 36 percent. But with growing frustration and impatience with the Barak government's lack of progress in the peace process, support for armed attacks against Israelis increased once again.

In the aftermath of the failure of the Camp David summit, in July 2000, 44 percent of the Palestinians believed that, despite the failure, talks would resume soon enough and no violence would erupt; only 21 percent anticipated that confrontations and an Intifada would break out in the West Bank and Gaza, and that the parties would not return to the negotiations. However, public support for violence increased to 52 percent, and, as a consequence of the Israeli unilateral withdrawal from Southern Lebanon in May, 63 percent believed that the Palestinians should emulate Hezbollah's violent methods. Moreover, 60 percent supported resorting to violent confrontations with the Israelis if no agreement was reached with Israel by September 13, 2000, the deadline for the end of the Oslo interim period. If confrontations erupted, 57 percent believed that they would help achieve Palestinian rights in ways that negotiations could not. These findings indicated that for the first time the Palestinian public had lost confidence in diplomacy altogether, and was willing to embrace violence as an alternative means of ending the occupation.

Since 2000: Two Belligerent Publics

The realities and overriding frames of "diplomacy failing" and "violence paying" paved the way for the outbreak of the second Intifada. The mutual bloodletting increased the perceptions of threat considerably and resulted in two belligerent publics. At the source of this belligerence were the rational strategic considerations concerning the use of force versus diplomacy as well as motives of psychological threat, fear, and revenge. The election of Netanyahu in 1996, the continued building of Jewish settlements in the West Bank and the Gaza Strip, and the Camp David failure in 2000 shifted Palestinian thinking regarding the role of diplomacy, leading to a swell of pessimism. Palestinian expectations that the peace process would soon lead to statehood and a permanent settlement dropped from 44 percent during the period when Shimon Peres was prime minister (1995–96) to 30 percent in the first year of Netanyahu's term of office. Four years later, with Ehud Barak having replaced Netanyahu and Jewish settlements continuing to expand, the expectation of a permanent settlement sank to 24 percent.[10] Once Ariel Sharon was elected as Israel's head of government in early 2001, a mere 11 percent of Palestinians clung to that hope. The perception that Hezbollah had been effective in forcing a unilateral Israeli withdrawal in 2000, and—as we discuss in the next chapter—that the Israeli unilateral withdrawal from the Gaza Strip in 2005 was the outcome of Palestinian use of armed struggle, fueled the belief that violence pays. Responding to the July 2000 failure of the Camp David summit, 57 percent of Palestinians believed that Palestinian "confrontations" with the Israelis would help them achieve national rights in ways that negotiations could not. One year after the eruption of the Intifada, 71 percent of Palestinians thought that the fighting had already produced this effect. Figure 6.2 tracks public opinion on this issue through 2005. An overwhelming majority of Palestinians, two-thirds on average, continued to view armed confrontations as helping Palestinians achieve national rights in ways that negotiations could not. In September 2005, following the Gaza disengagement, 73 percent thought so.

The Intifada, moreover, generated the perception of individual and collective threats caused by increased pain and suffering as a result of Israeli preventive and retaliatory steps aimed at curtailing Palestinian violence. These included the massive use of force, restrictions on movement by means of check points and closures, reoccupation of Palestinian areas in the West Bank, the demolition of homes, confiscation of land, and construction of settlements.

In July 2000, immediately following the failed Camp David summit,

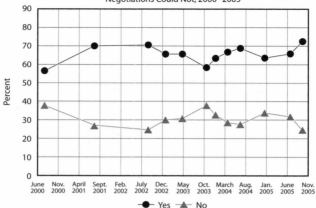

Figure 6.2. Belief That Armed Confrontations Have Helped
Palestinians Achieve National Rights in Ways That
Negotiations Could Not, 2000–2005

Note: In July 2000, the question was: "if Palestinian-Israeli *confrontations* were to erupt in the West Bank and the Gaza Strip, would they help achieve Palestinian rights in ways that negotiations could not?" After the eruption of the Intifada, the question was about the role of "*armed* confrontations."

the level of support for violence among Palestinians reached 52 percent. A year later, in July 2001, and again in December 2001, support for violence increased to 58 percent. Most Palestinians placed the goal of "ending occupation" as their top priority. The majority of Palestinians also believed that negotiations would not succeed and that armed attacks had so far achieved, and would continue to achieve, Palestinian national rights in ways that negotiations could not. A year into the Intifada, a clear majority believed that only violence would end the occupation. Figure 6.3 presents the Palestinians' support and opposition for "armed attacks against Israeli targets" between 2001 and 2004. Throughout this period, with one exception, more Palestinians supported than opposed these armed attacks.

Palestinians continued to support violent means in the conflict, although this support peaked during the first year of the Intifada. In the next polls the percentage declined somewhat, oscillating between 53 and 48 percent. The reoccupation of the Palestinian cities, the ongoing Israeli military operations in the West Bank, the beginning of the construction of the separation barrier, and the gradual evolvement of a political horizon by the U.S. call to establish a Palestinian state and the development of a Roadmap in that direction—all these may have played a role in undermining the belief that violence pays and that no benefit is to be gained from diplomacy. It is also worth remembering that support for negotiations remained high throughout the years of the Intifada, reaching 71 percent in December 2001 and 79 percent in December 2004, despite disbelief in their viability. In November 2002 more than three-quarters supported a

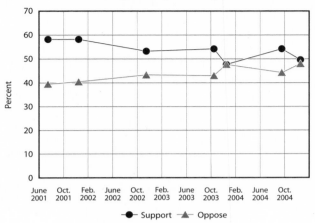

Figure 6.3. Support for and Opposition to Armed Attacks against
Israeli Targets among Palestinians, 2001–2004

mutual cessation of violence on both sides, and a majority of 54 percent supported the Roadmap plan.

The death of Yasser Arafat in November 2004 generated significant optimism in both publics, as he personified the dead end reached in the conflict. In December 2004 a majority of 53 percent believed that Arafat's death would increase the chances for a political settlement with Israel, whereas only 23 percent believed it would decrease those chances. Support for a cease-fire and for an immediate return to negotiations was high, reaching 80 percent for each. Support for armed attacks against Israeli civilians inside Israel dropped from 54 percent three months earlier to 49 percent. In March 2005 the suicide attack that took place in Tel Aviv received the support of 29 percent of those polled, and 67 percent opposed it; this compares to a level of support of 75 percent and 77 percent, respectively, for the suicide attacks at the Maxim Restaurant in Haifa in October 2003 and in Beer Sheva in September 2004.

The analysis of Palestinian public opinion regarding the use of force from the mid-1990s through the mid-2000s established that support for violence increased most significantly before the outbreak of the Intifada. Throughout the period we have studied, the viability of the diplomatic route versus the promise of violent means in the Palestinian national liberation struggle proved to be the most important element. When diplomacy proved effective, opposition to violence increased. Termination of negotiations when violence erupted left people dependent on violence as the only means to address grievances and deliver gains. Beyond the viability of the

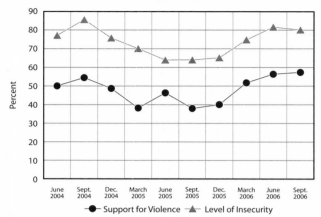

Figure 6.4. Threat Perception and Support for
Violence among Palestinians, 2004–2006

Support for Violence —▲— Level of Insecurity

Note: Figures for "support for violence" reflect support for "armed attacks against Israel targets."
Figures for "level of insecurity" reflect answers to the question about "feeling" of personal and family insecurity.

diplomatic route, threat and revenge motives seemed to further augment support for armed attacks. Public adoption of violent means increased in an environment of greater threat and insecurity, and decreased when the perception of threat was reduced, as our data from later on in the Intifada indicate (see Figure 6.4).[11]

Between May and October 2000 Israel retreated unilaterally from Southern Lebanon, the Camp David summit broke down, and the second Intifada erupted. The notions that diplomacy failed and that violence pays became firmly established in Palestinian public opinion. Consequently, as Figure 6.5 indicates, political support for Islamist hard-line groups promoting violent means—Hamas, Islamic Jihad, and independent Islamists—grew. These groups suffered a severe blow when the peace process first started; now they gained in popularity, rising from 17 percent support in July 2000 to 26, 25, 30, and 32 percent average support in the Intifada years through 2004. At the same time, support for Fatah decreased sharply following the outbreak of the second Intifada, from 37 percent in the July 2000 poll to less than 30 percent in the years 2001–2004. As we discuss at length in chapter 8, other factors also influenced this turnabout in the balance of power in the PA, but this was definitely a significant force in the process. Just before Arafat's death in November 2004, the Islamists became more popular than Fatah for the first time in Palestinian history.

Trends in public opinion similar to those we observed among Palestinians were also evident on the Israeli side. With the failure of diplomacy, the eruption of the Intifada, and the high levels of threat Israelis experienced,

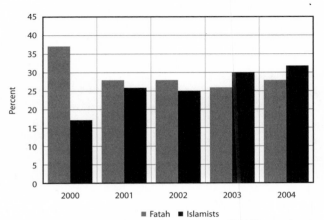

Figure 6.5. Political Support for Fatah versus the Islamists, 2000–2004

■ Fatah ■ Islamists

Note: 2000: poll taken in July 2000 before the eruption of the second Intifada. 2001–2004: averages for each year. Islamists include three groups: Hamas, Islamic Jihad, and independent Islamists

they overwhelmingly supported the use of military and violent means to counter Palestinian violence. At the same time they continued to support negotiations, despite disbelieving their viability. Politically, identification with the political right and electoral support for right-wing parties advocating these means increased.

Israel held an election in February 2001, following the disintegration of Ehud Barak's coalition after the collapse of the Camp David summit and the start of the Al-Aqsa Intifada. This was a special election only for the office of prime minister; Ariel Sharon from the Likud was victorious over the incumbent Barak from Labor, obtaining 62.4 percent of the ballots cast—the largest victory in Israel's electoral history. No election for the Knesset was held in 2001. In January 2003, more than two years into the Intifada, elections for the Knesset took place in which the left bloc declined from 46 to 33 seats in the 120-member Knesset and the right bloc increased from 33 to 47 seats. Based on ecological data on Israeli localities as well as public opinion polls, Berrebi and Klor (2006, 2008) established the role terror attacks played in the increase of support for the right-wing bloc of political parties.[12]

As we claimed earlier, the Palestinian-Israeli international game, involving a national liberation conflict and attempts to resolve it, entails different dilemmas for the two sides regarding the use of violence. The weaker side (the Palestinians) seeks to maintain by all means the use of force as a policy instrument, whereas the stronger side (Israel) seeks to deny its use as a legitimate instrument. Sharon's policy applied this notion consistently and forcefully throughout his term in office, both in the vigorous use of military means to "fight terrorism" and "dismantle the terror infrastructure," as well as in his Unilateral Disengagement Plan, explored in detail in the next chapter. Although Israelis obviously concurred with the delegitimation of the use of force by Palestinians, their agreement with Sharon's stance that negotiations should not be held as long as violence continues apparently eroded over time. In October 2000, 68 percent of Israelis were opposed to negotiations (27 percent thought negotiations should be stopped altogether and 41 percent thought they should be postponed until the violence ends), and only 26 percent thought that negotiations should be immediately renewed, even if Palestinian violence does not stop. In February 2003, 61 percent opposed the renewal of negotiations under the current situation of terror (53 percent thought Israel should wait until terrorism against Israelis stops, and 8 percent opposed negotiations altogether), but 34 percent supported the renewal of negotiations also under current conditions. In September 2004, 45 percent supported the Israeli government's position that negotiations should not be renewed as long as Palestinian terrorism continues, but 48 percent agreed with the position that putting an end to terrorism was more likely if negotiations with the PA were to be held.[13] Strict comparison of these figures is not warranted because the questions differed, but, as we discuss in the next chapter, Israelis (as well as Palestinians) preferred negotiations to unilateral steps in all the polls that presented this question.

Irrespective of the dilemma as to whether to negotiate under fire, a solid majority of Israelis—like Palestinians—supported negotiations between Israel and the PA throughout this period, even though only a minority believed that these negotiations would lead to peace between Israel and the Palestinians in the coming years.[14] They regarded negotiations as the most effective route to reach an agreement and understood the limits of force. For example, in December 2000, 74 percent thought that negotiations were more effective than confrontation in reaching an agreement, and only 13 percent preferred confrontation.[15] In February 2001, 37 percent thought that "letting the Israeli Defense Forces [IDF] win" will solve the ongoing Palestinian violence, but a majority of 55 percent rejected this commonly heard claim.[16]

During this period, support for military versus diplomatic means fluctuated,[17] but Israelis overwhelmingly supported the use of military means to quash Palestinian violence and terrorism. In a March 2001 poll, in response to a question about the appropriate use of military force against the Palestinians, 63 percent said that Israel should apply increased military force, and 64 percent supported closures of Palestinian cities and villages.[18] In October 2001, 60 percent supported the entrance of the Israeli military into Palestinian cities; in June 2002, 71 percent did so, with 77 percent anticipating that the IDF's reoccupation of Palestinian cities could significantly reduce terror, either for the short term or even in the long run.[19] On March 29, 2002, Israel initiated "Operation Defensive Shield," conducting major military incursions into most Palestinian cities. This followed the worst month of the Intifada in terms of suicide bombings and Israeli fatalities, culminating in the Netanya Park Hotel Passover Eve suicide bomb attack, in which thirty Israeli civilians were killed. Israeli public opinion overwhelmingly supported the operation (80% in the general population, 90% among Jews).[20] Over 60 percent supported targeted assassinations in surveys conducted in 2001, 2002, and 2004.[21] Majority support was also registered for the targeted assassination of Hamas leader Salah Shehade in Gaza in July 2002, in which a one-ton bomb dropped on his home killing him and fourteen other civilians, mostly children. This operation elicited a public debate in Israel over the morality and legality of such attacks where the civilian population is at risk. Fifty-five percent thought that even under these conditions Israel should continue targeted assassinations.[22]

The most important conclusion from our empirical analysis so far is the similarity of the public opinion trends in the two societies. With the failure of diplomacy and the outbreak of the Intifada, public opinion on both sides demanded and supported the use of violent means, and increased their support for political groups and parties advocating these means. Although the two publics continued to support negotiations, they did not hold out much hope for their success.

An Increased Willingness to Compromise

Despite the belligerence of the two publics and their growing support for the use of violent means and for hard-line groups and parties, the willingness to compromise increased on both sides. That this trend persisted even during the worst days of the second Intifada testifies to the deep nature of this development, and to the ability of public opinion to distinguish between violence as a means and conflict resolution as a goal.

Among Palestinians, we depicted the rise of the Islamists, the massive support for violence, the disillusionment with diplomacy, and the increased public confidence that violence pays. At the same time, however, willingness to compromise and support for reconciliation during the second Intifada were not negatively affected. Indeed, over time, the Palestinian public has become more moderate. By 2004 willingness to compromise was greater than it had been at any time since the start of the peace process.

Moderation and a willingness to support compromise can be seen in the consistent support for reconciliation based on a two-state solution, and in the moderation of views regarding the core issues of the permanent status agreement. When Palestinian respondents, between 2000 and 2006, assumed the existence of a Palestinian state—recognized by the State of Israel and emerging as an outcome of a peace agreement between Palestine and Israel—general support for reconciliation always exceeded 70 percent, with a single exception in April 2003, when support was 65 percent (see Figure 7.8).

Even more telling is the steady increase in support registered for the different compromise proposals for a permanent status settlement since the start of the peace process. Our data allow us to track the change in public opinion since 1996 with regard to core elements in the conflict, including a demilitarized Palestinian state, final borders with territorial exchange, Jerusalem, refugees, security arrangements, and an end to the conflict. Compromises in each of these issues were presented to the Palestinian public as part of different packages. The first package was the Abu Mazin–Beilin draft agreement from late 1995, negotiated in secret in Oslo by a team of Palestinian and Israeli negotiators, headed by Yossi Beilin for Israel and Abu Mazin (Mahmoud Abbas) for the Palestinian side. It was presented to the public in 1996. The second package was the one discussed after the end of the Camp David summit, in July 2000. The third was presented in our December 2003 poll as the Geneva Initiative, a package arrived at through nonofficial negotiations involving Palestinian and Israeli politicians and former negotiators. We discuss this initiative in the next chapter. In 2004, 2005, and 2006, we presented in our polls similar (but unlabeled) packages formulated along the Geneva Initiative and the Clinton parameters. Figure 6.6 demonstrates that although the first package received the support of a small minority of 20 percent in 1996, the Geneva package received the support of 39 percent in December 2003. In December 2004, following Arafat's death, this package, unlabeled, received the support of a majority of 54 percent, and in December 2005 and December 2006 the level of support stood at 46 and 48 percent, respectively. We present and discuss these data at length in the next chapter, but the major conclusion at this point is that support for the different compromise proposals for a permanent status settlement increased not only in the second half of the 1990s but also during the worst days of the second Intifada.

At the same time that Israelis were supporting hard-line political parties

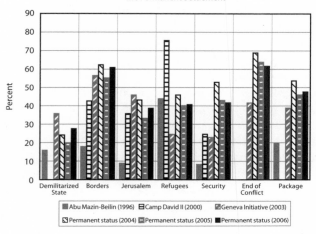

Figure 6.6. Support for the Compromises of the Core Elements of the Permanent Settlement

and policies, they also demonstrated that their willingness to compromise, and to support reconciliation during the second Intifada, were not negatively affected. General support for reconciliation never dropped below 70 percent; since mid-2003 it reached 80 percent most of the time (see Figure 7.8). The overall trend of this series during this period even indicates an increase in support for reconciliation over time.

Israelis' increasing moderation is indicated by their willingness to dismantle most of the settlements in the territories as part of a peace agreement with the Palestinians. We have been asking this question since the beginning of the Intifada,[23] and Figure 7.1 in the next chapter presents these data. Here, too, the trend is one of increasing willingness to compromise through the Intifada years. The number of Israelis willing to dismantle settlements increased up to the Gaza disengagement but dropped somewhat thereafter. Other data[24] show that agreement to the establishment of a Palestinian state did not drop during the Intifada but rather leveled off, fluctuating around the 55 percent figure reached in 1999 and 2000 (see Figure 8.1).

The Puzzle of Simultaneous Support for Compromise and Violence: Rational Choice and Political Psychology Perspectives

The two previous sections outlined the two foremost and simultaneous public opinion trends during this period: first, the swelling support for violence and military means and for the political forces that promote them;

and, second, the growing willingness to compromise. This puzzling pattern characterized both Palestinian and Israeli public opinion. We suggest piecing together this puzzle under the logic of rational choice in international relations, and also the role of violence and the use of force in two-level games presented earlier in the chapter, while taking into account insights from political psychology.

Political psychologists consider the psychological effects of violence on public opinion as significant and pervasive, and crucial in times of conflict, war, and terrorism (Crenshaw 1986; Long 1990; Huddy et al. 2005). Indeed, threat has often been found to be related to support for militant policies and groups among both Israelis and Palestinians (e.g., Arian 1989; Friedland and Merari 1985; Gordon and Arian 2001). However, the psychological impact of threat, violence, terror, and military operations on public opinion may be less straightforward and uniform than this body of work seems to suggest. Recent research has established concurrent, differing, and even opposite psychological reactions to external threat. Huddy and colleagues studied the effect of threat perception and anxiety (2005), and of anger and anxiety (2007), on Americans' support for military intervention in Afghanistan and Iraq post-9/11. They found them to be distinct reactions to terrorism with contradictory effects. Whereas perceived threat and anger increased a desire for retaliation and also promoted animosity toward the threatening enemy and support for military action, anxiety increased risk aversion and undercut support for military actions to curtail terrorism. Huddy et al. suggested that these distinct psychological effects may help explain why external threat conditions may sometimes foster support for belligerent policies but at other times lead to conciliatory or risk-averse behavior (2005, p. 594). Another recent study of Israeli Jews found no relationship between fear of Palestinians and support for compromise solutions (Maoz and McCauley 2005).

This political psychological research provides important insights as to the complex and multiform effects of external threat conditions. It suggests, in particular, opposite psychological effects on the individual level with contradictory policy reactions of different citizens. Applying these distinctions to our attempt to account for the simultaneous trends of belligerence and conciliation in public opinion, we recognize that external threat situations concurrently produce various negative emotions. During the period we examined, external threat was indeed high on both sides, and both Palestinians' and Israelis' personal experiences during this time could be expected to arouse a sense of personal vulnerability, thereby heightening anxiety.[25] Terrorism is designed to spread fear, and many

Israelis experienced physical proximity to a terrorist incident or personally knew terrorism victims. Palestinians lived through Israeli occupation policies and retaliatory measures, drastically aggravated since the start of the second Intifada. The unrelenting siege and closure of Palestinian territories, with the consequent debilitating restrictions on movement, have practically halted civil, social, and economic life. Use of military force including tanks, helicopter gunships, and F-16 bombers inside populated areas brought about a great deal of fear and suffering. Thus demand for military and terrorist retaliatory action may have been partly emotional, motivated by animosity, anger, and feelings of revenge in response to these threatening conditions. Anxiety about the future may have led people to be more averse to risk: less willing to take risks and more willing to reduce the threat and anxiety by becoming more moderate on the major issues of contention between the two groups. The psychological perspective, however, does not explain why being averse to risk would lead people to moderate their views with respect to their long-term goals rather than regarding the more immediate and concrete policy means they support, namely, growing opposition to the use of violence. Why do we observe this specific concurrence of the two policy reactions—belligerence on the means and conciliation on the ends? Why do they not cancel each other out, or why do we not observe an opposite pattern: increased hawkishness regarding the end goals in the conflict and moderation regarding the means? The distinction between the different negative emotions helps us account for variation in policy reactions among individuals, but less so for the two concurrent public opinion reactions.

Furthermore, emotional responses may only be for the short term. Our data from later on in the Intifada showed the close short-term relationship between public adoption of violence and increased threat and insecurity. That this effect may be short-term is suggested by a recent study which found that between 2000 and 2006, Palestinian fatalities shifted political support away from Fatah and lowered support for negotiations with Israel, but this was a short-term effect, disappearing within three months (Jaeger et al. 2008). A similar interpretation was also given to the fluctuations in support for the Oslo agreement in response to incidents of terror (Hermann and Yuchtman-Yaar 2002).

On the other hand, however, our rational choice perspective accounts for the observed pattern superbly, and the distinction between means and ends is crucial in this respect. We do not focus on variation in individuals' attitudes but rather on variation over time in collective public opinion as an actor in the two-level game. We regard public opinion, like other players in the two-level game, as guided by cost-benefit calculations and balance-of-power considerations, both in the short and long term. Clearly public opinion can distinguish between violence as a means and conflict resolution as a goal. The growing support for violent means resulted from consideration of the viability and promise of the alternative policy means of use of force and diplomacy in the two-level game. The increased willingness to compromise was based on long-term, cost-benefit analysis reflecting reality-based assessments of the other side to the conflict, the balance of power, and what is possible and feasible.

The analysis of Palestinian public opinion regarding the use of force from the mid-1990s through the mid-2000s established that support for violence increased most significantly before the outbreak of the Intifada. With the stagnation of the political process under Netanyahu (1996–1999), we observed a gradual increase in support for violence. Palestinians saw armed attacks as a tactic, and as a means of responding to perceived Israeli intransigence and violation of peace agreements. Moreover, this trend continued at a similar rate during Barak's term, and even following the collapse of the Camp David summit and the outbreak of the second Intifada in 2000, further supporting the rational choice interpretation over one based on psychological revenge and fear. On the other hand, Arafat's death in November 2004 heightened expectations that negotiations might be renewed and the dynamics of the conflict might change, along with declining support for armed attacks against Israelis. Throughout the period under study, the crucial factor in accounting for support of violence was the viability of the diplomatic route versus the promise of violent means in the Palestinian national liberation struggle, in which the Palestinian side, as the weaker side to the conflict, sought to maintain both the use of force and diplomacy as a policy instrument. When diplomacy proved effective, opposition to violence increased. Furthermore, unilateral steps, when taken amid violence, such as the Gaza disengagement which we discuss in the next chapter, strengthened public confidence in violence. All these trends are well explicated by a rational, strategic cost-benefit analysis of the viability of the alternative instruments of the policy at hand.

Israelis overwhelmingly supported the use of force following the failure of the diplomatic route and the eruption of the Intifada. In discussing "Operation Defensive Shield," Sharon was quoted as saying that "the Palestinians must be hit, and it must be very painful . . . We must cause them losses, victims, so that they feel a heavy price."[26] Sharon capably expressed Israeli public opinion on this matter. Although threat, anger, and revenge may have had a part in motivating support for such means, rational cost-benefit analysis within the framework of the two-level game drove the public and the leadership in the same direction. Obviously the major goal was to prevent, respond to, and deter Palestinian violence. A related consideration may have been the strengthening of one's position at the international table, which is an important determinant of the means considered along the game. As the stronger side in the conflict, Sharon's policy sought to deny the Palestinians the use of force as a legitimate policy instrument. Though public opinion concurred with this general notion, its agreement with Sharon's position that negotiations should not be held as long as violence continues eroded over time. Public opinion supported the continuation of talks, recognizing that only negotiations could lead to an agreement, and it also preferred negotiations to unilateral steps.

At the same time that public opinion on both sides increased its support for hard-line policies and groups, its willingness to compromise also rose. That this trend persisted during the second Intifada testifies to the profound nature of this development, and to the ability of public opinion to distinguish between violence as a means and conflict resolution as a goal. Indeed, the rational choice perspective calls for a fundamental distinction between ends and means,[27] and the short-term and long-term horizons may differ. The trend lines of the two need not and do not coincide. These differences are vividly illustrated in Figure 8.1, which presents Israeli public opinion concerning the establishment of a Palestinian state and the use of diplomatic versus military means for dealing with the conflict between 1987 and 2003. The figure demonstrates a long-term dovish trend of a growing willingness to compromise and accept a Palestinian state. On the other hand, the emphasis on diplomacy rather than on military means fluctuates significantly over time and is cyclical.

Events and developments pertinent to the conflict will have an effect on public opinion preferences and evaluations on both sides, within the frame of the two-level game. Not only policy means but also policy goals respond to assessments of the situation and power differentials, and are not static. The long-term goals to be achieved and a willingness to compromise may also change over time and as a result of new developments, and are related to expectations regarding the conflict, the sides to the conflict, and prospects for resolution. We have indeed established elsewhere that such expectations predicted both Israelis' and Palestinians' support for political compromise regarding Jerusalem, refugees, and the Palestinian state and its borders (Shamir and Shikaki 2002). Similarly, the death of Arafat in November 2004 had a significant effect on public opinion on both sides, raising optimistic expectations for a change in the course of the conflict, and, as we establish in the next chapter (see Table 7.1), increased the willingness of the two publics to compromise.

Public Opinion, the Domestic Political Arena, and Leaders' Room for Maneuver

We have argued that central players in the domestic political scene, including public opinion, play a major role in defining the leadership's policy options of violence versus diplomacy, and often determine the intensity of violence. This has been clearly demonstrated in the case of Yasser Arafat, whose room for maneuver following the Camp David failure was restricted. He was strongly influenced by the public demand for violence and Hamas's rise in popularity, and so, even if he wanted to, he could not put an end to violence or return to serious negotiations that would capitalize on the increased Palestinian willingness to compromise.

Israel, in its response to the second Intifada, focused on Yasser Arafat personally. Arafat, in the eyes of the Israeli government and, in particular, the eyes of Sharon, was responsible for the violence, using it as a strategic weapon to weaken Israel and force it to make political concessions. Israel sought to deny Arafat the use of force as a legitimate instrument and, by threatening him personally, hoped to force him to reverse this strategy and crack down on militant Islamists such as Hamas and nationalists such as the Tanzim, and to abandon violence completely.

This Israeli assessment of the nature of the Intifada overlooked the crucial sociopolitical transformation that had been taking place within Palestinian politics and society during the years before and immediately after the eruption of the Intifada. This transformation was the product of the public's perception of the failure of the peace process to end the Israeli military occupation discussed at length in this chapter, and the failure of the Palestinian leadership to deliver good governance discussed further in chapter 8. Therefore Israel's assessment of the Intifada missed the point. The policy Ariel Sharon adopted, based on this erroneous assumption, exacerbated the volatile situation even more, weakening Palestinian moderates and strengthening nationalist and Islamist hard-liners.

The Intifada was sustained from its earliest days by the determination of a young guard leadership in the national movement to seize the moment of a popular uprising in order to achieve two objectives: to increase pressure on Israel to end its occupation through the use of violence, and to marginalize and then displace the old guard of the PA. To improve their position vis-à-vis their older rivals, young guard militants also sought an alliance with the Islamists, while siding with refugees and the inner-city poor against the wealthy and the urban commercial class. Empowering these disenfranchised groups helped sustain the Intifada, despite the tremendous costs the uprising exacted on the Palestinian middle class. In other words, the nationalist young guard used the Intifada to undermine the prevailing Palestinian political system as much as to undermine Israeli security. By emulating Hezbollah's methods, the young militants wanted to force Israel to withdraw unilaterally from the occupied territories as it had from southern Lebanon in May 2000. But resorting to violence against the Israelis also brought the young nationalists popular legitimacy, free reign to carry arms and form militias, and a chance to intensify their fight against the old guard.

Meanwhile, the escalating attacks on Israel reduced Arafat's and the old guard's maneuvering room in its negotiations and diplomatic contacts with Israel and the international community, further damaging the PA's credibility. The young guard saw the Intifada as a means to disrupt negotiations rather than pursue them. The failure to achieve a breakthrough at Camp David affirmed these younger leaders' belief that the Palestinians could end the occupation on their own terms only through armed popular confrontation. The young guard did not consider negotiations a necessary part of the equation; a unilateral Israeli withdrawal or separation would be equally acceptable to them. The nationalist insurgents could not oppose a negotiated settlement supported by the majority of the Palestinians, should one ever emerge. But they realized that only the old guard could negotiate such a deal, for it alone had a unified national leadership and a well-articulated vision, as well as experience and connections with Israelis. Thus, for the young guard, as naturally it was for the Islamists, a unilateral Israeli withdrawal was a more attractive way of achieving Palestinian nationalist objectives: in bypassing the negotiations between the Israelis and the PA, it would render the old guard irrelevant and elevate the young guard to power.

Hoping initially to benefit from the Intifada, Arafat later found himself seeking to maintain a precarious leadership. He began to appease the young guard, tolerating its association with the Islamists and acquiescing in the face of its violence. But Arafat's dual policy of tacit approval of the young guard's methods, on the one hand, and solemn declarations of a cessation of violence, on the other, had shown him to be inconsistent and failed to project clear and decisive leadership. A prevailing perception of Arafat's inability to lead in the face of an uncertain future significantly damaged the PA's legitimacy, further emboldening the young guards. They now sought to achieve more transparency, greater accountability, a campaign against corruption, and a more direct confrontation with Israel. They had also called for the establishment of a national unity government that would include not only representatives from their own ranks but also senior members of Islamist and other opposition groups. And they strongly supported local and international demands for good governance, including respect for the rule of law, an independent judiciary, a larger role for the legislature, and stronger and more efficient public institutions.

Moreover, the young guard strenuously opposed any cease-fire agreement that would entail a crackdown on Palestinian nationalist or Islamist militants. Indeed, it had publicly condemned both the Mitchell Report (the conclusions of a fact-finding committee led by the former U.S. senator George Mitchell to look into the recent Israeli-Palestinian violence) and the Tenet Plan (the cease-fire and security plan put forth by the director of Central Intelligence George Tenet in June 2001). Rather than embrace these initiatives for ending the violence, the young guard wanted Arafat to "come out of the closet" by publicly endorsing the Intifada's goals and methods, and by ordering PA security forces to join the armed confrontations.

Arafat's lack of clear vision and leadership led many Palestinians to question his judgment. His popularity decreased from 47 percent before the Intifada to 35 percent by the end of its third year. In late 2003 and 2004, his popularity rating occasionally hit about 50 percent but only in response to Israeli threats to kill or expel him. His loss of control over the treasury in 2002—the result of increased scrutiny of PA finances by the international community—made it difficult for him to use money to secure his position. Those among the armed young guard who remained loyal to him began to grumble when he was unable to pay them regular salaries.

For all these reasons, Arafat and the old guard walked a delicate tightrope: the PA no longer enjoyed a monopoly over the use of force, its legitimacy was questioned by the street, the public was very supportive of violence and highly opposed to any clampdown on the Islamists or the young guard, and no viable political process was looming on the horizon. Arafat's choices were therefore limited. If he did what Israel asked him to do, and dismantled Hamas's military infrastructure and placed the militant nationalist leaders in jail, he risked, if successful, being seen by the Palestinians as an Israeli lackey, and, if unsuccessful, the specter of civil war. In the absence of a viable peace process, and as long as Israel continued its military incursions, assassination, and siege policy, Arafat and the old guard remained incapable of fully committing to the cessation of violence.

The initiative for changing the dynamics of the game was in the hands of Sharon, but it came only after the massive use of force and reoccupation of Palestinian areas in the West Bank, a civil society initiative designed to break the stalemate and present a diplomatic feasible alternative and, some say, a criminal investigation he was attempting to evade. We turn to these developments and the dynamics that took place between public opinion and leaders in the next chapter.

CHAPTER SEVEN

From Geneva to Disengagement
Opportunities and Constraints

Now the Palestinians bear the burden of proof. They must fight terror organizations, dismantle its infrastructure and show sincere intentions of peace in order to sit with us at the negotiating table.

—FROM PRIME MINISTER SHARON'S STATEMENT ON THE DAY
THE GAZA DISENGAGEMENT PLAN WAS IMPLEMENTED, AUGUST 15, 2005

I attach supreme importance to taking all steps, which will enable progress toward resolution of the conflict with the Palestinians. However, in light of the other challenges we are faced with, if the Palestinians do not make a similar effort toward a solution of the conflict I do not intend to wait for them indefinitely.

—FROM PRIME MINISTER SHARON'S SPEECH AT THE HERZLIYA
CONFERENCE, DECEMBER 18, 2003

A credible political process is essential for turning the tide of the last four years: a process that will lead to a permanent end to the Palestinian-Israeli conflict. A process that assures both peoples that they will not have to live again through the uncertainty and instability of another interim period. Only in the context of such a process will we be able to consolidate the security, democracy, and reform steps that we have been taking. . . . It is in this context of a credible political horizon that the Geneva Initiative is crucial.

—YASSER ABED RABBO, MEMBER OF THE PLO EXECUTIVE COMMITTEE AND
THE PALESTINIAN ARCHITECT OF THE GENEVA INITIATIVE,
SPEAKING AT THE HERZLIYA CONFERENCE, DECEMBER 16, 2004

The height of the Al-Aqsa Intifada in terms of violence and fatalities occurred in 2002. Suicide bombings peaked on the Israeli side, and Israel launched Operation Defensive Shield and reoccupied the West Bank. The year 2003 was still bloody but less so than 2002, and in addition to the ongoing fighting it also featured political and diplomatic initiatives. In March Abu Mazin was appointed prime minister of the PA. Soon after, the Quartet's Roadmap for peace was officially presented. In September Abu Ala was appointed to replace Abu Mazin after his resignation. In October the Geneva Initiative was publicized, and in December Ariel Sharon announced his Gaza Disengagement Plan.

The discussion in this chapter focuses on three important crossroads in the Al-Aqsa Intifada: the Geneva Initiative, Sharon's Disengagement Plan, and the consequent political turnabouts in Israel and the PA in the parliamentary elections in both societies in early 2006 (Shamir 2007). These events are intimately related; all three are a function of public opinion, though in different ways, and at the same time have shaped Palestinian and Israeli public opinion and the Israeli-Palestinian two-level game. The analysis supports our claim in chapter 3 that public opinion should not be viewed only as a constraint on policy, but that it can also create important opportunities to leaders involved in two-level games. Finally, we provide an in-depth analysis of public opinion on the permanent status framework and long-range prospects for normalization and reconciliation.

From Geneva to Disengagement

The Geneva Accord was a track II initiative led by a group of Israeli and Palestinian doves to draft a full-blown proposal for an Israeli-Palestinian peace agreement that would demonstrate that there is substantial common ground for a comprehensive peace agreement between Palestinians and Israelis.

The initiative was unveiled in mid-October 2003 and officially launched on December 1, at a ceremony in Geneva. Talks leading to the initiative were held over two years following the failure of the Taba talks in early 2001, while the Intifada was raging and hopes for a settlement were at a low point. Some of the participants were veterans from previous official and nonofficial negotiations. Building on those negotiations the two teams, headed by Yossi Beilin and Yasser Abed Rabbo, attempted to address the thorniest issues in dispute between the two sides, including the issue of the refugees and the status of Jerusalem.

The Geneva Accord was widely publicized in both societies and was further disseminated to the Israeli public by direct mail and to the Palestinian public through newspaper inserts. Public opinion was indeed a vital actor in this initiative. In two-level game terms, it was a bold move on the part of domestic players to interfere with the leaders' game in an attempt to expand their win-sets through public opinion. In fact, it went even further, offering a full-blown alternative game with different assumptions, different rules, and perhaps even different players. As such, it was perceived as a threat to Sharon and to Arafat, and a challenge to their leadership capacity, particularly since it appeared to be in conflict with their domestic political calculations and outside their acceptability-sets (Moravcsik 1993; Evans 1993).

The Geneva Initiative, coupled with a desire to renew the political process on the part of the Israeli public, a deteriorating economy, and protest groups refusing to serve in the territories, provided the impetus for Sharon's Disengagement Plan. In a revealing interview to the Israeli newspaper *Haaretz*, Dov Weisglass, Sharon's senior adviser, vividly explained the forces that motivated the Disengagement Plan:

> The economy was stagnant, and the Geneva Initiative garnered broad support. And then we were hit with letters of officers and letters of pilots and letters of commandos. These were not weird kids with green ponytails and a ring in their nose who give off a strong odor of grass. These were . . . really our finest young people.[1]

Obviously additional weighty considerations were involved in this decision. In this interview Weisglass also revealed Sharon's hope that his initiative would help deflect international pressure to move in undesirable directions and preserve the current situation for a long time. In any case, there can be no doubt about the central role of NGOs, grassroots protest, and public opinion in pressuring Sharon to come up with a new policy initiative. That Sharon's Disengagement Plan was announced in December 2003, two months after the Geneva Initiative, is not a coincidence.

In a speech given at the annual Herzliya Conference on Israel's national security on December 18, Sharon reiterated his commitment to the Roadmap but announced that if the Palestinians would not fulfill their part in its implementation soon, Israel would not wait for them indefinitely and would initiate a unilateral step of disengagement. Support for Sharon's Disengagement Plan was high and stable throughout this period, in most surveys over 60 percent. But the dynamics of public opinion are more interesting

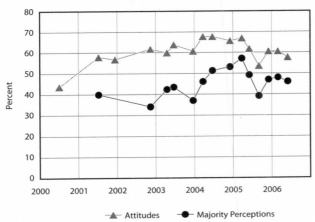

Figure 7.1. Percentage of Israelis Supporting the Dismantling of
Most Settlements for Peace, 2000–2006

—▲— Attitudes   —●— Majority Perceptions

and complex when viewed within the context of two-level games. Figure 7.1 provides an excellent illustration of these dynamics.

Since the beginning of the Intifada we have been tracing Israelis' willingness to dismantle most of the settlements in the territories as part of a peace agreement with the Palestinians.[2] But in addition to attitudes on this issue, we also trace the normative facet of public opinion. We do this by asking people not only what they think on the issue but also what they think the majority of the public thinks. People's perceptions of the majority opinion give us the prevailing norm about an issue—the climate of opinion.[3]

Figure 7.1, which shows both trend lines together, tells us a fascinating story. Since mid-2001 over 50 percent of Israelis already supported the dismantling of most settlements for peace, but this was still not perceived as a normative step. Only a minority of the public believed that this was the majority opinion, and the gap between the two lines was large. Only after Sharon's public declaration of his Disengagement Plan in December 2003 did this position become normative. Note the big jump in early 2004 in the climate of opinion line. It rises from 37 percent to 46 percent and even further to 51, 53, and 57 percent in the following months, bringing it close to the attitudes line. In other words, Sharon's announcement of his Disengagement Plan helped legitimize the dismantling of settlements in the eyes of the Israeli public.[4]

This case powerfully demonstrates the dynamic relationship between public opinion and leaders in two-level games. As with the first Intifada and the Oslo process (Hermann 2007; Shamir and Shamir 2000), here, too, the Israeli public was ahead of its leaders on a crucial policy issue, and provided an opportunity (and impetus) for Sharon's dramatic policy reversal. This policy move in turn transformed the "private" opinions into "public opinion" and legitimized them. Thus, contrary to common beliefs, wide support for a policy option is perhaps necessary for its implementation, but it is not always sufficient, as it does not always entail normative legitimacy. Obtaining normative legitimacy constitutes a crucial shift in public opinion from a mere favorable sentiment held privately by many people to actual collective readiness for the implementation of a specific policy option. This is where the role of leaders and other facilitating agencies in preparing public opinion becomes so important.

The Disengagement, the Israeli Settlers, and Public Opinion

In his Herzliya speech, Sharon did not specify the contours of the disengagement but the plan, as it shaped up in the following months and was implemented in August 2005, entailed the evacuation of all settlements in the Gaza Strip and four additional settlements in the northern part of the West Bank. From that point on, Sharon faced significant political and advocacy challenges put forward by disengagement opponents within his government, the Likud Party, and the Israeli settlers. While surviving all challenges, Sharon suffered a painful defeat in the Likud party members' referendum which rejected his plan. This was the culmination of a massive persuasion campaign by the settlers in which most Likud members were contacted in person and pressured to vote against the disengagement. With strong opposition continuing within his government, Sharon moved to form a national unity government with Labor which stabilized his regime in the short run. The scale of opposition to the disengagement was reminiscent of the opposition to the implementation of the Oslo Accord signed by Prime Minister Yitzhak Rabin in 1993, which led to his assassination in November 1995. The settlers' protest activities in 2005 were massive in numbers and concentrated on illegal activity, including confrontation with police and army forces.

Nevertheless, opponents to disengagement made little headway in persuading the Israeli public of their view, as indicated in Figure 7.2. Support for Sharon's Disengagement Plan was high and quite stable.[5]

These levels of support can be explained by a number of factors evident in our surveys. First, on the most fundamental level of societal values, territorial aspirations for "Greater Israel" have declined among Israelis since

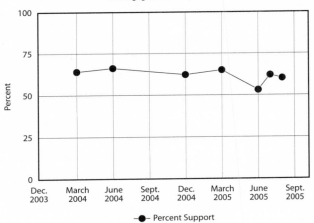

Figure 7.2. Percentage of Israelis Supporting Sharon's
Disengagement Plan, 2004–2005

the first Intifada in favor of the increased importance of maintaining Israel's Jewish identity and reaching a peace agreement. Second, Israelis have become less convinced that the settlements contribute to Israel's national security. Third, Israelis have become more critical of settlers' treatment of the Palestinians in the territories and of the undue share of national resources invested in the settlements. At the same time, a prolonged cease-fire with the Palestinians declared at the Sharm El-Sheikh summit in February 2005, between Abu Mazin and Sharon, suggested that Sharon's policy was reaping benefits.

In our June 2005 survey, carried out shortly before the actual implementation of the disengagement in August, we obtained a detailed account of the attitudes and behavioral intentions of the settlers and the general Israeli public with respect to the disengagement.[6] Sixty-five percent of the Israeli public and 46 percent of the settlers believed that the disengagement would eventually take place, and 29 percent of the Israelis and 46 percent of the settlers did not believe it would materialize. Moreover, 52 percent of the general public and 69 percent of the settlers believed that Sharon was planning to expand the disengagement in the future and evacuate more settlements in the West Bank. As to the long-term future of the settlements, 58 percent of the general Israeli public and 42 percent of the Israeli settlers believed that in the coming years the number of settlements in the West Bank would decrease. Eighteen percent of the general Israeli public and 34 percent of the settlers expected the number of settlements to increase in the future. In contrast, a majority of the Palestinians (52%)

feared that the number of settlements would increase in the future, and 33 percent thought it would decline.

In this poll we also attempted to understand what measures were considered justified in opposing the disengagement. Both the settlers and the general Israeli public in our sample were asked how one should respond to the disengagement decision. In the general public, 85 percent believed that the decision should be obeyed or resisted by legal means only (40% and 45%, respectively). A similar majority among settlers believed in abiding by the law, although 61 percent supported resistance by legal means and only 21 percent thought the decision should be obeyed. However, a significant minority in both samples—15 percent of the settlers and 14 percent of the general public—believed the disengagement should be resisted by any means possible.

As to perceptions of violence that might take place during the disengagement, the settlers apparently had succeeded in intimidating the Israeli public. Although 15 percent of the settlers thought that the proper response to disengagement was to resist the decision by all means, 38 percent of the Israelis questioned believed that the majority of the settlers would do so.

When inquiring more specifically about the means that would be justified in this type of struggle, 71 percent of the settlers and 46 percent of the general public believed that it was justified to bring down the government; 17 percent of the settlers and 11 percent of the general public said that it was justified to endanger oneself and one's family; and 9 percent of the settlers and 7 percent of the general public thought that it was justified to endanger other citizens in this struggle.

The low degree of legitimacy that settlers afforded to Israel's democratic institutions is noteworthy. Less than half the settlers in our June 2005 survey considered the government and the Knesset as having legitimate authority to decide on the evacuation of the settlements (49% and 48%, respectively). Fifty-two percent accepted the Knesset authority but only by a Jewish majority; 63 percent accepted the authority of a referendum; and 26 percent accepted rabbinic authority, and, of those, 5 percent considered only rabbinic authority as legitimate. Compared to a similar survey we carried out in June 2003, all these bodies have lost legitimacy among settlers. At the time of the disengagement, 8 percent of the settlers surveyed considered none of these bodies to be legitimate. This latter group, together with the 5 percent of settlers who accepted only rabbinic authority, provided the most radical and violent-prone responses in our survey.

Despite these attitudinal undercurrents, the evacuation of the Jewish settlers in the Gaza Strip and the four settlements in northern Samaria went more smoothly than expected. The most dramatic violent incidents in this context were two terrorist acts by Jews against Palestinians intended to provoke clashes between Jews and Arabs in the hope of preventing the evacuation of the settlers.[7] Both failed to achieve this goal. Among settlers and the troops performing the evacuation, a much smaller number of injuries occurred than expected and no casualties. The disengagement thus became a major success for Sharon and his policy and set an important precedent for the future. Still, the settlers' threat and their delegitimization of Israel's democratic institutions should not be taken lightly. It would be a mistake to assume that the Gaza precedent would also apply to the West Bank, where religious sentiments and historical attachments might fuel a much more violent resistance. The evacuation of Amona—an illegal outpost in the West Bank—in February 2006 proved to be a bold reminder of such a possibility. In Amona, several thousand Israeli soldiers and policemen, recruited to evacuate the settlement, faced thousands of determined settlers, many of them teenagers. The settlers tried to blockade the roads to the settlement and fortified themselves in buildings and on rooftops. The ensuing clashes turned out to be among the most violent between Jewish civilians and the Israeli security forces, much more so than those that took place during the disengagement. Apparently, in this incident, settlers tried to establish their own precedent to signal that further evacuation attempts in the West Bank might inflict an unbearable toll on Israeli society.

From Disengagement to Kadima

Sharon's unilateral disengagement in Gaza was a bold attempt to redefine the rules of the game played between Israel and the Palestinians and, as such, has been a key formative event in charting the course of the Israeli-Palestinian game at both domestic and international tables. At the Israeli domestic table, it was significant in that it shattered the perceived omnipotent position of the settlers. It further triggered the restructuring of the Israeli party system with the establishment of the Kadima Party and its victory in the 2006 election (analyzed in depth in the next chapter). The disengagement also laid the foundation for Olmert's Convergence Plan, announced just prior to the March 2006 election. The plan proposed to evacuate most of the settlements in the West Bank within a few years, while consolidating them into large blocks of settlements along the line of the separation fence. As to the Palestinian domestic table, the disengagement was a major factor behind Hamas's rise to power in the January 2006 parliamentary elections (also explored in the following chapter) and consequently the divided government in the PA. As a result, the makeup of the international table was completely overturned.

A momentous offshoot of the fierce political battle within Israel over the disengagement came about on November 21, 2005, when Sharon called for early elections and announced that he was leaving the Likud and establishing a new party—Kadima. Shortly thereafter, Sharon suffered two strokes; following the second and more serious one, on January 4, 2006, he slipped into a coma. In the elections that followed on March 28, Kadima, without Sharon and with Olmert as its new leader, became the largest party in the newly elected Knesset. This political "Big Bang," as Israeli politicians and political analysts described it, was the culmination of a dramatic but long-expected realignment process. The Israeli political continuum and the parties aligned along it, frozen for many years, now realigned to concur with their constituencies' policy positions and value priorities, which had shifted considerably in the last decades. This shift began a while back, during the first Intifada, and continued throughout the Oslo years and into the second Intifada, which ultimately shaped the circumstances that triggered the realignment process. The change in Israelis' support for a Palestinian state provides just one striking illustration of the magnitude of this shift. Before the first Intifada about 20 percent of Israeli Jews expressed a willingness to accept a Palestinian state (Shamir and Shamir 2000, pp. 189–191); in 2006 about 60 percent supported it.[8] These figures, and those above documenting the willingness to relinquish settlements for peace, indicate Israeli Jews' preference for a state with a Jewish majority over the dream of Greater Israel and holding on to the occupied territories.

As previously noted, Israeli political culture incorporates several fundamental values that underlie the conflict with the Palestinians—the values of peace, democracy, a Jewish state with a Jewish majority, and Greater Israel. These values are in conflict, and in the last two decades Israeli Jews have come to understand that they cannot successfully attain them all (Shamir and Shamir 2000, chap. 9).

Figure 7.3 traces these value preferences among Israeli Jews during the second Intifada period, showing that the choices have become clear. "Jewish majority," followed by "Peace," consistently rank highest, with "Greater Israel" ranking the lowest. In other words, Israeli Jews understood that they had to trade off the dream of Greater Israel if a state with a Jewish majority and attaining peace are important to them.

These value priorities begin to tell the story of the disintegration of the Likud and the success of Kadima in the 2006 election, although not fully.

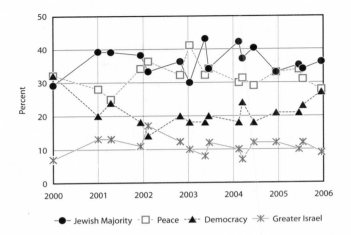

Figure 7.3. Israeli Jews' Value Priorities, 2000–2006

—●— Jewish Majority -□- Peace -▲- Democracy —✳— Greater Israel

Given these priorities, it is evident that the Likud's ideological and policy positions of adherence to the territories and the settlement project were far off from the electorate's ideal point. On the other hand, the Labor Party and the Israeli Left did not have a chance to capitalize on Israelis' yearning for peace, the second most preferred value.

As discussed in the previous chapter, the failure of the Camp David summit, its framing in Israeli public discourse, and the ensuing Intifada managed to obliterate any trust the Israelis had in a political settlement with the Palestinians. We observed consistent despair among Israelis in our surveys regarding the prospects of such a settlement. For example, in March 2006, just before the elections, only a quarter of the Israelis polled believed a settlement with the Palestinians might be reached in the next few years. Fifty percent of the public thought it might take at least another decade if not generations. Another quarter thought a political settlement with the Palestinians was not possible. Similar results were obtained in our June 2006 poll. The frame that there is no Palestinian partner for making peace asserted itself in the Israeli public discourse.

Clearly, then, the two big dreams that defined and polarized the Israeli political scene have been shattered: the Right's idea of a "Greater Israel" and the Left's desire for "peace now," or at least soon. As a result, the two traditional camps in Israeli politics lost their ideological and electoral appeal, and Israelis began to gravitate to the center, as documented strikingly in Figure 7.4. The regression lines in the figure chart the trends: the right-wing line moves down while the center line moves up. The Left remains

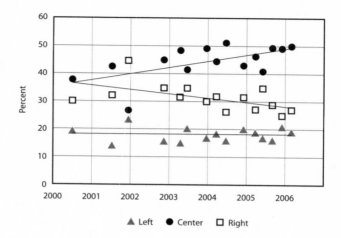

Figure 7.4. Israelis' Left-Right Identification, 2000–2006

▲ Left ● Center □ Right

virtually flat over the entire period. Note that, in the last polls in Figure 7.4, approximately 50 percent of the Israeli electorate defined themselves as centrist; this figure, together with the percentage of those identifying with the Left, amounted to almost 70 percent of the voters.[9]

It is important to stress that this process, while being gradual, was not linear, as the regression lines perhaps suggest. Figure 7.5 plots the mean values of the Left-Right scale ranging from 1 (extreme Left) to 9 (extreme Right) and the best-fit polynomial function. As the figure shows, the political realignment process was quite sensitive to the progression of the conflict with the Palestinians. Following the eruption of the Intifada, mean values increased, indicating a shift to the right, as we saw in the previous chapter. As the Intifada progressed further, the mean values began to decline, marking a gradual shift in the dovish direction, basically to the center.

The combination of the Left's willingness to compromise and the Right's focus on Jewish in-group orientation, together with pessimism, distrust, and despair over the Palestinians as a partner, caused this move to the center. Separation and unilateralism became the logical conclusion, embodied in the notions of a separation wall and the Disengagement Plan. Politically the establishment of Kadima was a direct consequence of the disengagement, and of Sharon's difficulties within his Likud Party and the Right. The party would not have emerged, however, without these political preferences of the electorate. Kadima thus restructured the Israeli party system in accordance with the electorate's placement along the Left-Right continuum.

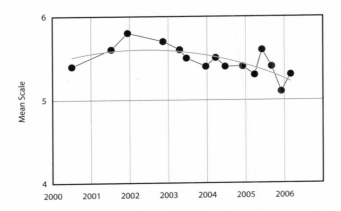

Figure 7.5. Israelis' Mean Left-Right Identification, 2000–2006

From Disengagement to Hamas

Let us turn now to the role that the disengagement played in the Palestinian turnaround and Hamas's rise to power in the PA. The Israeli disengagement in Gaza had a profound effect on Palestinian public opinion and the elections in two ways: it boosted the popularity of Hamas in the Palestinian public at the same time that Israel's insistence on a unilateral process considerably weakened the Fatah leadership and eroded Abu Mazin's political assets in the eyes of the Palestinians.

Israel's unilateral retreat in Gaza was largely interpreted by Palestinians as a sweeping victory of Hamas's doctrine of violent resistance to the Israeli occupation. When Prime Minister Sharon first presented the Israeli Unilateral Disengagement Plan, two-thirds of the Palestinians viewed it as a victory for armed resistance. As demonstrated in Figure 7.6, this perception was further consolidated throughout 2004 and 2005, reaching 84 percent in September 2005 during the actual withdrawal. Highly remarkable is that the respondents' attitudes, as the figure shows, are almost identical with their perception of the prevailing public mood. In other words, the view that the disengagement is a Palestinian victory reflects not only the attitudes of individual respondents but also the normative sentiment of the society as a whole.

The disengagement was seen, moreover, as a replay of Hezbollah's success in Southern Lebanon, and it only reinforced the widespread Palestinian belief that Israel understands only force. In fact, in our first joint poll in July 2000, 63 percent of Palestinians believed that Palestinians should

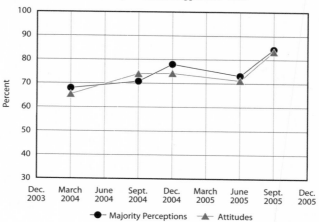

Figure 7.6. Palestinians' Perception of Disengagement as a Victory for Armed Struggle, 2003–2005

emulate the methods Hezbollah used in Lebanon; only 28 percent disagreed. More generally, a majority of Palestinians have consistently agreed that armed confrontations have helped them achieve national rights in ways that negotiations could not (see Figure 6.2).

Our September 2005 poll demonstrated that the public mostly credited Hamas for the Israeli withdrawal. From that moment on, Hamas's popularity continued to rise. Three months after the disengagement, in December 2005, results of a PSR exit poll conducted during the local elections in four main cities in the West Bank, Nablus, Jenin, Ramallah, and al Bireh, showed that Hamas's lists received 59 percent of the vote compared to 26 percent for Fatah and 15 percent for all other lists. But, more important, the results showed that, in predicting voters' intentions in the legislative elections set for January 2006, Hamas would most likely be victorious receiving 41 percent of the vote compared to 21 percent for Fatah and 15 percent for all other lists, with 23 percent of the voters remaining undecided.[10]

The erosion in Abu Mazin's standing was a direct outcome of the unilateral nature of the disengagement and should be understood in the context of the two-level game Sharon played with the Palestinian leadership. The unilateral component in the disengagement was an essential part of Sharon's political calculus. First, functionally it allowed full implementation of the Israeli interest with no strings attached by negotiation. Second, and even more important, a unilateral approach was meant to threaten the Palestinian leadership politically to yield to Israeli demands to crack down by force on the "terrorist infrastructure"—a term Sharon favored. Depriving the Palestinian leadership of the opportunity to negotiate with Israel was meant to strip Fatah and Abu Mazin of their most important political asset in the eyes of the Palestinians: that only they and not Hamas hold the key to the Israeli lock and can reach a peaceful solution. Indeed, this explains Sharon's refusal to boost Abu Mazin's standing even after the disengagement. Risking Hamas's rise to power was not an issue for Sharon, as he believed that Hamas was bound to take over anyway, unless Abu Mazin disciplined the Islamists by force. Moreover, a belligerent and extremist regime in the PA seemed to ably serve the Israeli government's interest in the short run by substantiating its reservations regarding the Roadmap and shielding it from an internationally imposed solution. In terms of two-level games, Sharon's unilateral paradigm provides a fascinating and rare example of a game in which one leader threatens the political survival of the other side's leader by implementing a policy that will erode the latter's standing among his domestic public.

Although the disengagement contributed to Hamas's victory in the PA, it was by no means the primary cause. Just as with the Israeli realignment, the growing support for Hamas was gradual, driven primarily by domestic issues rather than conflict-related causes. Most analysts (Shikaki 2006a; Shomali 2006) attribute its rise in power to Fatah's colossal failure in the state-building project ever since the establishment of the Palestinian Authority in 1994. Palestinian disillusionment with the PA regime focused specifically on two areas. Most important was the widespread corruption of the regime coupled with its neglect to fight it. Also at issue was the failure to enforce law and order so as to end the chaos created by the many armed groups ruling the streets.[11] These processes are analyzed at length in the next chapter.

On the surface, these developments in the Israeli and Palestinian domestic political scenes seemed to have validated the Israeli logic of unilateralism, Sharon's most conspicuous legacy. However, a deeper examination of this logic and its consequences, especially at the international table of the two-level game, offers different conclusions.

The Disengagement and the International Table

At the international table Sharon wanted the notion of unilateralism and the Gaza disengagement to redefine the rules of the game. Since the beginning of the Oslo process—and as often occurs in similar international disputes—the international table simultaneously entertained diplomatic and violent means. Clearly this is in the interest of the side that wants to alter the status quo, the Palestinian side in this case. The Roadmap from

2002, in its sequential phases, required the Palestinians to renounce terrorism and violence before moving on to the next phase of a Palestinian state with provisional borders and negotiations on a final status settlement. The Roadmap, however, failed to bring the sides beyond the first phase. Sharon's policy of unilateralism was similarly an attempt to break from the logic of simultaneous negotiation and violence, and try to force the Palestinians to choose between them. It went beyond the declaration that as long as the Palestinians do not do away with the "terrorist infrastructure" there will be no dialogue to suggest that, without any negotiations taking place, a solution will be imposed unilaterally. This was designed to produce a political threat for the Fatah leadership at its domestic table, as described above. Further, Sharon hoped for wide international support for the new reality he meant to create in the region, thus reducing international pressure on Israel. The most significant outcome turned out to be the end of Fatah's dominance in the PA and Hamas's ascent to power, continued violence, and only lukewarm acceptance by the international community of Sharon's step. Ultimately Sharon's hopes did not materialize, leaving the international game as it was until the disengagement.

The makeup of the international table was completely overturned, however. On the Palestinian side, a fierce struggle developed over the question of who would sit at this table with Israel. The issue arose not only because of a government divided between a Fatah president and a parliament ruled by Hamas but mainly because of a Hamas retraction of all previous agreements with Israel. All subsequent political maneuvers within the PA were tied to these questions, including the politics around the Prisoners' Document and the unity government. There was confusion in this regard on the Israeli side. The two-level game had regressed to the pre-Oslo period, when mutual recognition and the existence of a willing and capable partner for peace were the major issues on the international table.

Here it is worthwhile to examine concurrent public opinion with regard to negotiations on each side. Both Israelis and Palestinians supported negotiations, and overwhelmingly supported negotiations over unilateral moves. In our March 2006 poll, about three-quarters of the Palestinians (73%) and Israelis (76%) preferred to see further disengagements in the West Bank negotiated between the PA and Israel, and only 23 percent of the Palestinians and 17 percent of the Israelis preferred that these further disengagements are unilateral. Moreover, majorities in both publics—59 percent of the Palestinians and 63 percent of the Israelis—also believed that taking the unilateral path decreased the chances to eventually reach a final status settlement.

Within the Israeli political establishment, Abu Mazin was widely regarded as an incompetent player, and Hamas as an unwilling partner. Nevertheless, in the same March 2006 poll carried out shortly after the Hamas victory in the PA elections, a considerable majority (60%) among the Israelis supported entering talks with Abu Mazin over a final status settlement. At the same time they were not optimistic regarding the results of these talks. Forty-six percent believed it was possible to reach such a settlement with Abu Mazin and the Fatah leadership, and 51 percent thought it was impossible. Even more surprising was the level of support in Israeli public opinion for negotiations with Hamas. As Figure 7.7 shows, through 2005 and 2006 about half the Israelis thought that Israel should talk to Hamas if this is what is needed to reach a settlement with the Palestinians. In March 2006 this figure even rose to 62 percent. This level of support for talks with Hamas coexisted with a high level of mistrust of Hamas: 58 percent of Israelis believed that the aspirations of the Hamas leadership eventually were to conquer the State of Israel, or to conquer it and annihilate a considerable part of the Jewish population in the state. Only 38 percent believed that Hamas's aspirations were to take back part or all of the pre-1967 territories. Moreover, a majority of the Israeli public believed that there was little or very little chance that Hamas would moderate over time; 44 percent thought that the chances for this to occur were medium or high.

At the same time most Israeli politicians opposed negotiations with Hamas. The discrepancy between the political leadership and public

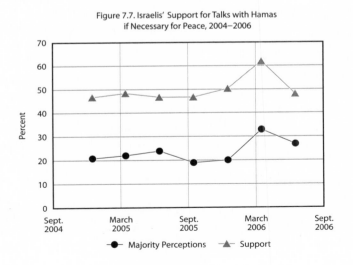

Figure 7.7. Israelis' Support for Talks with Hamas
if Necessary for Peace, 2004–2006

opinion on this issue is similar to the context of the early 1990s, when Israeli public opinion indicated a willingness to talk with the PLO long before its mainstream politicians did (Shamir and Shamir 2000, p. 191). Public opinion was split in its attitudes on this issue, as illustrated in Figure 7.7, but note that negotiations with Hamas were not normative, and only a small minority thought that support of talks with Hamas constituted the majority opinion. These data thus present another example of public opinion providing opportunities to its leaders, as well as waiting for them to successfully overcome this hurdle.

A similar situation could be identified in the Palestinian Authority, where the Hamas government was ambiguous about negotiations with Israel, as this would imply the government's recognition of Israel. However, Palestinian public opinion in support of such a move was overwhelming. In our June 2006 poll, 70 percent of the Palestinians thought that if Israel agreed to enter into peace negotiations with Hamas, then Hamas should agree to do so, and only 26 percent disagreed. Thus both publics opened opportunities to their leaders in the two-level game in terms of entering into negotiations.

The Permanent Status Framework

A necessary condition for the success of international negotiations is an overlap in the players' domestic win-sets. We may then ask whether there is a permanent status proposal that simultaneously wins the support of the two publics. In such a case, public opinion on both sides provides a most meaningful opportunity for its leaders.

Many ideas and plans for a permanent settlement in the Israeli-Palestinian conflict have been floating around for years. Since the Oslo process began, however, several more concrete proposals reached the public agenda, mostly in off-the-record versions. Of these, most prominent are the Beilin–Abu Mazin understandings from 1995; Clinton's parameters from December 2000; the Moratinos non-paper on the January 2001 Taba negotiations; and, during the Intifada, the Geneva Initiative mentioned earlier. Though differing on specifics, almost all the proposals addressed the most crucial components underlying the conflict: territory, statehood, sovereignty, security, Jerusalem, refugees, and the end of conflict.

In December 2003, following the official launching of the Geneva Initiative, we presented the framework to our respondents as the Geneva package. One year later, shortly after Arafat died, we asked these questions again. Here the package was presented unlabeled, simply as a permanent status package, and we repeated the questions in December 2005, after the disengagement in Gaza; in June 2006, after the electoral reversals in both societies; and again in December 2006. The questions in these surveys were phrased along the lines of the ideas President Clinton presented to both sides in late December 2000 and the Geneva Initiative from December 2003, and they cover the six most important components of a permanent status framework as listed below:[12]

The end of conflict component suggests that the permanent status agreement will mark the end of conflict, with neither side making any further claims. Mutual recognition of Palestine and Israel as the homelands of their respective peoples will also be in place.

The demilitarized state component entails the establishment of a Palestinian state with no army but with a strong security force. Its security and borders will be protected primarily by a multinational force.[13]

The sovereignty/security component suggests that the Palestinian state will have sovereignty over its land and airspace but that Israel will have the right to use this airspace for training and will maintain two early-warning stations in the West Bank. The multinational force will monitor the implementation of the agreement and the territorial integrity of the Palestinian state and its border crossings.

The borders component concerns the Palestinian state spanning the entire West Bank and Gaza Strip apart from several blocks of settlements on no more than 3 percent of the West Bank; in return, Palestinians would receive territory of similar size alongside the Gaza Strip.

Jerusalem will be the capital of both states. The Arab neighborhoods, including those in the Old City as well as the Temple Mount, will come under Palestinian sovereignty. The Jewish neighborhoods, including the Jewish Quarter and the Western Wall, will be under Israeli sovereignty.

The refugees component included reference to UN resolutions 194 and 242, compensation, and the following five options for permanent residency:

- Return to the Palestinian state.
- Return to areas in Israel that will be transferred to the Palestinian state in a territorial exchange.
- Residency in their current states.
- Immigration to third countries.
- Return to Israel that will be restricted and at Israel's discretion.

Following questions about each of the individual components, Israelis and Palestinians were asked to state their support or opposition for this version of the permanent status agreement as a combined overall package. The results of these surveys, shown in Table 7.1, are revealing in several respects. First, and most meaningful, at least at one point in time, there is majority support for the Clinton/Geneva framework as a combined overall package. In December 2004, 64 percent of the Israelis and 54 percent of the Palestinians supported this framework as a combined overall package, up from 47 percent of the Israelis and 39 percent of the Palestinians who supported this package a year earlier in December 2003. Second, considerable changes clearly occurred in the two publics over this period. Third, large differences are apparent in the levels of support for the different items within each public and between them. And, finally, the pattern of support for the overall package is more than the sum of its parts, suggesting, specifically, that people's calculus is compensatory and trade-offs are considered.

The lowest level of support obtained for the Clinton/Geneva permanent status formula was in December 2003, and the highest level was observed a year later, in December 2004, shortly after Arafat's death, probably the major factor behind the change. Arafat personified the dead end reached in the conflict, and his death raised high expectations as to the feasibility of the diplomatic route and of reaching a settlement. Arafat's death was followed by a surge of optimism and considerable moderation in both publics. This optimism was evident in most of the other questions we asked

TABLE 7.1. Support for Clinton's Permanent Settlement Framework, 2003–2006

	Israelis					Palestinians				
	Dec. 2003	Jan. 2005	Dec. 2005	June 2006	Dec. 2006	Dec. 2003	Dec. 2004	Dec. 2005	June 2006	Dec. 2006
1) Borders and Territorial Exchange	47%	55%	53%	47%	44%	57%	63%	55%	54%	61%
2) Refugees	35%	44%	43%	43%	38%	25%	46%	40%	41%	41%
3) Jerusalem	41%	39%	38%	37%	38%	46%	44%	33%	35%	39%
4) Demilitarized Palestinian State	61%	68%	69%	63%	62%	36%	27%	20%	25%	28%
5) Security Arrangements	50%	61%	62%	52%	51%	23%	53%	43%	40%	42%
6) End of Conflict	66%	76%	80%	70%	68%	42%	69%	64%	58%	62%
Overall Package	47%	64%	64%	55%	52%	39%	54%	46%	44%	48%

in our December 2004 survey. Another factor that could account for the large difference between the two polls is that the first survey presented the framework to our respondents as the Geneva package, which might have lowered its level of support, given the ongoing delegitimization of the Geneva Initiative by officials and the media in both societies at that time.

Among Israelis, majority support for this package was also obtained in the three later polls held in 2005 and 2006. In December 2005, after the disengagement and the establishment of Kadima, the same level of support for the package was registered as in January—64 percent. In June 2006, however, after Hamas's rise to power and the continuous shelling of Kassam rockets from the Gaza Strip into southern Israel, support fell to 55 percent; in December 2006, it declined further to 52 percent.

Among Palestinians, December 2004 was the only time when a majority of the public (54%) supported this permanent status framework package. In December 2005, following the disengagement, and in June and December 2006, after the political reversals in both societies, only 46 percent, 44 percent, and 48 percent, respectively, supported the overall package.

These data reiterate the degree to which public opinion is affected by political and military circumstances in the time frame our data examine: the disengagement and Hamas's rise to power. Notably Palestinian support for this permanent status framework package seems to have been affected more by the disengagement and the disappointment from it than by Hamas's rise to power. Israeli support only fell following the Palestinian political turnabout and does not seem to have been affected by the disengagement.

Support for individual items varied significantly within and between the two publics. It is important to see, however, that despite strong reservations regarding some of the components the overall package always received greater support in both publics, and the gap between the least-liked component and the support for the overall package varied between 12 and 27 percentage points. This indicates that people's calculus in this respect is compensatory. The desirable components and the chance of reaching a permanent status agreement seem to compensate for the undesirable parts, and therefore the size of this gap varies significantly over time and is bigger when there is reason for optimism.

The significance of these findings cannot be overestimated. They suggest that a permanent status framework which could be endorsed by both publics is not out of reach. On the other hand, these findings and their practical implications must be treated with caution. Not only does the level of support fluctuate, but, even more important, so far we have examined only attitudes. When we look at other dimensions of public opinion such as the prevailing norm and people's short- and long-range expectations for a settlement, we obtain a much more pessimistic reading.

Regarding the short term, our surveys repeatedly show that both publics expect negotiations to resume but with some continuing violence. Their expectations as to the feasibility of a permanent status agreement are gloomy and provide a completely different reading from their level of endorsement of such an agreement. In our June 2006 survey we asked the two publics to estimate how soon a political settlement between Israel and the Palestinians would be achieved. Only 26 percent of the Israelis and 13 percent of the Palestinians expected it to be reached in the next few years; 45 percent of Israelis and 26 percent of Palestinians believed it could be achieved only in the next decade, in the next generation, or in many generations to come; and 23 percent of the Israelis and 51 percent of the Palestinians believed a political settlement would never be achieved.

Furthermore, Clinton's ideas and a Geneva-like permanent status framework have not acquired legitimacy and normative approval in the two publics. In December 2005 we asked our Palestinian and Israeli respondents not only about their opinion on the combined package for a permanent status settlement but also about their perceptions of the majority opinion on this package in both societies. At that point, almost two-thirds of Israelis and 46 percent of Palestinians supported this package. Among Palestinians and Israelis alike, more respondents perceived majority opposition than majority support for such a package in the PA. Palestinians similarly perceived majority opposition to the package among Israelis. More Israelis perceived majority support than majority opposition to the package in their society, but they were still a minority (46%).

The Palestinian and Israeli publics have been assigned direct ratification power and thus a decisive role regarding the permanent status solution, with the leaders of both sides committed to advancing any final status agreement for approval in a public referendum. Thus the overall picture of public opinion we charted thus far gains added significance to be considered when we set out to translate these findings into operational steps. Of particular importance is an in-depth understanding of the policy constraints and opportunities that public opinion presents to the Israeli and Palestinian leaders. That both publics, at least at some point within the context of the second Intifada, were shown to support a concrete permanent status package structured around the Clinton parameters, suggests that a permanent-status framework that could be endorsed by both publics is viable.[14] Moreover, the compensatory nature of the individual components affords opportunities to policy makers. It suggests that in order to move forward on this path of compromise, it is important and worthwhile to emphasize the overall benefits of a comprehensive package and the necessity of trade-offs it implies. The role of framing in this context is clear, especially on issues of symbolic importance such as the refugees' problem. We return to these issues in the concluding chapter.

Long-Range Prospects—Normalization and Reconciliation

From the outset, the joint Palestinian-Israeli public opinion project made a deliberate decision to move beyond the daily events and developments to longer-range and more profound dimensions of the conflict. The question of Palestinian-Israeli reconciliation is significant in this respect. In recent years, there has been increasing understanding that conflict resolution cannot be truly achieved without conflict transformation that promotes social and cultural change and transforms societal relations in order to attain lasting peace. This entails not only a redefinition of economic and political interests but, even more, a long-range process of fundamental changes in the most basic threads holding societies together—societal beliefs, value systems, collective memories, and identity perceptions (e.g., Kelman 1997, 1999; Lederach 1997; Rasmussen 1997).

In our surveys we have attempted to tap Palestinians' and Israelis' sentiments toward reconciliation and their expectations as to when this can be achieved (Shamir and Shikaki 2002a). For this purpose, we devised a reconciliation scale composed of normalization and reconciliation steps, often mentioned in the reconciliation literature as prerequisites for successful reconciliation following protracted conflicts (Calleja 1994; Gordon 1994; Kelman 1999; Krepon, McCoy, and Rudolph 1993; Lederach 1997). They vary in terms of difficulty and commitment, ranging from normalization measures such as open borders and economic cooperation, through steps toward political alliance, to transformative steps intended to change the national ethos such as fundamental modifications in school curricula. Two additional items tap social rather than policy-oriented sentiments and ask respondents about their willingness to maintain social ties with someone from the other side. We also inquired about reconciliation sentiments in general. All these questions were presented in the context of having reached "a peace agreement and the establishment of a Palestinian state that is recognized by Israel."

As is evident from the graph in Figure 7.8, support for reconciliation in general is very high in both publics. However, we should not be overly

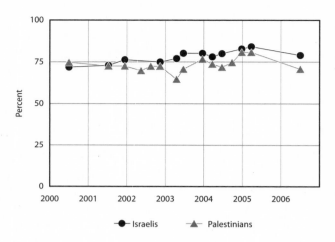

Figure 7.8. General Support for Reconciliation, 2000–2006

●— Israelis   ▲— Palestinians

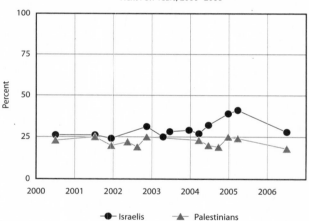

Figure 7.9. Reconciliation Will Be Achieved in the Next Decade or
Next Few Years, 2000–2006

●— Israelis   ▲— Palestinians

impressed with these figures, given that high levels of support are typical for general questions inquiring about highly desirable values. Indeed, when we asked respondents to estimate when this reconciliation might be achieved, optimism began to fade. As indicated in Figure 7.9, no more than one-quarter of the Palestinians believe that reconciliation will be reached in the next decade or in the next few years. All the others believe it will take longer. In June 2006 half the Palestinians thought that reconciliation was impossible. Israelis have become more optimistic in 2005, but even then only about 40 percent expected reconciliation in the next decade or

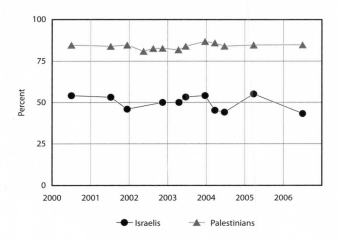

Figure 7.10. Reconciliation Scale — Open Borders, 2000–2006

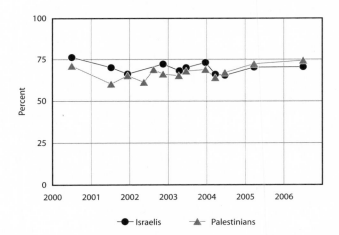

Figure 7.11. Reconciliation Scale — Joint Economic Ventures, 2000–2006

sooner. In the June 2006 poll this figure was down again to 28 percent. The rest of those polled believe that reconciliation will take more time, and 28 percent of the Israelis think it will never happen.

Some of the more specific normalization steps are presented in Figures 7.10 and 7.11. It is important to stress, as noted above, that these and all subsequent questions assume a state of peace between Israel and an independent Palestinian state. Figure 7.10 demonstrates that Palestinians overwhelmingly support open borders. Israelis are more reluctant, with levels of support oscillating between 43 percent and 55 percent over time. Both

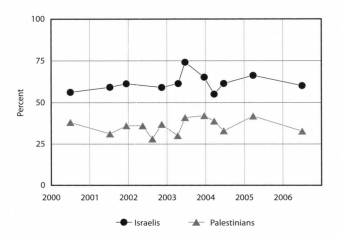

Figure 7.12. Reconciliation Scale — Take Measures against Incitement, 2000–2006

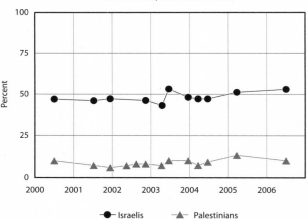

Figure 7.13. Reconciliation Scale — Socialize Against
Irredentist Aspirations, 2000–2006

publics support joint economic ventures in high and similar percentages, as shown in Figure 7.11.

Turning from normalization to reconciliation measures, greater differences begin to appear between Israelis and Palestinians. Figure 7.12 shows support for measures to prevent incitement against the other side, and it is apparent that Israelis consistently give this item majority support, but only a minority among Palestinians support it.

Finally, the greatest difference between Palestinians and Israelis became apparent with regard to taking steps to make cultural changes. Whereas about half the Israelis agree that school curricula should be revised to socialize children against irredentist aspirations, no more than 13 percent of Palestinians support this change (Figure 7.13). Relinquishing such aspirations is obviously easier for Israelis who have their own state than for Palestinians who are struggling for a state. Nevertheless, here again, we stress that responses were given under the assumption of a state of peace and the existence of an independent Palestinian state.

The overall conclusion drawn from these reconciliation data is that, even under the best possible scenario, reconciliation sentiments are quite superficial at this time. Goodwill exists for normalization steps that promise clear and tangible benefits, but less so for the more fundamental steps to change the state's ethos. Moreover, among both publics, the expectations of reaching reconciliation in the foreseeable future are meager.

CHAPTER EIGHT

Political Turnabouts
The Electoral Connection

Public opinion exerts its influence as a player in the Israeli-Palestinian two-level game by means of various mechanisms and institutions, but, among those, elections are fundamental. Elections are considered the key instruments of democracy that "forge connections between the wishes of citizens and the behavior of policy makers. Because of these connections, the policy makers take account of citizens' preferences more fully than they would otherwise" (Powell 2000, p. 14). These may provide public opinion indirect ratification power in the terminology of two-level games. Elections allow citizens to select their leaders and choose between policy alternatives; they make it possible to hold elected officials accountable for their performance in office by "throwing the rascals out," and they motivate the elected representatives to engage in a reciprocal process, paying attention to their publics in anticipation of the next election. The electoral connection may thus be retrospective as well as prospective. These are normative but also well-substantiated empirical claims in the political science literature (e.g., McDonald and Budge 2005; Powell 2000; Stimson, MacKuen, and Erikson 1995; Erikson, MacKuen, and Stimson 2002).

From our point of view of the public imperative, we focus in this chapter on the correspondence between the public's policy preferences, elections, and the behavior of the elected leaders on both sides. On the Israeli side, we establish the long-time primacy of the conflict issue in voters' considerations. We trace voters' preferences regarding the handling of the conflict from the start of the first Intifada, corresponding government turnover, party positions, and policy adjustments under different governments. We then focus on the March 2006 Knesset elections, which highlighted the importance of public opinion in the Israeli-Palestinian two-level game on two counts. First, they denoted a politically significant realignment of the Israeli party system in step with public opinion; and, second, they exhibited a bold attempt on the part of Olmert to secure an electoral mandate for his Convergence Plan for further disengagement in the West Bank, attesting to the significance he conferred to public opinion.

On the Palestinian side, democratic elections are a novelty and occur infrequently. We sketch the history of elections and democratization in the PA, the changing public agenda, and the balance of power between Fatah and Hamas. Here, too, we concentrate on the 2006 Legislative Council elections. These elections did not focus on the conflict but rather on internal Palestinian issues, but the Palestinian-Israeli two-level game was intrinsic to their dynamics. We provide an in-depth analysis of these elections that brought Hamas to power, introducing a profound change in the rules of the Palestinian-Israeli game on its two levels: the international and the domestic Palestinian game.

Dynamic Representation in Israeli Elections since the First Intifada

Israel is a well-established democracy, and its electoral history includes seventeen Knesset elections and one additional direct election of the prime minister through 2006. We begin with a longitudinal examination of the electoral connection since the first Intifada as "dynamic representation," a term referring to the responsiveness of government to public preferences in the sense that "if public opinion changes . . . then public policy responds" (Stimson, MacKuen, and Erikson 1995, p. 543). Elections may bring about such responsiveness in two ways: the direct route, through the selection of leaders and change in the makeup of government; and the indirect route, where the political actors who wish to be reelected must take their publics into account through rational anticipation. As discussed previously in chapter 3, the common rational choice logic for the leverage that public opinion holds over leaders is their fundamental drive to seek office—to maximize their chances for reelection (Bueno de Mesquita and Siverson 1995; Schultz 1998; Stimson, MacKuen, and Erikson 1995).

In studying dynamic representation we examine voters' electoral behavior, their preferences and changes therein, government turnover, party positions, and policy under different governments throughout the six elections that took place between 1988 and 2003. A special section is devoted to the 2006 election.

In order for public opinion regarding the Israeli-Palestinian conflict to influence electoral outcomes, certain factors are required: the public must have coherent preferences regarding peace and security; this issue dimension must be salient in the elections so that these attitudes may be accessible and affect the vote; and the major parties must offer alternatives that are distinct enough on these issues so that there is actual choice (Aldrich et al. 2006, p. 478; see also Trumbore 1998). We have seen throughout our analysis that both the Palestinian and the Israeli publics maintain coherent preferences on peace and security issues. Moreover, the cleavage over these issues is at the center of Israeli politics and constitutes a highly salient dimension in elections. The Israeli party system has been defined primarily along the security and foreign affairs divide for many years, particularly since the 1967 Six-Day War. The "Left" and "Right" labels are associated in Israel with positions relating to the Arab-Israeli conflict, the Palestinians and the territories occupied in 1967, and not, as in most democracies, along socioeconomic lines. The Right defined itself as the national or nationalistic camp, and the Left as the peace camp. Since the 1980s, following the 1977 realignment that brought the Likud to power for the first time, the Israeli party system has been characterized by a two-bloc competitive structure, with the Likud and Labor parties at the nucleus of the Right and Left party blocs, respectively.

The data in Table 8.1 establish that voters see differences between the competing parties on these issues, and that they vote on them. Here we rely on preelection surveys of the Israel National Election Studies (INES),[1] which provide voters' perceptions and vote considerations. In the first panel in the table we can see that in all elections, at least in the voters' minds, identifiable options are available. The electorate views the differences between the major parties on this issue dimension as follows: over 50 percent and up to 80 percent say they perceive large or very large differences on peace/territories; 40–67 percent perceive differences on how to deal with terrorism. It is worthwhile to compare these figures to other policy areas, and, indeed, in line with experts' assessments, many more voters perceive differences on this dimension than on economic and social policy (30–44%).

Furthermore, as evidenced in the next panel, voters say that conflict-related issues are significantly affecting their votes, and consistently more than other domestic issues.[2] Finally, the last two panels in the table present logistic regression coefficients measuring the impact of voters' positions on the conflict, state-religion, and socioeconomic issues, and of their performance evaluations in the security and economic realms on their vote for the Left versus the Right blocs or candidates.

TABLE 8.1. Israeli Voting Behavior, 1988–2003

	1988	1992	1996	1999	2001	2003
Perceived Differences between Parties (%)[1]						
Peace/territories	51	61	79	59	72	61
Terror	n.a.	n.a.	61	38	67	51
Jerusalem	n.a.	n.a.	54	27	73	48
Economy	44	43	30	35	35	34
Social policy	n.a.	n.a.	n.a.	38	41	40
State-Religion	n.a.	n.a.	n.a.	47	47	49
Vote Considerations (%)[2]						
Peace/territories	29	71	74	67	54	67
Terror	n.a.	82	68	62	66	66
Jerusalem	n.a.	n.a.	55	42	61	46
Economy	14	n.a.	34	58	54	63
Social policy	n.a.	77	n.a.	51	48	51
State-Religion	n.a.	56	n.a.	48	41	52
Corruption	n.a.	70	n.a.	n.a.	n.a.	53
Issue Voting[3]						
Peace/territories	1.23	.92	1.07	1.10	.92	1.03
Socio-economic	.62	.34	(.20)	(.23)	.30	.56
State-Religion	(.06)*	(.20)	.24	.49	(.03)	(.35)
Performance Evaluations[3]						
Security performance evaluation	1.07	1.51	1.28	1.52	1.99	2.13
Economic performance evaluation	.78	.67	.93	2.44	1.29	1.76

Source: Data from INES pre-election surveys; Jewish voters only (see note 1):

* Figures within parentheses are non-significant.

[1] *Perceived differences:* "In your opinion, are there or aren't there differences in the major parties' positions on the following issue?" Reported here are the percentages of "very large differences" and "large differences" (the other categories were "some differences," "small differences," "almost no differences"). In 2001 the questions referred to prime ministerial candidates. Instead of peace and territories, the item referred to the agreement with the Palestinians. In 1992 the item referred to territorial compromise (giving up territories); in 1988—to security policy.

[2] *Vote considerations:* "To what extent will each of the following issues affect or not affect your vote?" Reported here is the percentage of "will have much effect" (the other categories were "will have some effect," "will have little effect," "will have no effect at all"). In 1992 this series of questions was asked in a somewhat different format than in the other election years, so the figures are not strictly comparable across elections but of course can be compared within the election. In 1992 only two alternative responses (affect / not affect) were offered, and respondents were given a much longer list of factors. The category "Peace and Territories" was omitted; instead, the report here is of the average effect response for three items: beginning of peace talks, government handling of peace talks, and the Likud's settlement policy. There was no "Terrorism" category but rather "Intifada." The "Social Policy" category was also omitted, and in its place we present the "Unemployment" category. The "Corruption" category read "Corruption in Government and the State Comptroller Report." In 1988 the question referred only to territories. In 2001, instead of "Peace and Territories," respondents were asked about "Agreement with the Palestinians."

[3] *Issue voting and performance evaluation:* b estimates from multivariate logistic regression models predicting the left/right bloc vote in 1992 and 2003, and the prime ministerial vote in 1996, 1999, 2001. The estimates are partial coefficients indicating the unique impact of issues and performance evaluations, controlling for all other demographic and attitudinal variables in the models. The figures are taken from Shamir & Arian (model III: 1999, table 2, p. 269; 2002, Table 2, pp. 48–49; 2005, Table 1.2, p. 7).

The results demonstrate that individuals vote on the basis of the conflict issue, although this is not the only consideration, of course. The conflict, however, is a much more significant factor in their vote calculus than other domestic issues. In all elections it is the most important consideration, both in terms of position and performance evaluation (with the exception of 1999, when performance evaluations in the domestic domain overrode performance considerations on the conflict, but it was still the most potent issue in terms of position).

Having established the primacy of the conflict issue in voters' considerations, we proceed to look at dynamic representation in terms of the substance of the conflict. We follow voters' preferences and changes therein, corresponding government turnover, party positions, and policy under different governments.

Unlike Israel's early electoral history, beginning in the 1990s turnover in government has been high, and Israelis have consistently used the elections to transfer power and choose between leaders of opposite camps. In fact, in 1992, 1996, 1999, and 2001 there was a complete changing of the guard: the office of prime minister, the leading party, and the ruling coalition. All elections with the direct election of the prime minister provision (1996, 1999, and 2001) were turnover elections, but turnover also occurred under the old Proportional Representation system in 1992.[3] Figure 8.1 places these elections together with policy landmarks and public opinion data[4] on two survey questions. The first question asked what means Israel should emphasize to prevent war: peace talks or military power. The second asked about agreement or opposition to a Palestinian state as part of a peace settlement as a long-term solution to the conflict. These two questions may be taken, respectively, as indicators for means and ends in the Israeli-Palestinian conflict. They are not unrelated, but they exhibit two very different trends over the period of study, in line with the rational choice perspective discussed in chapter 6.

It is apparent from Figure 8.1, as previously mentioned, that there is a long-term dovish trend of a growing willingness to compromise and accept a Palestinian state since the start of the first Intifada, continuing through the Oslo years, and seeming to level off toward the end of the 1990s and on into the second Intifada. This trend line denotes the significant value change in Israeli society, to which we referred in chapter 7, where the values of the Jewish state and peace take clear precedence over the vision of a Greater Israel. The other item that measures the public's preference for either diplomatic or military means for dealing with the

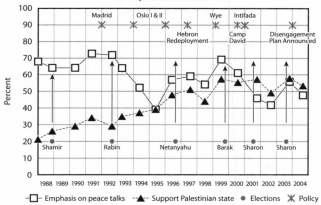

Figure 8.1. Israeli Elections, Public Opinion, and
Policy since the first Intifada

-□- Emphasis on peace talks --▲-- Support Palestinian state ● Elections ✗ Policy

Note: Data are from the "Public Opinion and National Security" project of the Jaffee Center for
Strategic Studies at Tel-Aviv University and are based on representative samples of the
Jewish adult population.

Peace Talks Emphasis is measured by the percentage responding "Concentrate on peace
talks" to the question, "What do you think Israel should emphasize in order to avoid war
with Arab countries?" (rather than "Increase its military power")
Palestinian state is measured by the percentage of respondents who agree and definitely
agree (rather than disagree and definitely disagree) with the question, "In your opinion
should Israel agree or not to the establishment of a Palestinian state in Judea, Samaria and
the Gaza Strip as part of a peace settlement?"

conflict demonstrates significant fluctuation over time and is cyclical. This
is indeed what one would expect from such a question about policy means,
which should be highly responsive to the measures governments are taking
as well as to developments in the conflict.

How do the election results and policy correspond to these public opinion preferences? Clearly the dynamic element is the public's preference for
negotiations versus military means for dealing with the conflict. Following its trend line, we can see that the growing yearning for peace talks led
to the election of left-wing Labor governments (Rabin in 1992 and Barak
in 1999). These are the two high points in terms of public preferences
for peace talks over military means. Hawkish trends with an increasing
emphasis on military power led to the election of right-wing Likud governments (Netanyahu in 1996, Sharon in 2001 and 2003, and the reelection
of Shamir in 1988, almost a year after the eruption of the first Intifada).
The elected government indeed acted in the direction of the public opinion shift concerning negotiations. The Labor governments of Rabin and
Barak initiated and immersed themselves in negotiations. The governments of Shamir (at the head of a National Unity government and a right-
wing government), Netanyahu, and Sharon emphasized military means
and shied away from negotiations. Shamir's National Unity government

with Labor fell on this issue, and in October 1991 Prime Minister Shamir was practically coerced into participating in the Madrid Conference following the First Gulf War. Similarly Netanyahu was dragged along by developments on the ground, public opinion, and international pressures into the Hebron Redeployment and the Wye River Agreement, whereas Sharon took the unilateral path. Figure 8.1 also demonstrates that, following the elections, this trend as to which means are preferable is reversed in conjunction with policy change, and even only in anticipation of it, as in a thermostat model (Erikson, MacKuen, and Stimson 2002; Wlezien 1995). Following the electoral victories of Rabin, Netanyahu, and Barak, the public adjusts its preferences for more or less diplomatic (versus military) emphasis in response to what it expects of the new government and of actual policy moves.[5]

Does the public's increased willingness to compromise, as indicated by its slowly growing acceptance of Palestinian statehood, register in politics? Indeed it does (Shamir and Shamir 2007). Party platforms and their policy moves while in office indicate that Labor moved more significantly and more quickly than did the Likud, but the Likud also moved, adapting itself to the Oslo reality. In 1992 Labor's platform acknowledged the national rights of Palestinians, hinted at a willingness to talk with the PLO, and provided greater details of peace terms and a willingness to compromise. The Likud's platform reflected no significant change relative to 1988, and it still emphasized the Israeli claim and right to sovereignty in Judea, Samaria, and Gaza. In 1996 both platforms exhibited change. Labor's platform no longer held any explicit opposition to a Palestinian state and did offer recognition of the Palestinian people. The Likud adjusted in response to the changes dictated by the Oslo Accord and accepted the Oslo reality. It still mentioned sovereignty over the Land of Israel but did not include an explicit claim to this sovereignty. It also did not speak about the importance of holding on to all the territories, and for the first time no reference was made to the settlements' contribution to security. In 1999 Labor's platform indicated a willingness to accept a Palestinian state. The Likud's platform showed no further significant change and emphasized demands from the Palestinians such as giving up the right of return and certain security measures (Oren 2005, chap. 13).

It is evident, then, that both parties moved to the left, that is, in the compromise direction, but in an uneven manner. The major policy move during this period was obviously the Oslo Accord signed by the Rabin government in 1993.[6] The next moves were incremental, and as part of the

Oslo process, both parties, when in power, relinquished territory and sovereignty to the Palestinians, including during Netanyahu's term of office. This is also true of Sharon's Disengagement Plan, announced in December 2003 and implemented in August 2005. The Gaza disengagement, however, represented a different approach to the conflict because of its unilateral logic. Most interesting from the perspective of representation and of public leaders' interrelationships is that in the January 2003 election the electorate actually voted against a similar proposal that had been put forward by Amram Mitzna, then leader of the Labor party. Nevertheless, as discussed in the previous chapter, by the end of 2003 the desire among the public to end the stalemate, together with other considerations, motivated Sharon to initiate his Disengagement Plan. In terms of the electoral connection of the public imperative, clearly it was not the public that pointed in the direction of unilateral disengagement. It was Sharon's leadership and his political outlook that made unilateral disengagement a viable policy agenda and a reality. The public imperative at the time, discussed in chapter 7, was more diffuse, consisting more of an urge to rectify the difficult and disadvantageous situation, thereby primarily opening policy opportunities to its leadership. The Gaza disengagement was not the result of an electoral mandate. A short, straight line connects it to the 2006 election and Olmert's explicit attempt to secure a mandate for his planned convergence or disengagement policy in the West Bank, to which we turn in the next section.

Whoever is in power alters the two-level game in the Palestinian-Israeli conflict, and those in power change in accordance with changing public preferences. This is the direct route in the electoral connection of representation. During the period we examine, elections have fostered representation on the conflict dimension by means of this direct route, where in four of the six elections the voters "threw the rascals out" and changed the government's makeup. In 1988 and 2003 the electorate returned the Likud governments of Shamir and Sharon to power, ostensibly in approval of their Intifada policies. Consequently the elected governments acted according to public preferences for an emphasis on negotiation and movement at the international table of the two-level game.

Above and beyond the turnabouts in government, we witnessed an overall shift of the party platforms and of policy toward compromise, corresponding to the change in public opinion. Both Labor and the Likud moved in this direction and away from the vision of a "Greater Israel" since the first Intifada. They did so differentially, with Labor governments implementing the major moves (the Oslo breakthrough and Barak's negotiations at Camp David) and the Likud taking smaller steps. This is indicated by the changes in their platforms as much as by the actual policy that each implemented while in office. Policy is incremental, and after the major policy innovation of the era, the Oslo Accord, both parties in government continued in this direction, albeit at a different pace and probably with different motives. In any case, this points to the indirect route to representation, where elected officials anticipate their constituency's reactions. All in all, the electoral connection seems to be working in Israel, and supports a rational choice analysis of Israeli leaders' policy making in the context of the conflict with the Palestinians. Elections in Israel during this period were a meaningful instrument in bringing about government responsiveness to public opinion on this fundamental issue, and in making public opinion a major imperative in the two-level Israeli-Palestinian game.

The 2006 Knesset Elections

The March 2006 Knesset elections further buttress the electoral connection and provide several additional and unusual angles in this regard.

Kadima and Party System Realignment

In the previous section we demonstrated turnover in election results, as well as changes in party platforms and policy in correspondence with changing public opinion. In 2006 the electoral connection manifested itself in the establishment and success of a new political party, Kadima, which positioned itself at the median voter location in terms of the Israeli-Palestinian conflict. The 2006 election realigned the Israeli party system in accordance with public opinion. In chapter 7 we discussed the movement of Israeli public opinion to the center, and the resulting colossal success of Kadima at the polls. Indeed, a pending "Big Bang" was being discussed in the corridors of power for quite some time before the elections. Haim Ramon,[7] in an article published in *Yediot Aharonot* in March 2005,[8] forecast this "Big Bang," arguing that Israeli politics and political parties were anachronistic, and the time had come for them to realign and offer voters real alternatives.

This took place following the Gaza disengagement and Sharon's consequent political troubles within his Likud Party. Sharon called for early elections and deserted the Likud to establish Kadima, a step widely interpreted as an indication of his future political plans. Shortly thereafter he suffered two strokes, as noted earlier, and Ehud Olmert replaced him as the head of Kadima. Despite Sharon's incapacitation, the few-months-old newly established center party became the largest party in the Knesset, and Ehud Olmert became the prime minister. Only a popular and forceful leader like Sharon could have founded Kadima, and probably the party would not have come about were it not for his leadership and vision. At the same time, however, Kadima would not have succeeded were it not in tune with voter preferences. It was a timely response to the changing value priorities and policy positions of the electorate, and the vote for it had a solid policy base of moderate and middle-of-the-road views on the Israeli-Palestinian conflict. This reservoir of votes accumulated as the combined product of two vectors accelerated by the second Intifada: A vector of *pragmatism* and one of *despair*. On the one hand, the Intifada pushed Israelis toward pragmatism. On the other, it taught Israelis that they cannot hope for a negotiated breakthrough with the Palestinians in the short term. This is the substantive meaning of the center, one that combined the willingness of the Left to compromise with the pessimism and distrust of the Right. In this regard, the combination that Kadima offered to the Israeli electorate was closest to its ideal point: a mixture of unilateralism, concessions, and bold in-group orientations of strong emphasis on a Jewish state and much distrust in the Palestinian partner.

Figure 8.2 presents Israeli voters' self-identification in terms of the Left-Right continuum according to their voting intention in our March 2006 poll conducted just before the elections. As illustrated in the figure, Kadima comes out as the ultimate centrist party, with 70 percent of its supporters identifying as centrist, and 12 percent and 15 percent, respectively, identifying as belonging to the Left and the Right. Also noteworthy is the relative similarity of Labor to Kadima, with more centrist than left-wing voters. Here again we see the pervasive movement to the center of the Israeli political continuum, where close to 60 percent of leftist Labor voters identify as centrist and only a third as left-wing.

Tables 8.2 and 8.3 provide further insight into the phenomenon of Kadima and the 2006 Israeli realignment by examining the voters who switched to Kadima from the Likud and Labor compared to those who remained loyal to these parties. The two tables compare four groups of voters based on our March 2006 poll.

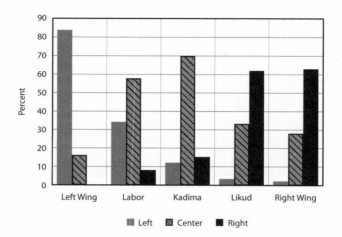

Figure 8.2. Left-Right Identification by Party (March 2006)

1. *Likud loyalists* who voted for the Likud in 2003 and intended to vote for the Likud again in 2006 (n = 21).
2. *Likud switchers* who voted for the Likud in 2003 but said they will vote for Kadima in 2006 (n = 46).
3. *Labor loyalists* who voted for Labor in 2003 and intended to vote for Labor again in 2006 (n=38).
4. *Labor Switchers to Kadima* (n = 19).

   Clearly the switchers overwhelmingly define themselves as being of the center (74% and 82%). It is noteworthy, however, that quite a few among the Likud and Labor loyalists also define themselves as centrist (38% and 45%, respectively).

TABLE 8.2. Left-Right Identification by Vote — Likud and Labor Loyalists and Switchers

2003 Vote	Likud		Labor	
2006 Vote	Likud	Kadima	Kadima	Labor
Left	3%	5%	12%	43%
Center	38%	74%	82%	45%
Right	53%	16%	5%	9%
	(n=21)	(n=46)	(n=19)	(n=38)

Table 8.3 establishes the political basis for the Kadima vote, by focusing on the policy positions of these four groups of voters. These positions pertain to some of the most important issues at the heart of the conflict and the efforts to resolve it. The first two rows list the issues that served as the direct trigger of the political "Big Bang": the disengagement and dismantling of settlements. Here we see a huge difference between the Likud loyalists and voters who switched to Kadima. Not surprisingly, there is no difference on these two issues between Labor loyalists and switchers, reflecting Kadima's shift to the center and closer to traditional Labor positions. The same pattern is evident regarding both Clinton's final status package and support for the mutual recognition of identity. The last two issues, however, provide an indication of the growing despair and sinking belief in the Palestinian side, which is evident in the differences between Labor loyalists and switchers. Switchers are noticeably less supportive of negotiations and more skeptical with respect to the feasibility of reaching a political settlement.

Table 8.4 focuses on the Likud, whose disintegration epitomizes the "Big Bang." The two middle columns (shaded) describe the Likud loyalists and switchers to Kadima analyzed in Table 8.3. Here they are compared to voters

TABLE 8.3. Policy Positions by Vote—Likud and Labor Loyalists and Switchers

2003 Vote	Likud		Labor	
2006 Vote	Likud	Kadima	Kadima	Labor
Support disengagement	24%	93%	86%	85%
Support dismantling of settlements	27%	77%	86%	85%
Support mutual recognition of identity	48%	77%	82%	74%
Support Clinton's package	29%	80%	97%	91%
Support negotiations	53%	73%	66%	90%
Believe political settlement is possible	38%	49%	55%	66%
	(n=21)	(n=46)	(n=19)	(n=38)

TABLE 8.4. Policy Positions by Vote

2003 Vote	Right and Religious Parties	Likud		Labor
2006 Vote		Likud	Kadima	
Support disengagement	16%	24%	93%	85%
Support dismantling of settlements	23%	27%	77%	77%
Support negotiations	49%	53%	73%	68%
Believe political settlement is possible	32%	38%	49%	52%
Support mutual recognition of identity	53%	48%	77%	74%
Supporting Clinton's package	27%	29%	80%	94%
Support Jerusalem Component	6%	14%	39%	67%
Support Refugees Component	16%	12%	34%	64%
Left	—	3%	5%	32%
Center	36%	38%	74%	61%
Right	55%	53%	16%	6%
	(n=96)	(n=21)	(n=46)	(n=75)

for Labor and to the combined voters for the right-wing and religious parties. The results are remarkable in that they show that those who remained loyal to the Likud have essentially the same policy positions as those who vote for the right-wing and religious parties. On the other hand, former Likud voters who voted for Kadima are strikingly similar to Labor voters. The dividing line now appears to run between the religious, right-wing, and Likud parties, on one side, and what may be called the center and the Left, which places Kadima with Labor and the Left. On this issue dimension, Kadima's electoral base is much closer to the Left than to the Right.

In sum, the establishment of Kadima along with the 2006 elections restructured the party system in accordance with the electorate's placement along the Left-Right continuum. The policy preferences of its voters now constitute the center in Israeli politics—the combination of the Left's willingness to compromise and the Right's in-group orientations stressing separation, a Jewish state, and pessimism and distrust in the Palestinians as a partner.

Olmert's Campaign Quest for a Mandate

Of special interest in terms of our focus on the role of public opinion in two-level games was Ehud Olmert's attempt during the 2006 election campaign to secure a mandate for his Convergence Plan of further disengagement on the West Bank. Olmert's campaign initiative provides a powerful example of the role of public opinion as a central player in the Israeli Palestinian game. Previous bold moves by Israeli leaders such as the Oslo interim agreement signed by Rabin and the Gaza disengagement implemented by Sharon encountered a furious delegitimization campaign by the Israeli right wing aimed at denying their capacity to take these decisions. Olmert's initiative was probably contemplated as a preemptive measure against the opposition.

Olmert disclosed his Convergence Plan in interviews to all the major newspapers on the weekend of March 10, eighteen days before election day. Ideas and parts of the plan were leaked during the previous week, probably in an attempt to gauge public response before the official launch. In his interviews Olmert connected his plan to the rise of Hamas, emphasizing that Israel will not be hostage to terrorists and will determine its borders on its own and according to its own time frame. He outlined in detail his Convergence Plan that called for withdrawal from most of the West Bank. The new border would include the blocs of the large settlements (Ariel, Ma'ale Edumim, and Gush Etzion), the Old City of Jerusalem and adjacent neighborhoods in East Jerusalem, more or less along the separation barrier, and military control of the Jordan valley. Settlements beyond the separation barrier would be evacuated, and the blocs of settlements would be fortified. Israel would wait for the new Palestinian government to allow it to accept the minimum conditions of relinquishing terrorism, recognition of Israel, and acceptance of previous agreements. If the Palestinians did not concur, however, Israel would then unilaterally determine its borders based on internal consensus and international backing.

At that point it looked as though Olmert's plan succeeded in capturing the election campaign agenda; indeed, the Likud's leader, Benjamin Netanyahu, defined the elections as a referendum over the "second disengagement plan." According to sources in the Likud campaign headquarters, the decision to use this line was based on their assessment that the majority of the public opposed further unilateral withdrawal. They suggested that Olmert's plan was beneficial to the Likud campaign, because until then it was not clear what the elections were about, whereas now a clear choice existed between Olmert's plan for a large-scale withdrawal and the Likud's plan.[9] Olmert's move raised interest and approbation among journalists, amazed at the publication of a detailed policy plan, unique in the absence of ambiguity commonly practiced in election campaigns.[10] The Convergence Plan became a major issue in the campaign. An editorial in *Haaretz* on the Friday before the election, titled "Indeed a Referendum," called on the voters to come to the polls and participate in "the first national referendum on the future of the occupation."[11]

Olmert's strategy is unusual among candidates in electoral contests in most democratic elections. The accepted approach is to blur messages, evade issues, and use vague language and "catchall" tactics, as Ariel Sharon did in the previous two election campaigns. In stark contrast, Olmert specified for the voters, in remarkable detail, precisely what their prospective choice would be. The considerations behind this move were probably diverse and complex,[12] but it is inconceivable that he would make such a move were he not seriously contemplating this policy, which is how it was interpreted. Having learned the lesson from Sharon's difficult experience in leading the Gaza disengagement, Olmert was concerned with the settlers' challenge to his legitimacy to implement another far-reaching disengagement in the West Bank. As argued in chapter 7, the settlers' campaign against Sharon was essentially a battle over public legitimacy. Sharon was accused of retreating from election promises to protect the integrity of the settlement project, and he was under tremendous pressure to hold a referendum over his Disengagement Plan. To preempt a similar scenario, Olmert put his Convergence Plan before the voters, hoping to secure a mandate.

It is difficult to estimate the impact of Olmert's move on the electorate. A comparison of INES preelection data before and after Olmert's media blitz detects no change whatsoever in voters' support for the Convergence Plan nor in their assessment that further disengagement and settlement evacuation would take place. According to this survey, a minority of about 46 percent of the general public (and 40% of Jewish voters) supported further unilateral disengagement and settlement evacuation in the West Bank, while the majority opposed it. Approximately 50 percent of the general public and 57 percent among Jews, however, gave it high odds, and almost 30 percent more gave it certain odds. In other words, there was no majority support for Olmert's suggested plan, but an overwhelming majority expected it to happen—before and after Olmert put his plan at the center of the election campaign. As to voting intentions, it is difficult to assess the impact of Olmert's move. Comparing before and after forecasts of eight media organizations, five indicated an increase in the Kadima vote varying between one and four Knesset seats, two demonstrated a decline of one and two seats, and one provided exactly the same prediction twice. It appears overall that the immediate impact was positive, but thereafter the decline in the Kadima share of the vote continued. In the final analysis,

Kadima obtained twenty-nine seats, significantly fewer than the thirty-four to thirty-six seats projected in the latest polls. Yet it was still the largest party in the 120-member Knesset, with Labor, the second-largest party, trailing far behind with nineteen seats.

Our interest, however, is not in the effect of Olmert's move on the electorate's voting intentions and issue preferences, but rather in the act itself. The major point is that the prospective winner of the elections resolutely placed his policy agenda before the public with the hope of obtaining a mandate for it. An electoral mandate provides particularly powerful authorization, legitimacy, and credibility to a leader's policy initiative, one that is especially needed when it involves a bold and innovative approach, as with conflict resolution efforts. Olmert's campaign initiative thus provided a vigorous manifestation of his appreciation of the public imperative in the two-level Palestinian-Israeli game. It also displayed the role of elections in this complex reciprocal process between leaders and publics.

But the mandate Olmert sought was not to be. In order for a mandate to materialize, the mandate's message must be identifiable, and there must be ability and commitment to carry it out. Olmert's Convergence Plan caught the public's attention, and his media blitz turned into a defining moment in the campaign. However, the election campaign in terms of media coverage, party advertisements, and the public focus was split between socioeconomic and peace and security issues, with domestic issues prevailing most of the time. Most crucial, although Kadima won the election, its share of the vote and Knesset seats (twenty-nine) was much smaller than expected, and so it did not achieve a sufficient advantage in terms of size or political weight. Although it occupied the central position in the policy space, it was not dominant enough. Olmert's victory speech and his coalition government agreement diffused the "convergence" concept. Later political developments in Israel removed the Convergence Plan from the political agenda altogether. As noted above, Olmert's quest for a mandate was probably based on the lesson he seems to have learned from the experiences of Rabin and Sharon, who both faced a fierce battle of legitimacy—Rabin over the implementation of the Oslo Accord and Sharon over the Gaza Disengagement. But the real lesson to be learned from Rabin and Sharon was that campaign promises accrue audience costs, as discussed in chapter 5. Ironically, having to back down from his Convergence Plan, together with other unsubstantiated statements during the second war in Lebanon, fatally hurt Olmert's credibility and contributed to his image as a cynical spin doctor.

Palestinian Democratization and Balance of Power since the First Intifada

Until the eruption of the first Intifada in 1987, Fatah dominated Palestinian politics. There were several other nationalist factions, but they were significantly smaller and marginal. The Intifada gave birth to the Islamist Resistance Movement, Hamas, that came to challenge the hegemony of Fatah. Two major differences separated Fatah and Hamas. First, the nationalists sought a two-state solution to the Palestinian-Israeli conflict, whereas the Islamists rejected the existence of the State of Israel and sought its destruction. While Fatah was willing to engage in negotiations with Israel, Hamas believed that only violence could end the Israeli occupation of Palestinian territories. Second, the nationalists sought the creation of an independent secular and democratic state, where state and religion were separate. The Islamists, on the other hand, wanted an Islamic state and rejected the separation of religion and state. Moreover, Islamists cared more about the nature of the state than merely its creation.

Throughout the early 1990s the balance of power between Fatah and Hamas remained unclear, as no general national or local elections took place between 1987 and 1996, when the first parliamentary election was held in the West Bank and the Gaza Strip. Furthermore, solid survey data are lacking for this period. Results of professional, student, and trade union elections show a tight race between the two factions, with Fatah maintaining a small lead, but these probably do not mirror the actual factional balance of power in public opinion, since they are too small and too particular to reflect the mood and interests of the general public.

The Oslo peace process transformed the domestic balance of power between 1993, when the Oslo process began, and 2000, when the second Intifada broke out and Hamas went into decline, with support decreasing from approximately 25 percent to approximately 15 percent. The peace process created a political system that rewarded Palestinian nationalists while marginalizing the Islamists. By linking participation in the 1996 Palestinian national elections to the acceptance of the peace process, and by selecting a majoritarian electoral system rather than the more popularly accepted proportional representation system, the Islamists were discouraged from participating in the first Palestinian parliamentary elections.[13] The Islamists viewed the peace process as illegitimate, because, in their opinion, it made unnecessary concessions to the Israelis. Fatah, who headed the PLO and had signed the peace agreements with Israel that led to the creation of the Palestinian Authority (PA), gained electoral legitimacy once a

Palestinian parliament was elected in January 1996. Seventy-five percent of eligible voters participated in the election, despite the call for a boycott by Hamas and other opposition groups. In addition to the nationalists' desire to exclude Hamas, the most important factor contributing to this development has been the failure of the Islamist faction to understand and engage the new domestic dynamics unleashed by the peace process. Palestinian public focus shifted during this period from fighting Israeli occupation to state building. The public punished Hamas, which continued to carry out violent attacks against Israelis and was detached from the daily needs of the public. Hamas was perceived as undermining the peace process which, at that time, the overwhelming majority of Palestinians supported. Despite the fact that the peace process went into a gradual decline in the second half of the 1990s, and even though, by 2000, the authoritarianism and corruption of the PA was overwhelmingly apparent, Hamas was unable to benefit from this because it failed to take the initiative during this period.[14]

Between 1996 and 2004 elections among professional associations and student bodies, as well as public opinion surveys, provided the only electoral indicators of the domestic balance of power. In 2005 presidential and local elections provided significant input as to the direction of the balance of power. While associational elections never mirrored the actual factional balance of power as we suggested previously, polls conducted by about half a dozen polling centers have been highly inconsistent, and the public and the factions viewed their results with skepticism.

Whereas associational elections demonstrated significant polarization among highly educated and politicized professionals and students, PSR polls among the public at large during the 1996–2004 period showed significant political alienation with an average of about 40 percent favoring none of the existing factions.[15]

The immediate aftermath of Yasser Arafat's death in November 2004, and the optimistic environment generated by that event and by the anticipation of the Israeli withdrawal from Gaza in 2005, created hopes for Fatah that turned out to be false. Without Arafat, the balance of power indeed shifted in favor of Fatah, increasing its popular support from an average of 28 percent in PSR's quarterly surveys in 2004 to an average of 39 percent in 2005. The Islamists dropped from 31 percent in September 2004 to 24 percent in December 2004, one month after Arafat died, but increased their strength to 35 percent by December 2005. In these same polls, Fatah obtained 40 percent and 45 percent, respectively, thereby maintaining its advantage over the Islamists.

Hamas boycotted the January 2005 presidential elections, but approx-

TABLE 8.5. Distribution (%) of Popular Vote in Four Rounds of Local Elections, 2004–2005*

	First Round (Dec. 2004–Jan. 2005)	Second Round (May 2005)	Third Round (Sept. 2005)	Fourth Round (Dec. 2005)
Fatah	30%	39%	45%	35%
Hamas	31%	32%	31%	44%
Others**	39%	28%	20%	18%

* Authors' calculation based on the official results released by the Palestinian local elections commission.
** Most other candidates were "independent" Fatah members or Fatah allies.

imately 67 percent of the eligible voters participated, and seven candidates representing the full national spectrum competed. Mahmoud Abbas won the elections with 63 percent voting for him and 19 percent for Mustafa Barghouti, representing independent and leftist forces such as the Popular Front for the Liberation of Palestine (PFLP). Local elections took place over four rounds of voting that began in December 2004–January 2005 and ended in December 2005. The combined results of the four rounds of local elections demonstrated Hamas's growing power, winning 34 percent of the popular vote to Fatah's 37 percent; 28 percent went to other candidates, mostly family and independent candidates (Shikaki 2006a). In the January 2006 parliamentary elections Hamas won 44 percent of the popular vote and Fatah won 42 percent. But the Palestinian electoral system—in which 50 percent of parliamentary seats were contested at the national level based on proportional representation, and the other 50 percent were contested in sixteen districts based on a majority system—rewarded party discipline and members' obedience and severely punished fragmentation. Hamas's discipline and Fatah's fragmentation skewed the distribution of seats in favor of Hamas, giving it 58 percent of the seats to Fatah's 37 percent, with the remaining seats going to third parties and a few independents (Shikaki 2006a).

That Fatah decisively won the presidential elections and the popular vote in all rounds of local elections except the last one (see Table 8.5) encouraged negligence and sloppiness in Fatah's performance throughout 2005. Fatah failed to take serious steps to deal with its own fragmentation and the lack of discipline among its rank and file. The postponement of Fatah's sixth convention until after the parliamentary elections indicated that Fatah did not view the prevailing divisions and fragmentation within the movement as posing a serious impediment to its ability to win future elections.

Most fatal, Fatah failed to take notice of public demand regarding the need to deal with corruption within its ranks. Throughout 2005 Fatah believed that with Mahmoud Abbas heading the PA, the peace process would soon resume, restoring public confidence in diplomacy, and that the public would then continue to look to Fatah to lead the process of peacemaking and drop its anti-corruption demands. Until December Fatah was doing well in these elections, which enabled its leaders to believe that they would be even more successful in the parliamentary elections.

The Second Intifada: The Changing Public Agenda and the Rise of Hamas

The second Intifada that erupted in 2000 changed the domestic balance of power, weakening the ruling party, Fatah, and strengthening Hamas and other Islamists. Three developments shifted public support in favor of Hamas: first, the shift in public attention to issues of governance such as corruption; second, the perceived demise of diplomacy and the declining prospects for progress in the peace process, accompanied by an increased confidence in violence as the most effective means of ending the occupation; and, third, the increased role of traditional values in shaping public behavior, a development produced by the mounting lawlessness, poverty, and overall political and security instability.

Stagnation in the peace process and the weakening of central government contributed to shifting the focus of the Palestinian public to domestic issues. In the aftermath of Arafat's death, the Palestinian political system became more open and inclusive, leading to Hamas's decision to participate in formal domestic political processes such as elections. With local elections beginning in December 2004, public attention began increasingly to focus on the legitimacy of the nationalists' state building. Issues such as corruption and good governance, which until then were being deferred to the post-independence era, gradually came to dominate the domestic agenda and party platforms, particularly those opposing Fatah, the ruling party. The net effect of this development was a diminishing of the PA's legitimacy in the eyes of the public and increased support for alternative sources of legitimacy. Groups and activities relying on "revolutionary" or Islamist legitimacy gained additional public support.

Legitimacy has been measured since 1996 by observing public responses to four issues: the status of PA democracy measured by the level of positive evaluation among the public, PA performance measured by the public's level of positive evaluation of overall performance, the perception of corruption in the PA measured by the public's belief that corruption in PA institutions exists, and the popularity of the president of the PA. Although not always occurring in parallel, shifts in the domestic balance of power showing disapproval of nationalists were associated with a depreciation of PA legitimacy. The year 1996, which witnessed the first Palestinian national elections, was the best year for PA legitimacy. By 2000, however, just before the eruption of the second Intifada, all indicators were negative, with the PA losing much of its popular legitimacy. With the Intifada unfolding, further erosion in PA legitimacy could be detected (Shikaki 2006b).

The perception of corruption seems to have been the nationalists' and the PA's Achilles' heel, with the overwhelming majority of voters in the different rounds of local elections in December 2004, January 2005, and May 2005 indicating that the incorruptibility of candidates was their first and foremost consideration; the candidates' political affiliations were listed in fifth place after education, religiosity, and position on the peace process. Voters in these contests elected more Hamas than Fatah candidates in the Gaza Strip and slightly fewer in the West Bank.[16]

Figure 8.3 demonstrates the relationship between PA legitimacy and the domestic balance of power. The dramatic decline in support for Fatah between 1996 and 2000 is accompanied by a significant decrease in public appreciation of Palestinian democracy and PA performance. Support for Arafat dropped by one-third, and the perception of PA corruption increased by 55 percent. The significant shift in the balance of power favoring the Islamists one year after the second Intifada erupted is also accompanied by a continuation of the same pre-Intifada trends.

Figure 8.3. Legitimacy and Balance of Power, 1996–2004

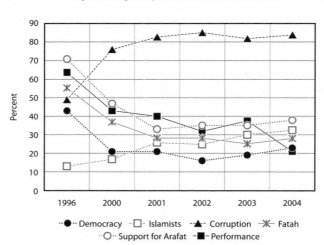

As the public lost confidence in the viability of diplomacy and in the peace process as the means to end the occupation, it began to reassess the utility of violence as a means toward achieving national rights. The failure of the Camp David summit in July 2000 was a major turning point in shaping public perception of the role of diplomacy, as discussed in chapter 6. The outbreak of the Intifada, and Palestinian exposure to violence and resorting to it, further increased demand for violence against Israelis. Unilateral withdrawal steps taken by Israel in 2000 from South Lebanon, and in 2005 from Gaza, consolidated public belief that "violence pays" and indeed helps to achieve national rights in ways that diplomacy and negotiations cannot.

The factions that were able to meet public demand were rewarded by increased support. Despite the fact that Fatah also engaged in violence against Israelis, it was Hamas that was more responsive to public demand, as it managed to carry out many more suicide attacks against the Israelis than Fatah or any other faction. Between 2000 and 2001 we witnessed the greatest increase in support of the Islamists (see Figure 8.3).

During 2003 and 2004 calls for a mutual cessation of violence increased significantly. After some hesitation, both Fatah and Hamas were quick to realign their behavior according to public demand: beginning in 2003 both began to express support for the mutual Palestinian-Israeli cessation of violence or Tahdia. By January 2005 the cessation of violence was in place.

Prolonged violence and the failed peace process contributed greatly to a stagnant economy and a highly unstable domestic environment, where the central government was weak, law and order hardly existed, and a sense of safety and security was generally absent among the population. In this environment, traditional, religious, and family values reasserted themselves, as people were no longer willing to take the risks involved in embracing liberal and secular values. Large families provided financial support and protection for their family members; tribal rules of dispute and conflict resolution substituted for the normal functions of police and courts; and membership in organized armed factions provided jobs and other financial rewards as well as social status and physical security.

The Road to the 2006 Turnabout Elections

Developments in the years and months leading up to the January 2006 parliamentary elections provided the backdrop for clear party differentiation in the minds of the public. These dynamics led an increasing number of people to abandon Fatah and support Hamas. Support for third parties remained limited, never exceeding 15 percent. Comprehending the process of party differentiation helps us understand the rise of Hamas and the decline of Fatah during the 2000–2004 period, the short-lived increase in support for Fatah and the decline in support for Hamas during 2005, and the eventual Hamas electoral victory in January 2006.

Determinants of Party Affiliation

In determining one's party affiliation and vote, three dynamics have been found to come into play during the past decade: preference for violence versus diplomacy; a focus on traditional values versus secular and liberal values, and the attention in state building on gaining independence and building a state versus fighting corruption and building good governance.

When Palestinians believe that diplomacy is viable and can help them attain independence and end the occupation, they support and vote for Fatah because they expect it to deliver a peace agreement with Israel. Therefore, if there is a viable peace process—the prevailing perception in the mid-1990s—people turn to Fatah. If the peace process is not viable and, equally important, if one believes that violence pays, he or she is not likely to turn to Fatah or third parties but will turn instead to Hamas. Supporters of third parties distinguish themselves from those voting for Fatah by taking a more hard-line view on the issues of negotiations. In the second half of 2000 Palestinians were convinced that diplomacy was failing them. In the aftermath of the Israeli unilateral withdrawals from South Lebanon and later from the Gaza Strip, and in the aftermath of the Israeli war with Hezbullah in the summer of 2006, Palestinians became convinced that violence pays and that Israel best understands the logic of force.

The second reason why people chose Hamas over Fatah is linked to the role of traditional values in politics and society. If individuals maintain that traditional values are important, they turn to Hamas. If, however, they want more liberal political values and a more secular political system, they are likely to turn to Fatah. Voters of third parties tend to seek not only a more secular and liberal political system, but a more secular and liberal social order as well. Fatah represents those Palestinians who value traditional social values but tend nonetheless to seek a modern and Westernized political system. Supporters of Hamas are those who seek to consolidate the conservative nature of society and reduce the impact of secularism and Westernization on the political system. When domestic stability, tranquility, and economic prosperity prevail, the tendency among voters to take risks and go beyond traditionalism increases. A combination of economic prosperity, domestic security, and political stability leads people to seek liberal, secular values, whereas increased poverty, violence, and political uncertainty lead people to seek refuge in traditional values, to return to family and religion. In other words, the increased levels of instability and poverty during the second Intifada benefited Hamas and reduced support for Fatah.

The third factor that motivates people to vote is how they view Palestinian state building. At stake for those who support Fatah is the attainment of independence and sovereignty in a state in the West Bank and Gaza; clean and good governance can be achieved later on. In their mind, therefore, state building tends to be very much about creating an independent and sovereign state. For those who support Hamas, on the other hand, the question of establishing a state, though important, is not sufficient. The nature of the state and the pre-state entity, the PA, matters. Hamas voters focus on clean governance; they want a pre-state authority and a post-independence state free of corruption. Third-party voters share Fatah voters' passion for independence and sovereignty, and do not disagree with Hamas voters on the critical need for a clean Palestinian Authority, but they add to that the need for the creation of a liberal democratic political system. Fatah voters therefore seek first and foremost the creation of an independent state, Hamas voters focus on fighting corruption, and third party voters tend to focus on building liberal democratic state institutions. Today most Palestinians continue to associate Fatah with corruption and fragmentation, whereas Hamas is viewed as clean and cohesive. The growing conspicuousness of corruption benefited Hamas and hurt Fatah.

The 2005 Presidential Elections

The death of Yasser Arafat in November 2004, as pointed out, temporarily changed public perception of the future of Palestinian-Israeli diplomacy, along with Palestinian state building and economic recovery. This change was significant and influenced the outcome of the presidential elections in which Fatah's candidate received 63 percent of the popular vote, as well as the local elections in which Fatah won the popular vote in all but the last round in December 2005. However, this change in the climate of opinion was short-lived. The unfolding events during 2005 brought about significant public disillusionment, and the focus shifted to state-building failures such as corruption and lawlessness, and to the unilateral Israeli policy in the Gaza Strip and the West Bank, like the unilateral disengagement from Gaza and the building of the separation barrier in the West Bank.

As Table 8.6 demonstrates, one month after Arafat's death a majority of Palestinians (53%) believed that his death would increase the chances

TABLE 8.6. Public Expectations regarding Violence and Diplomacy before and after the Death of Yasser Arafat

Expectations	September 2004 (before Arafat's death)	December 2004 (after Arafat's death)
Expect continued violence and no return to negotiations	37%	12%
Expect negotiations to resume soon and violence to stop	17%	30%
Expect negotiations to resume but some violence to continue	39%	53%
Believe reconciliation between the two peoples is never possible	47%	34%
Popularity of Islamists	31%	24%
Popularity of Fatah	29%	40%
Popularity of other forces	12%	11%
Undecided	29%	25%

for progress in the peace process. Two months before his death, 37 percent expected continued violence and no return to negotiations, and only 17 percent expected a return to negotiations and continued violence. Forty-seven percent believed that reconciliation between the Israelis and Palestinians is never possible. In December 2004 public expectations changed significantly, and along with that the popularity of Hamas fell while Fatah's rose. This dramatic change in expectations regarding the peace process contributed to the high level of participation (67%) in the presidential elections, despite Hamas's boycott, and the large percentage of support (63%) for Mahmoud Abbas, Fatah's candidate in those elections.

In addition to peacemaking, three other issues came to dominate the Palestinian public agenda during this time: the need to improve economic conditions, the need to address corruption, and the need to enforce law and order. Despite poll findings showing considerable public interest in the issue of corruption at the time of the presidential elections, and in spite of this issue playing a critical role in increasing the appeal of Hamas, they also indicate that the considerations of the voters in the presidential race were different from those in the local elections. In the presidential elections, voters wanted a president who was able to improve the economic conditions and resume the peace process. In the local elections, the integrity and incorruptibility of the candidates was the primary consideration. In the presidential elections, Mahmoud Abbas was the candidate most perceived as meeting voters' requirements, something he fully understood, as his election campaign focused on the big national issues: the economy and the peace process. He declared his intention to revitalize the economy, reduce unemployment, and pursue the peace process with Israel based on the two-state solution. He repeatedly asserted his opposition to Palestinian use of violence during the Intifada, knowing that the overwhelming majority supported an Israeli-Palestinian mutual cessation of violence.

Our exit poll on the day of the presidential elections indicated that the main issue on voters' minds was not corruption. Instead, the public was focused on poverty, unemployment, and the need to improve the economy; the Israeli occupation measures and the need to revive the peace process; and lawlessness and chaos, and the need to restore law and order. For 23 percent of the voters, the top priority was the ability of the presidential candidate to improve economic conditions. (One week before the presidential elections, 61% believed that Abbas was the individual who could do that.) The ability to reach a peace agreement with Israel came second, with 19 percent (with 71% believing that Abbas was the one most able to make peace). Most important, 52 percent believed that it was possible to negotiate a compromise agreement with the Israeli leadership of Ariel Sharon, and 58 percent believed that, if such an agreement was reached, the leadership would be able to convince the Israeli public to accept it. In third place was the ability to enforce law and order, according to 16 percent of voters (with 60% believing that Abbas was the one most able to accomplish this).[17]

The 2004–2005 Local Elections

PSR exit polls throughout 2005 showed that, in the local elections in 264 localities in the West Bank and the Gaza Strip, the vote for Hamas was primarily a vote against corruption, whereas a vote for Fatah was first and foremost a vote to improve economic conditions and end the Israeli occupation. Hamas and its candidates, who won more votes than Fatah only in the last round in December 2005, were perceived as honest, whereas Fatah's candidates, who did better than Hamas's in the first three rounds, were seen as corrupt. Fatah was able to withstand the corruption charges in the first three rounds only because the public at that time placed corruption as the third most important problem confronting Palestinians. Economic issues and Israeli occupation were identified, respectively, as the first and second most important problems in the first three rounds. Only in the fourth round did voters identify corruption as the most important problem confronting

Palestinians. For Hamas voters, the need to fight corruption was the most significant priority in all rounds. But even for Hamas voters, improving economic conditions was viewed in the first round as equally important to that of fighting corruption. As for those supporting Fatah's candidates, improving economic conditions came first in all rounds, followed by the need to reach a peace agreement with Israel. Fighting corruption came last in all rounds. In other words, the Hamas victory in the last round of the local elections, just one month before the parliamentary elections, came about primarily because most Palestinians at that time viewed corruption as the most important issue confronting Palestinians. Notably voters in the Gaza Strip, where Hamas consistently did better than Fatah in all rounds, were more concerned about corruption than voters in the West Bank.[18]

The Palestinian 2006 Parliamentary Elections

By January 2006 the optimistic post-Arafat climate of opinion had dissipated, and public expectations once again were pessimistic. The newly elected president, Mahmoud Abbas, failed to address most of the public's expectations, as Israel refused to engage him in serious peace negotiations while he failed to deliver on ending Palestinian violence against Israelis. Equally important, Abbas failed to restore domestic law and order, a development that inflicted considerable damage on his party, Fatah, which was viewed by the public as the primary culprit in the anarchy and chaos that increased considerably during this period. Moreover, Abbas took no action whatsoever to diminish public perceptions that the PA was corrupt and that this corruption would increase or remain the same in the future. Fatah continued to believe that a promise of progress in the peace process would convince the public to remain loyal to the party. Its election platform focused on independence and the creation of a sovereign Palestinian state. In addition, in the post-Arafat era, fragmentation within Fatah increased considerably, leading to a split within the movement one month before the elections. At the official level, Fatah managed in the end to present the public with one official list for the party and its candidates, but, in reality, the split was too deep and could not be addressed solely with superficial camouflage.

In contrast, Hamas was unified and highly disciplined. During its election campaign it focused on Fatah's weaknesses, bringing up issues such as corruption and the failure of the PA and Fatah to deliver law and order or end the occupation. Its election platform avoided taking clear positions on issues it knew the public opposed, such as Hamas's opposition to the peace process. It did not seek a mandate to reverse the peace process, despite its clear ideology and previous positions. It made no mention of its refusal to accept the two-state solution, to accept existing agreements with Israel, or to recognize the State of Israel in a permanent peace agreement. In other words, Hamas sought to avoid having the elections serve as a referendum on the peace process. For this reason, many new "third parties" were created in the few weeks before the elections. They hoped to capitalize on the failure of the two major parties to meet public expectations in vital areas of peace and governance. Ultimately, however, Hamas's campaign strategy proved highly effective and third parties were perceived as too weak to deliver on any of the issues.

Hamas's mission to win hearts and minds was facilitated by the prevailing gloomy climate of opinion during the months and weeks before the election. Public expectations that violence would prevail and negotiations would not resume increased from 12 percent during the optimistic days in December 2004 to 28 percent in January 2006. Belief that a political settlement was never possible increased from 34 percent to 44 percent. During those thirteen months, the popularity of the Islamist factions increased by more than 50 percent, from 24 percent to 37 percent, whereas that of Fatah remained almost unchanged.[19]

Public perception of the nature of the problems confronting the Palestinians changed significantly in one year, given these developments in the Israeli-Palestinian conflict and in domestic Palestinian politics, as well as a result of Hamas's efficient campaign. The issue of the peace process and economics now attained the lowest priority, with corruption and lawlessness dominating the agenda. This hierarchy of priorities increased Islamists' popularity and significantly influenced electoral behavior leading to Hamas's electoral victory. The emergence of corruption as the most important issue served Hamas's interests, as the public perceived the Islamist movement as clean and truthful. Moreover, public feelings of the loss of security and safety hurt Fatah's popularity, since most people viewed Fatah as responsible for the lawlessness. Similarly the decline in the importance of the peace process caused a great deal of damage to Fatah, since it was this movement that presented itself to the public as the owner of the peace process and the two-state solution.

Table 8.7 is based on exit poll results[20] and demonstrates how all the above-mentioned considerations affected the vote in the legislative elections. Voters' behavior was considerably affected by their own priorities, expectations, and perceptions of their personal safety and security. For example, 71 percent of those who identified corruption as their top priority voted for Hamas, whereas Fatah received only 19 percent of their vote. By contrast, 69 percent

TABLE 8.7. Vote by Priorities and Other Factors Influencing Selection of Electoral Lists

Vote on Election Day	*Voters' Priorities, Expectations, and Perceptions of Safety*						
	Ability to fight corruption was the primary consideration when voting	Expectation of continued violence and no return to negotiations	Feels no safety or security at all	Between optimism and pessimism	Feels full safety and securty	Optimistic about the future	Ability to reach a peace agreement was the primary consideration when voting
Hamas	71%	64%	56%	47%	35%	26%	19%
Fatah	19%	25%	31%	38%	53%	59%	69%
Third parties	11%	11%	13%	16%	12%	15%	12%
Total	100%	100%	100%	100%	100%	100%	100%

of those who identified the ability to reach a peace agreement with Israel as the most important factor in the selection of the party voted for Fatah, and Hamas received only 19 percent of their vote. The more unsafe and insecure voters felt, the more they voted for Hamas, and the more safe and secure they felt, the more they voted for Fatah. Support for Hamas among those feeling the least safe and secure reached 56 percent and for Fatah 31 percent. In contrast, among those feeling safe and secure, votes for Hamas dropped to 35 percent but increased to 53 percent for Fatah.

Voters were able to identify factions based on their abilities to deal with the issues that concerned them, as well as their positions on the issues. Results of the January preelection surveys and the exit poll have shown that Hamas was always selected as the party most able to fight corruption, whereas Fatah was always selected as the party most able to reach a peace agreement with Israel. In a January 2006 PSR preelection poll, 50 percent of the Palestinians believed Hamas was the party most able to fight corruption, and only 34 percent believed that Fatah was the most able to do so. Similar results were obtained on the day of the election: 50 percent believed that Hamas was most able to fight corruption, and 37 percent believed that Fatah could best do the job. The preelection survey found 59 percent of the Palestinians believing that Fatah was most able to reach a peace agreement with Israel, with only 24 percent believing that Hamas could do it best. On the day of the election, 61 percent of the voters thought that Fatah was most able to deliver progress in the peace process, and only 27 percent believed that Hamas was most able. Voters were also clear about their own priorities: most important was the need to fight corruption, with one-quarter of the voters selecting it. In contrast, only 9 percent selected the need to reach a peace agreement as their top priority.[21]

Three major conclusions emerge from our findings and analysis. First, the outcome of the legislative elections was primarily influenced by public perceptions and demands regarding governance. The outcome reflected public preferences for policy changes in governance, making Hamas more attractive to voters, while public distrust of diplomacy neutralized Fatah's greatest asset. Hamas understood this long before the elections took place; Fatah, on the other hand, did not understand or chose to ignore it, hoping to meet public needs in areas other than governance such as the peace process. Fatah lost the elections because voters believed that Hamas was more able to deliver better governance in the area of fighting corruption. PSR polls during the preceding five years showed that an average of approximately 80 percent of the public believed that the PA was corrupt. Hamas's success in elevating the status of corruption to a top priority constituted a magnificent achievement, ensuring its victory in the elections.

Second, voters' behavior was influenced by their pessimism about the future of Palestinian-Israeli relations. The stagnation of the peace process destroyed Fatah's chances by removing the issue from voters' cost-benefit calculations. In other words, the lack of confidence in diplomacy rendered Fatah's greatest asset irrelevant to voting behavior, with only 9 percent of the voters placing the peace process on top of their agenda, according to PSR's exit poll. Although the majority of voters shared Fatah's views on the peace process, and indeed viewed Fatah as the party most able to advance the cause of the peace process, as indicated earlier, the overwhelming majority seemed to have lost confidence in the viability of the peace process. The only sign of hope was the Israeli disengagement, as reflected in the dismantling of all settlements in the Gaza Strip and a few in the West Bank, but it was decided and implemented unilaterally, thereby only reinforcing the perception of Fatah's helplessness to renew the peace process. Moreover, that was a step the Palestinian public viewed as a victory for armed struggle, giving Hamas most of the credit for this achievement. In September 2005, 84 percent of the public viewed the Israeli disengagement as a victory for armed resistance, and a plurality of 40 percent believed that Hamas deserved most of the credit for that achievement. Only 11 percent gave the credit to Fatah. A negotiated peace process was the centerpiece of Fatah's national agenda; therefore the collapse of diplomacy dealt a heavy blow to the national movement.

Although a majority viewed Hamas as more able than Fatah to ensure the "continuation of the armed Intifada," the vote for Hamas was not an expression of support or a demand for violence, as the Intifada was literally the last thing on voters' minds (only 5% viewed it as the most important consideration in their vote). The overwhelming majority of Palestinians (always more than 80%) indicated support throughout 2005 for a Palestinian-Israeli cease-fire. As we saw in chapter 6, support for violence among the Palestinians during the last decade should be understood in terms of their aim to maintain the use of force as a policy instrument, their assessment of the viability of violent versus diplomatic means, as well as an emotional response to threat—not an indication of political extremism. It fluctuated depending on developments on the ground such as collective punishment, settlement activities, home demolition, the building of the separation barrier, and steps to isolate Jerusalem and sever links between Palestinian Jerusalemites and Palestinians living in the rest of the West Bank and the Gaza Strip. But the Israeli decision to unilaterally disengage and pull out of the Gaza Strip—a decision perceived as a victory for violence by an overwhelming majority of Palestinians, as indicated above—enhanced Palestinians' perception of the role of violence as an instrument of policy. Hamas's declared commitment to armed struggle, though not a major attraction, no longer troubled voters. As discussed earlier, the adoption of armed struggle as an instrument of policy has been well understood and overwhelmingly supported by the Palestinian public.

The third conclusion is that, given what we know about the role of corruption and peace in voters' calculations, the vote for Hamas cannot be interpreted primarily as an embrace of its value system or its ideological and political views. Religion was a factor, but in no way can the vote for Hamas be interpreted as a vote for Islam. Based on the exit poll, it is evident that Hamas voters tended to be more religious than Fatah supporters: Hamas received the support of 52 percent of the more religious voters, and Fatah and the other eleven lists were backed by only 48 percent. Yet, equally important, 38 percent of the "somewhat religious" and 19 percent of the "not religious" voted for Hamas.

Moreover, and probably most important in terms of our concerns with the public imperative in the Palestinian-Israeli two-level game, only a minority of the voters identified with Hamas's views on the peace process; the majority identified with Fatah's. For example, in our January 25 exit poll, a majority of 60 percent viewed themselves as supporting the peace process, and 23 percent saw themselves somewhere between supporting and opposing the process. Only 17 percent defined themselves as opposed to the peace process. Attitudes regarding three critical (long-, mid-, and short-term) issues of the peace process were also examined in PSR's exit poll. All three received majority support from the voters: the two-state solution with Palestinians recognizing Israel as the state of the Jewish people, and Israel recognizing Palestine as the state of the Palestinian people;

TABLE 8.8. Voting Groups' Position on Various Issues relating to the Peace Process

	Hamas Voters	Fatah Voters	Voters of Other Parties
Support the peace process	40%	79%	62%
Support collecting arms from armed factions	32%	65%	57%
Support the implementation of the Roadmap	32%	70%	50%
Support mutual recognition of Israel as a Jewish state and Palestine as a Palestinian state in a two-state context	34%	60%	63%

implementation of the Roadmap; and collection of arms from all armed groups whereby the PA security services would be the only armed force in PA areas. Indeed, as Table 8.8 shows, even among Hamas voters, one-third or more (32–40%) identified themselves as supporters of the peace process and supported the three positions outlined above.

These results pose a challenge to Hamas in terms of maintaining public support: a clear attitudinal gap exists between its positions and the public majority regarding the peace process. As long as the Palestinian public continues to view the peace process as deadlocked, Hamas has little to fear. This explains why, in the post-election period, the public increased its support for Hamas while simultaneously becoming even more moderate. The March PSR post-election survey found support for the peace process increasing, with 72 percent wanting the cease-fire to continue, 75 percent wanting Hamas to negotiate peace with Israel, and 53 percent wanting Hamas to implement the Roadmap. Sixty-seven percent supported a two-state solution even when the formula presented was one in which Palestinians recognize Israel as the state for the Jewish people and Palestine as the state for the Palestinian people, once all issues in dispute have been settled. That 58 percent, as the survey found, believed that a majority of Palestinians support this formula for a two-state solution was a clear indication that despite the Hamas victory, the public did not think Palestinians have embraced hardline attitudes regarding the peace process. Surprisingly this percentage was the highest Palestinian percentage ever recorded in our polls, indicating that it was the normative attitude of the society. If and when the public believes that progress in the peace process is possible, Hamas will find it difficult to maintain its current peace policies and still remain in power.

Indeed, the post-election period witnessed important changes in Hamas's behavior and positions indicating that it was aware of its predicament, and that it may be responsive to public opinion. By agreeing to the Prisoners' Document and the Mecca Agreement of February 2007, Hamas has introduced important changes in its declared positions. For example, whereas Hamas insisted that it can only agree to a "hudna"—a truce or armistice with Israel that would not rule out a return to violence in the future—some of its leaders have not ruled out conducting negotiations over a permanent peace once a hudna is in place. On the question of the recognition of Israel, Hamas has consistently denied Israel's legitimate right to exist but has not rejected the acceptance of Israel as a reality and a "fact on the ground." Even while denying Israel's legitimacy, under the conditions of a hudna, Hamas was willing to allow a Palestinian state to engage in normal relations with the State of Israel. Hamas still rejected an agreement that would end the conflict with Israel, as it sought to keep some issues on the table, such as the refugees' Right of Return. Nonetheless, Hamas did not rule out the possibility that the severity of conflict over these issues might diminish over time. Finally, as part of the Mecca Agreement, Hamas agreed to "respect" those same Oslo agreements which until then it considered illegitimate.

The Electoral Connection in the Israeli-Palestinian Two-Level Game

Israel is a well-established democracy with an entrenched party system delineated primarily by the cleavage over the Palestinian-Israeli conflict. Its electoral history includes seventeen Knesset elections between 1949 and 2006 and one more election only for the office of prime minister (in 2001). The history of elections in the PA is much shorter. The first presidential and parliamentary elections were held in January 1996, as one of the high points of the Oslo peace process. Arafat and his Fatah movement, having dominated Palestinian politics long before the establishment of the PA, won both contests by a landslide. Turnout reached 75 percent, but Hamas, as well as other opposition groups, did not participate in these elections. The next elections in the PA took place almost a decade later. Following the death of Arafat in November 2004, presidential elections were held in January 2005. Hamas boycotted these elections as well, but two-thirds of the eligible voters participated, several candidates representing the full national spectrum competed, and Mahmoud Abbas won the elections with 63 percent of the vote. In the January 2006 elections to the Legislative Council, Hamas participated and won. Before these critical turnabout elections, Hamas also took part in the local elections held in several rounds in the West Bank and Gaza between December 2004 and December 2005.

Our analysis of Israeli elections compellingly exposed the public imperative in the Palestinian-Israeli two-level game. We corroborated the notion of dynamic representation and the role of the electoral connection in this process. Changes in public opinion resulted in corresponding changes in policy, and elections were a major tool in forging this linkage. We have established the salience of the conflict issue in electoral politics and have shown that Israeli voters, to a considerable extent, cast their ballots based on this issue. We have further established the correspondence between public opinion shifts, government turnovers, platform accommodations, and the establishment of new parties and policy adjustments over the period since the first Intifada. The 2006 Knesset elections provided particularly notable manifestations of the importance of public opinion in the Israeli-Palestinian two-level game. The establishment and success of Kadima, and the realignment of the Israeli party system in step with public opinion, were one aspect. Another was Olmert's quest for an electoral mandate for his Convergence Plan in the West Bank. Olmert put his policy agenda before the public in detail, hoping to obtain an electoral mandate and the authorization, legitimacy, and credibility that would accompany this mandate. Even though the election did not end up a mandate election as he had hoped, this case provides a powerful manifestation of a leader's appreciation of the public imperative in the two-level Palestinian-Israeli game, especially when bold and difficult policy initiatives are necessary.

In the Palestinian 2006 elections Hamas's strategy was exactly the opposite, seeking to avoid having the elections serve as a referendum on the peace process. Indeed, our analysis suggests that good governance issues lead voters' electoral considerations. Unlike referendums, in elections voters select leaders and parties and not policy directly, with many issues usually placed on the agenda of the voters and the competitors. Moreover, campaign strategy often dictates blurring messages and evading issues. Because voting is a low-information form of participation and the meaning of elections is often elusive, interpretations of elections are debatable. However the indirect ratification power that elections afford is not defined by any one election; it stems from the institutionalization of elections and the extent to which elected leaders believe in the reward and punishment efficacy of the electorate. The higher the salience or intensity of an issue, the more likely that leaders will consider public preferences (Trumbore 1998), and the Palestinian-Israeli conflict is, without question, highly intense and salient.

The Palestinian electoral experience suggests that there is an institutional and civic learning process of the electoral connection, probably for citizens and policy makers alike. It takes time for a party system to institutionalize, for party affiliation to be acquired, and for civic culture to develop. Elections allow the public to hold those elected accountable for their performance in office by "throwing the rascals out." The Palestinian electorate in 2006 did precisely that, primarily because of corruption and lawlessness. Elections should allow the voters to select their leaders and choose between policy alternatives. Palestinians hold coherent views on the Palestinian-Israeli conflict and the peace process, and this is obviously a salient dimension in politics; but in the brief Palestinian history of elections, important party and policy alternatives were missing until recently because central actors boycotted the elections. In the 2006 parliamentary elections, the electoral priorities, structured by Israeli policy and domestic state-building failure, muted the potency of this crucial dimension by removing it from voters' cost-benefit calculations. Elections should also engage the public and its leaders in a reciprocal process, where the elected leaders heed their publics in anticipation of the next elections. In other words, the need to be reelected should motivate the elected representatives to be attentive to public opinion. However, as we have demonstrated, the Fatah leadership did not seem to have internalized this feature of elections—either for lack of ability or lack of will. As a result of the longtime uncertainties about the balance of power, and from its position of long-term dominance, it neglected the need to take into account its electorate's preferences. It did not correctly assess the changing public agenda and the growing criticism of its failure in state and good governance building, and was ousted from power in the January 2006 parliamentary elections. Our analysis uncovered signs that Hamas might have learned the importance of responsiveness to public preferences in the framework of electoral democracy, but the jury is obviously still out on this, as well as on the question of Hamas's commitment to electoral democracy altogether. The question as to whether Fatah and Hamas, the major Palestinian political actors, will draw both the normative and instrumental democratic conclusions from the 2006 electoral reversal remains to be seen.

The outcome of the 2006 Palestinian elections dramatically changed both the Palestinian domestic table as well as the international table of the Palestinian-Israeli two-level game, reminding Israeli and international participants in the game that it is indeed a two-level game. The lack of progress in the peace process may have damaging consequences for the Palestinian domestic balance of power. Helping Palestinian "moderates" regain the initiative and win public confidence by restoring public confidence in diplomacy has become a major theme in regional and international diplomatic contacts.

Conclusion

Public opinion is a central imperative in two-level games. This is the major tenet of this book, and the rationale behind the Joint Israeli-Palestinian Poll (JIPP) which we have been conducting together since 2000. Our aim in the book was to highlight the role public opinion plays in the context of the Israeli-Palestinian conflict, through conflict resolution and management phases as well as through outbursts of violence during the Al-Aqsa Intifada.

Domestic publics in democracies may constitute crucial veto actors of international agreements. This is evident when the public has the power to directly ratify international agreements under certain institutional arrangements. But public opinion is also an essential actor in two-level games when no such institutional arrangements apply where high-intensity and salient issues are involved, even in autocratic systems. Public opinion confers or denies political legitimacy. This is highly valued by autocratic leaders precisely because they cannot draw upon institutional legitimacy. However, public opinion and its unique characteristics as a domestic player have been largely neglected in the body of theoretical and empirical research building on Robert Putnam's two-level game metaphor. This book sought to fill this lacuna. The cases and critical events analyzed provide theoretical insights central to the two-level game paradigm regarding the role of public opinion in these games, as well as policy-relevant lessons for the future. These observations have been drawn based on the unique data set produced by the Joint Israeli-Palestinian Poll.

Public Opinion as a Domestic Imperative: Theoretical Insights from the Palestinian-Israeli Conflict

Tracing the Palestinian-Israeli conflict since 2000, we analyzed several modalities of the role of public opinion in the two-level game that exhibit public opinion involvement in conflict resolution efforts and in the management of the conflict. The first modality of public opinion involvement was documented during the July 2000 Camp David summit, where public opinion on both sides severely constrained the bargaining options of Ehud Barak and Yasser Arafat.

Evidently the summit failed. As we argued in chapter 5, contrary to Schelling's conjecture, the respective constraints did not provide a bargaining advantage to either side. In fact, the outcome corresponded to a greater extent with Tarar's analysis which shows that domestic constraints are not necessarily a bargaining advantage when both sides are constrained and the outcome depends, among other things, on the leaders' respective beliefs regarding their own and the other side's constraints. We suspect that these were flawed at the time the summit took place. Moreover, as Tarar also demonstrates, in cases where both sides are highly constrained, delay in reaching an agreement may result in losses for both sides, where they receive discounted payoffs compared to what they would respectively be receiving if neither side were constrained.

Unfortunately both Barak and Arafat went to Camp David with their lips closed, avoiding any attempt to obtain more slack from their constituencies by preparing their publics for the depth of concessions required to reach an agreement. Apparently this "closed-lips syndrome" is not unique to the game Arafat and Barak played at Camp David. It stems from the dynamics inherent in many two-level games of this kind. These dynamics often suggest a trade-off between the leaders' need to expand their own and the other side's win-sets, and their desire to retain their bargaining edge. This dilemma is particularly relevant concerning public opinion constraints. Interactions between leaders and their publics are necessarily a matter of public record. Acts or statements designed to mold public opinion in more conciliatory directions risk the disclosure of credible information on the leader's reservation price. Such statements are taken to be credible given the domestic political risk the leader is taking by revealing unpopular policy positions. On the international table, these statements expose leaders to further demands from the other side and can spoil the deal they were hoping to achieve at the outset. As a result, leaders tend to keep their lips closed, and consequently their hands remain tied by their unprepared constituency, which again might undermine an agreement. This vicious circle is characteristic of many two-level games where public opinion is a decisive player at the domestic table.

The second modality of public opinion involvement in the Israeli-Palestinian conflict arose when an accommodating Israeli public opened new policy opportunities that came into effect in Sharon's Gaza Disengagement Plan. The case of the disengagement, examined in chapter 7, powerfully demonstrates the dynamic relationship between public opinion and leaders in two-level games, and the viability of our view of public opinion as a multifaceted phenomenon. Similar to the first Intifada and the Oslo process, the Israeli public moved ahead of its leadership on a crucial policy issue—that of relinquishing Palestinian territories. As far back as mid-2001, a majority of Israelis supported the dismantling of most settlements for peace, whereas even after the 2003 election Sharon still insisted that "the fate of Netzarim (a settlement in the Gaza Strip) was the fate of Tel-Aviv."[1] The willingness evidenced in public opinion to relinquish settlements provided an opportunity and impetus for Sharon's dramatic policy reversal. In turn, his policy declaration regarding the disengagement in December 2003 transformed Israelis' "private" opinions into "public opinion" and legitimized the Disengagement Plan. This was a crucial phase shift in public opinion from a mere favorable sentiment held privately by many people to actual collective readiness and legitimacy for the implementation of the plan.

The third and more intricate expression of the significance of public opinion in the Palestinian-Israeli two-level game was the leaders' ability to use the other side's public, in addition to their own, as leverage in their game. This is what Putnam calls "reverberation strategies": the reverberation of international pressures within domestic politics, often intended to tip the domestic balance in order to influence the international negotiations. As we contend in chapter 7, this intricate move came to the fore with Sharon's implicit threat directed at Abu Mazin to shatter his political support among Palestinians unless he cracks down on Hamas. The unilateral component in Sharon's Disengagement Plan was meant to be just that: denying Abu Mazin the opportunity to negotiate the disengagement threatened to deprive him of the only political asset he held over Hamas— the ability to promise Palestinians a peaceful rather than a violent path to a settlement with Israel. Withholding negotiations also threatened to deny Fatah's leadership from claiming credit for Israel's withdrawal and to leave Hamas as the sole victor in the eyes of the Palestinian public.

Ironically, using the opponent's public opinion as leverage to achieve political goals has long been a major objective of terrorism. Indeed, the fourth modality of public opinion involvement in the game—on both sides—was its support of the use of violence as an instrument in the game and the expectations it transmitted to leaders in this regard. Our conception of aggregate public opinion as an informed player actively involved in the domestic game is consistent with the preferences of the Palestinian and Israeli publics regarding the management of the conflict in terms of the extent to which violent or diplomatic means should be used. This depiction of public opinion also helps to decipher a long-standing puzzle that we encountered in our longitudinal research of the Palestinian-Israeli conflict, going back to the first Intifada. As we discussed in detail in chapter 6, we observed simultaneous trends of support for violence and compromise. Among Palestinians—as the weaker side in a national liberation conflict—the adoption of armed struggle as an instrument of policy has been well understood and overwhelmingly supported. Their support for the use of violence increased when diplomacy failed or did not promise progress toward achieving Palestinian national goals; it was also correlated with mounting threat. Israelis understood this mechanism and feared that, in the absence of any progress in the negotiations with the Palestinians, a third Intifada was bound to erupt. However, following the flare-up of the Intifada, their support for violent measures intended to quash the Intifada was staggering. Concurrently we observed support in both publics for the continuation of negotiations between the parties and growing support for compromise involving long-term goals. This seemingly contradictory pattern is explained by the two publics' ability to distinguish between violence as a means and conflict resolution as a goal, and to apply different cost-benefit calculations to each within the context of the two-level game.

Public opinion on both sides, even in the bloodiest and most desperate periods, continued to support negotiations, and was even further moderated on the basic parameters of the conflict. At the same time, however, it was transmitting expectations for the use of violence, thus becoming deeply involved in the two-level game, in stages of conflict management just as in conflict resolution efforts. Throughout the Intifada we could observe this classic dispute that has long characterized national liberation conflicts and attempts to resolve them, where the weaker side seeks to maintain, by all means possible, the use of force as a policy instrument, and the stronger side seeks to deny its use as a legitimate instrument.

At this point we can classify the four modalities of public opinion involvement in the Israeli-Palestinian game into a two-by-two matrix in which one dimension delineates the type of effect—whether public opinion exerts constraints or opens opportunities; and the second dimension refs to the arena in which the effect takes place—in one's own side or the other. The Camp David case exemplified constraints exerted by public opinion in the domestic arena and aimed at narrowing down the leaders' win-set. The case of public opinion support for the use of violence as an instrument of the game deals with public opinion attempting to constrain the other side's policy. In this instance the application of violent means is meant to force the other side's public to pressure its leaders to expand their win-set and modify the policy instruments they apply in the game. The disengagement case falls within the same rubric of constraints targeted at the other side in terms of Sharon's logic of unilateralism. It exemplifies beautifully the exertion of pressures within the other side's political arena, generating reverberations geared to changing the political balance on the other side in ways that will affect international negotiations.

The disengagement case also falls under the rubric of opening domestic opportunities to facilitate the expansion of the domestic leadership win-set. The Israeli public's readiness to compromise and relinquish settlements provided fertile soil and incentive for Sharon's policy reversal, as expressed in the Gaza disengagement. The consistent support of the Israeli and Palestinian publics for negotiations also belongs in this category.

The fourth rubric is opening opportunities for the other side to help that side's leadership consolidate its political standing and expand its win-set. We have not analyzed such cases here, but relevant examples falling beyond the time scope of this book may be the support of the Israeli public for steps designed to boost Abu Mazin's political standing among Palestinians—a mirror image of Sharon's threat to weaken Mazin's standing. This entails, for example, Israeli public opinion support for military and economic aid for Abu-Mazin and the Fatah government in the West Bank.

The central role of public opinion in the Israeli-Palestinian conflict and the attempts to resolve it can be appreciated all the more by acknowledging the status it has acquired over the years as a critical domestic veto player in the Palestinian-Israeli two-level game. The Palestinian and Israeli publics have been assigned a decisive role regarding the permanent status solution, with the leaders of both sides committed to putting any final status agreement for ratification to a public referendum.

Since the beginning of the Oslo process, all Israeli leaders have committed themselves to a public referendum if they reach an agreement that would transfer territory under Israeli control to Arab sovereignty. In 1999 the Knesset passed legislation that requires a majority vote of the Knesset and a referendum for approval of any agreement that would involve relinquishing territory that is under Israeli jurisdiction (this applies to the Golan Heights and

Jerusalem but not to the West Bank and the Gaza Strip). However, no referendum legislation was enacted at that time. In 2008 the Knesset opted for an amendment of the original law that would provide the referendum details. On June 30, 2008, this amendment passed the first of three calls and was transferred to the Constitution and Knesset committees in charge of preparing it for the final vote. The fierce political debate in Israel over a referendum on Sharon's limited Disengagement Plan demonstrated how entrenched the notion of a referendum had become, but it also focused the spotlight on the political leaders' ability to manipulate its actual enactment. Similarly the third draft of the Palestinian Constitution, drawn up in 2003, requires a constitutional amendment (by means of a public referendum) for any agreement that falls short of establishing a Palestinian state on all pre-1967 territories. Another indication of the entry of this concept in the Palestinian political discourse as well was Abu Mazin's threat to use a referendum to pressure Hamas to accommodate the Prisoners' Document in 2006.

One fundamental instrument by which public opinion has been exerting its influence as a player in the Palestinian-Israeli two-level game is elections—in Israel since independence and in the PA since 1996. This electoral connection was discussed at length in chapter 8. Elections may bring about responsiveness by way of two routes: the direct route, through the selection of leaders and change in the makeup of government; and the indirect route, where the political actors who wish to be reelected must take into account their publics through rational anticipation. We demonstrated this responsiveness in the Israeli domestic political system since the first Intifada and through the second. In both societies, we focused in particular on the two critical elections that took place during the second Intifada and dramatically altered the Israeli-Palestinian game and the management of the conflict by both leaderships.

Hamas participated and won in the elections to the Legislative Council held in the Palestinian Authority in January 2006. As pointed out in chapter 8, this Hamas victory was mainly a result of the public's disappointment with the Fatah leadership based on domestic issues, particularly corruption. In terms of the international game, however, Sharon's game was "successful" in that it deprived Fatah's leadership of its most important political asset—being able to promise a peaceful rather than a violent path to a settlement with Israel. It also denied Fatah credit for Israel's withdrawal, leaving Hamas the sole victor in the eyes of the Palestinian public. Hamas was also more responsive to public demands to resort to violence and was rewarded for this, too. In sum, the stagnation of the peace process and the lack of confidence in diplomacy downgraded this issue in voters' electoral considerations. The Hamas victory completely changed the rules of the game on its domestic and international levels, imposing a new political reality for the leaders and constituencies on both sides—the reality of a divided government in the PA. Eventually Hamas's victory came to its full realization in its violent takeover of the Gaza Strip, establishing an independent Hamas government there in June 2007.

In Israel the March 2006 election also resulted in a political reversal—the culmination of a long-term trend of greater willingness to compromise and a significant change in values in Israeli society (pointed out in chapter 7), where the values of the Jewish state and peace took clear precedence over the vision of a "Greater Israel." The establishment of the Kadima Party, positioned at the median voter location in terms of the Israeli-Palestinian conflict, provided an attractive outlet for the reservoir of voters that accumulated with the Israeli public's move to the center, and realigned the Israeli party system in accordance with public opinion.

Policy Implications and Recommendations

Our study of the Israeli-Palestinian conflict during the second Intifada has significant short- and long-term implications for the management and resolution of the conflict. We assess these implications within the context of the Palestinian-Israeli two-level game on its international and domestic tables, taking into account the special nature of public opinion as a player in this game. In the next section we discuss implications for conflict resolution and focus on the feasibility of a final status agreement, the role of track II initiatives in achieving such an agreement, and the need to apply strategic framing for this purpose. We then turn to the implications of managing the conflict in the hope of returning to a peace process with prospects of success. We begin by analyzing Israelis' and Palestinians' assessment of the Intifada, its achievements and impact. We then discuss how the use of violence should be further managed and evaluate the prospects of unilateral steps in bringing the derailed peace process back on track. Finally, we explore ways to reinstitute a unified Palestinian player in order to boost the prospects for reaching a permanent agreement, along with the Arab League initiative for a comprehensive Arab-Israeli peace.

Conflict Resolution
IMPLICATIONS FOR A PERMANENT STATUS SOLUTION

Most important in this context is the issue of joint Palestinian-Israeli support for an overall permanent status package that addresses the most crucial components of the conflict. The JIPP survey data show that, at least at one point during the second Intifada, both publics appeared to demonstrate mutual support for a concrete permanent status package structured around the Clinton parameters. The significance of this cannot be overstated, despite fluctuations and a later decline in the level of support. It suggests that a permanent status framework—endorsed by both publics—is not beyond reach.

A second important finding stems from the attitudinal structure of both publics regarding the permanent status framework. It is evident that, despite strong reservations about the issues of the refugees and Jerusalem (and, among Palestinians, the issue of sovereignty), the overall package could receive majority support in both publics. This indicates that people's calculus in this respect is compensatory. The desirable components and the chance of reaching a permanent status agreement seem to compensate for the undesirable parts. This suggests clear operational recommendations for all players in the game interested in conflict resolution. To move forward on this path of compromise and increase the chances that a permanent status agreement will be ratified based on the Clinton parameters, it is important to emphasize the general benefits of a comprehensive package and the necessity of trade-offs it implies. The role of framing in this context is clear. Framing can suggest alternative modes of information integration to determine overall support or opposition to international agreements.[2] We expand on the promise of strategic framing for future conflict resolution attempts below.

The issue these findings raise is how to translate these attitudes realistically into actual policy. We have seen that Clinton's ideas and the ensuing Geneva package may fall within both publics' win-sets—the range of possible solutions that stand a chance to be ratified. Yet the mutual support for this permanent status package occurred only once during the period we studied. Moreover, and even more important, if we take into account the full sense of public opinion, it would be overly optimistic to suggest that the two publics may be ripe for a permanent status agreement. People's individual policy preferences reflect only one, albeit important, dimension of public opinion. Other aspects of public opinion suggest an even bleaker outlook. Expectations of future developments indicate a more pessimistic reading. The JIPP surveys repeatedly showed that both publics expect negotiations to resume but with concurrent violence. Moreover, expectations as to the feasibility of a permanent status agreement were gloomy and provided a completely different outlook from the endorsement of such an agreement. No less problematic in this regard was the dominance of groups and voices opposed to compromise in the political arenas in both societies. Finally, Clinton's ideas and a Geneva-like permanent status framework did not seem to have acquired sufficient legitimacy and normative approval, as read in the climates of the two publics. Measured by majority perceptions, at no time did we observe perceived majority support for the Clinton package simultaneously among Palestinians and Israelis. Another indicator for this reserved climate of opinion was the low level of support in the two publics for making societal changes on the reconciliation scale. But one does not necessarily need survey data to reach this conclusion; listening to the ongoing public discourse and the public statements of the two leaderships is sufficient. In neither society did the leadership promote public debate on the measures that would constitute an acceptable agreement, which left the public unprepared for necessary compromises and trade-offs. If anything, in the discourse with their publics, leaders on both sides tended to raise rather than lower the acceptability thresholds. With Hamas's covenant on the agenda following its electoral victory, and Israeli right-wing opposition demanding unconditional recognition of Israel as a Jewish state, this discourse seemed to have regressed all the way back to long-forgotten, pre-Oslo themes, including doubts regarding mutual recognition, the viability of a two-state solution, and the existence of a willing and capable partner for peace.

Consequently there is still a long way to go to turn the one-time joint Israeli-Palestinian majority support for a final status package into a viable, politically relevant policy option. For example, the idea of offering Palestinians the right of return—even if it is only symbolic—is currently entirely off-limits in Israeli public discourse. Similarly Israelis are hardly prepared to face the far-reaching implications of full Palestinian sovereignty in an independent Palestinian state, conforming even to the minimal expectations of the Palestinian leadership. Palestinians, on the other hand, have yet to come to grips with the idea that Israel will not fully and completely retreat to the 1967 borders. The notion that an actual massive return of refugees to Israel proper will never happen, at least not in the way it has been idealized, is completely missing from the Palestinian discourse. It is also unrealistic to expect Hamas to retract unequivocally from its core ideology in the immediate future. Clearly neither side is ready for the profound changes that are needed in their national narratives, Palestinians even less so than Israelis. Indeed, anyone advocating these ideas risks severe social and political sanctions in the PA and, to a lesser extent, in Israel. Only when the concessions and trade-offs, such as those outlined in the Clinton package, become an integral part of public debate and discourse can one begin to consider the possibility that those ideas have made normative inroads in public opinion in its fullest sense.

It is not far-fetched to suggest that the range of permanent solutions that stand a chance to be jointly ratified will almost necessarily have to resort to some variation of the Clinton ideas and the Taba understandings, particularly the ideas on the core issues of territory, refugees, and Jerusalem. This entails the preparation of public opinion, moderating expectations among the two publics with respect to what a permanent status solution holds for them: legitimizing options such as sovereignty-sharing in Jerusalem, a Palestinian state in the pre-1967 occupied territories with some minor border modifications, the presence of settlement blocs in the West Bank, a symbolic recognition of the right of return devoid of practical implications, and some declaration stating an end to the conflict.

ON THE ROLE OF TRACK II INITIATIVES IN CONFLICT RESOLUTION

Preparing the ground for a permanent status agreement and its ratification is not easy to implement, even for leaders who may sympathize with the Clinton ideas, for the following two reasons. First, the process of legitimizing unpopular policy options that shatter hopes, dreams, and cherished values is long and hazardous for a political leader on the domestic front. Second, acts or statements designed to mold public opinion in more conciliatory directions may weaken a leader's position in the international game. Given the "closed-lips" orientation inherent in two-level games, other players, such as NGOs, opposition parties, and international players, have an important role, and indeed sometimes step in to shatter inhibiting norms and prepare public opinion for compromise. Their role becomes even more crucial when leaders in power do not seem willing or able to opt for costly and painful steps to resolve the conflict, which seems to be the case in the Israeli-Palestinian game during the period of this study. The Geneva Initiative, discussed in chapter 7, exemplifies such a quite successful move. Significant international players, such as the United States or the United Nations, may play a similar role in terms of public-opinion dynamics, and their actions and statements may be especially effective in shaping people's expectations as to future developments, viable policy options, opportunities, and constraints.

STRATEGIC FRAMING FOR A PALESTINIAN-ISRAELI SETTLEMENT

Negotiating a permanent status agreement and preparing the Israeli and Palestinian publics for it will most likely resort to practices of strategic issue framing, used often in politics and international relations. Issue framing and framing theory in general have been found effective both in negotiating agreements as well as in persuasion campaigns (Mintz and Redd 2003; Riker 1986).[3]

Negotiations often take place as a sequence of turns in which offers and counteroffers are exchanged between interlocutors. Such exchanges obviously involve profit maximization considerations, but they necessarily also involve strategic framing intended to maximize the suggestive power of the offer to the other side. Equivalent offers and counteroffers can be framed in many different ways, such as "an absolute value, an incremental adjustment, or an act of reciprocation" (Blount and Larrick 2000, p. 44).

International negotiations usually involve two types of discourses: "arguing," which appeals to norms of fairness and equity, and "bargaining," which abides by rules of rational utility maximization (Ulbert, Risse, and Muller 2004). Case studies of negotiations demonstrate that the key factor in producing an agreement are moral concerns such as the accommodation of competing standards of justice, and not the efficiency of the distributive outcome (Muller 2004, p. 401; and see Hampson 1995). Similarly analysis of international law suggests that an element of fairness is present in many international agreements and constitutes the essence of their legitimacy (Frank 1995).

Arguing in negotiations leaves ample room for issue framing, which often resorts to fairness and equity claims. In the context of the Israeli-Palestinian conflict, and as discussed in chapter 4, a "just solution" has become a key phrase in Palestinian official statements and declared opening positions in landmark negotiations with Israel. A justice frame is used consistently by Palestinians to express their grievances and pleas to the international community.[4] It reflects a discourse that centers on morality rights and entitlement rather than on utility gains and benefits. Israelis, on the other hand, tend to frame negotiations in rational cost-benefit utility terms revolving around security and territorial considerations. Nevertheless Shlomo Ben-Ami, Israel's foreign minister during the July 2000 Camp David summit, acknowledged the need to recognize the Palestinians' justice frame: "It is important," he wrote, "that we understand that in such an agreement which involves historical memory, cumulative frustrations and open wounds due to uprooted populations, it is impossible to reach an agreement unless it is based on granting moral compensations in certain areas and an honorable solution regarding the material demands" (Ben-Ami 2004, p. 159). It is important that Israeli negotiators internalize Ben-Ami's insight in anticipation of future negotiations with the Palestinians.

Prospect theory (Kahneman and Tversky 1979; Levine, Schneider, and Gaeth 1998; Levy 1996) suggests that people think more in terms of gains and losses than in terms of net wealth and welfare. Losses and gains are defined relative to a reference point that shifts along with the description of the situation. The theory further suggests that people are loss-averse, less preferring outcomes perceived as losses than equivalent results presented as gains. One of the most difficult factors burdening the Palestinian-Israeli negotiations at Camp David was the vast discrepancy between the reference points of the two sides. For Israel, the reference point for many years has been the status quo whereby Israel rules the Palestinian occupied territories. The Palestinians, in turn, set an extremely high reference point for themselves in assessing the gains or losses of a settlement: the pre-1948 reality and the concessions they made previously in the Oslo Accord.[5] Such a high reference point is bound to render most concessions on their part as further losses. We believe that, from the Palestinians' point of view, a state that would justify a final status agreement cannot compromise on Jerusalem as its capital, on territorial contiguity,[6] and on sovereignty symbols. These must entail substantive Israeli concessions if Palestinians are to perceive them as actual gains. To make this happen, Israel must also shift its status quo reference point considerably.

Finally, we reiterate our recommendation to frame the settlement in a way that emphasizes the overall benefits of the comprehensive package and the achievements for one's side in the trade-offs it required, given our findings that people's calculus is compensatory.

With the continuation of violence and the difficulties involved in reaching a final settlement, efforts should turn to formulating coherent principles to manage the ongoing conflict in ways that would facilitate a quick return to a dynamic and effective peace process (Bar-Siman-Tov 2007a, 2007b). For this purpose it is essential to understand Israelis' and Palestinians' assessments of the Intifada and its outcome. These may serve as indicators for the evolution of the conflict into the future and as a guidepost of how further use of violence should be managed.

Conflict Management
PUBLIC ASSESSMENT OF THE AL-AQSA INTIFADA

Throughout the period we covered, Palestinians believed that the Intifada was achieving goals for them that negotiations could not. Between July 2001 and June 2005 an average of 66 percent thought so; immediately following the Gaza disengagement in August 2005, in our September poll,

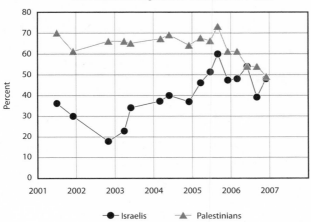

Figure 9.1. Percent Believing That the Intifada Achieved Goals for Palestinians That Negotiations Could Not, 2001–2006

the figure peaked at 73 percent (Figure 9.1). The majority of Israelis did not concur during most of this period, but as the disengagement was nearing, an increasing number agreed that indeed the Intifada had been beneficial to the Palestinians, with 60 percent supporting this assessment in the September 2005 poll, immediately after the disengagement was implemented.

Subsequently, however, this belief weakened among both Israelis and Palestinians. Among Israelis, it averaged 47 percent, oscillating between 39 percent and 54 percent. More important, belief in the success of the Intifada steadily declined among Palestinians, less than 50 percent in the December 2006 poll. After six years of the Intifada the two publics appear to have converged in their assessment of its success. Early on in the Intifada, Palestinian public opinion overwhelmingly considered the Intifada to be a success, and Israeli public opinion did not. By 2006, however, after years of mutual bloodletting, the drastically aggravated Israeli (re)occupation of the West Bank, the disengagement from Gaza, and the divided government in the PA between Fatah and Hamas, the two publics seem similarly ambivalent and weary of the Intifada.

Since mid-2004 we have also been asking another question in our polls: "Who came out the winner in the ongoing armed conflict between Israel and the Palestinians?" The most common answer among Israelis (52%, on average) was "neither side." Few thought that both sides had won. Among the remaining Israeli respondents, up to the disengagement, more said that Israel had won; after the disengagement this changed, and more Israelis said that the Palestinians had won. Among Palestinians, through 2004 and 2005, the most common answers were either that "neither side" had won or that the Palestinians had been the victors; in September 2005, right after the disengagement, a record high of 49 percent thought the Palestinians had won. But by the end of 2006 Palestinian answers were quite evenly divided between the four options: for the first time more Palestinians thought that Israel had come out the winner (27%), and only 24 percent said the Palestinians had won; 29 percent said that neither side had won, and 18 percent thought "both" had won. A majority of Israelis (52%) thought as before that neither side had won, 28 percent said the Palestinians had won, and a record low of 5 percent thought that Israel had won. These data offer an important perspective on the Intifada and its consequences, providing a picture of two publics worn out and disillusioned with the Intifada and its consequences.

THE USE OF VIOLENCE AND ITS REWARD

The most important policy implication in terms of conflict management, based on our analysis of the Intifada period in this book (especially in chapters 6, 7, and 8), as well as the public opinion assessments of the Intifada presented above, is that violence should not be rewarded and diplomacy should.

The belief that violence pays was a major source of Palestinians' high level of support for the use of violence throughout the Intifada, justifying and rationalizing this position. It was also a factor behind the growing support for the militant factions in the PA. As we maintained in chapter 6, this view was not detached from reality but rather was based on a rational cost-benefit analysis of the viability of the alternative instruments of policy at hand. Any conflict management steps currently being contemplated should bear this consideration in mind. Policy moves that reward violence should be avoided, and policy moves that negate rewarding violence and encourage negotiation tracks should be advanced. For example, the release of Palestinian prisoners ought to be conceived according to this thinking.

A third option in the context of conflict management that received much attention and has been implemented by Israel during the period of our study is that of meaningful unilateral steps. We turn now to an assessment of Sharon's Gaza Disengagement Plan and later proposals for unilateral disengagement along these lines.

UNILATERAL DISENGAGEMENT

Sharon's unilateral Gaza Disengagement Plan was a critical policy move of great consequence. As discussed at length in chapter 7, Sharon's plan received the support of a majority of the Israeli public, despite the set-tlers' fervent resistance to the plan. However, the concept of relinquishing territory unilaterally suffered a severe blow in the Israeli domestic scene, including public opinion, because of its failure to reduce violence—especially that involving the shelling of civilian communities—which only intensified after the disengagement was completed. Consequently Olmert's unilateral Convergence Plan to evacuate most of the settlements in the West Bank within the next few years, while realigning into large blocks of settlements along the line of the separation wall, was not endorsed by the Israeli public.[7] Following the second war in Lebanon in the summer of 2006, this option further lost favor in Israeli public opinion. In fact, as we have seen, the Israeli public as well as the Palestinian public preferred negotiations over unilateral steps throughout this period, although a solid majority of Israelis supported the dismantling of most settlements as part of a peace agreement with the Palestinians. Probably even more significant in terms of conflict management, Palestinians saw the unilateral disengagement as a sign of victory and an indication that violence paid off, in the same way that Israel's unilateral withdrawal from Southern Lebanon in May 2000 was viewed. Indeed, most Palestinians thought at that time that Hezbollah's violent methods should be emulated. These events also helped bring Hamas to power in the January 2006 parliamentary election. As we argued in chapter 6, such unilateral steps, when taken amid violence, reinforce public support for, and confidence in, violence.

Given all these considerations, unilateral steps such as the Gaza Disengagement are not recommended even as conflict management steps, and a negotiated settlement should continue to be the preferred goal.

REINSTATING A UNIFIED PALESTINIAN PLAYER

Following Hamas's victory in the parliamentary elections, the Palestinian domestic game immersed itself in a fierce political struggle taking place within a structurally divided government, and the acute weaknesses of the Palestinian political culture and political system came to the fore. This impinged on the international game, shattering Palestinians' ability to present a legitimate and potent partner for negotiations with Israel. Moreover, Hamas's popularity in the Palestinian domestic arena allows it to act as the spoiler of any peace initiative it opposes. In other words, Hamas acquired the status of the main veto player in the PA. The international players interested in the success of a political process—notably the United States and the Quartet—must maneuver carefully within the parameters of this new reality. Most important, actions taken must be conducive to facilitating the political crisis in the PA in a manner that will reinstitute a unified Palestinian negotiating partner for the political process with Israel, and one that is also acceptable to Israel. This is not easy to achieve, given the need to refrain from rewarding violence. The chances for establishing such a partner depend largely on the domestic political struggle in the PA but also on the political route chosen for the resumption of negotiations.

Within the domestic political struggle, the role of public opinion and bottom-up grassroots initiatives assumes utmost importance. Hamas government policy, which provoked the international boycott and the financial crisis in the PA, has encountered some social protest and labor strikes. The National Conciliation Document of the Prisoners, and Abu Mazin's threat to put it to a referendum in mid-2006, pressured Hamas to blur its initial unequivocal political platform. Since Hamas took over the Gaza Strip, its grip on Gaza has tightened, considerably curtailing grassroots opposition activity. Nevertheless, quite remarkable is that both Hamas and Fatah understand that the political struggle is, in fact, a struggle over legitimacy, and that public opinion bears the role of the major arbiter in that struggle. In this regard, it is important to stress that this legitimacy struggle is primarily affected by each side's ability to claim credit for improvements in Palestinian living conditions, and for solving acute problems such as that of Palestinians imprisoned in Israeli jails. The ebbs and flows in the popularity of Hamas and Fatah attest to this, and the connection between the domestic and international games is manifestly clear.

Regarding the routes for the resumption of the peace process, it is extraordinary that the Quartet's Roadmap first presented in 2002 was still on the international agenda, having been revived by the Annapolis summit in November 2007. The Roadmap is obviously favored by Israel, the stronger side in the conflict, but is unpopular among Palestinians, the weaker side in this national liberation conflict, because of its demand to disarm the militant factions. The Roadmap was stripped of any chance to be implemented following Hamas's rise to power, given Hamas's official doctrine and policy of armed resistance.

Given the strong inroads Hamas has made in Palestinian society and the balance of power in the PA, no peace process can be envisioned that leaves Hamas altogether out of the game. As discussed in chapter 7, Israeli public opinion is divided about talks with Hamas, but it does not rule out the possibility of such talks should they be necessary to reach a political settlement. However, a creative configuration of a Palestinian partner such as a national unity government may secure greater support among Israelis, and may provide an international player with better chances to proceed.

The role of the international community in reinstating a unified Palestinian player is essential. Such a reinstatement should be based on principles of inclusion rather than exclusion of the central political forces in the PA and the Palestine Liberation Organization. It should also insist on a long-term truce and cessation of violence, thereby adhering to the principle that violence should not be rewarded. These efforts should also involve both political as well as economic incentives to the parties concerned, the removal of the boycott on the Hamas government, a massive package of financial assistance, and pressure on Israel to yield to demands to relieve the acute social needs of Palestinians, including the release of prisoners and the opening of the passage between Gaza and the West Bank. Though Palestinians may view international involvement in these matters as meddling in the PA's internal affairs, thus making it counterproductive, recall that international pressure has proven effective in the past, for example, in convincing Arafat to introduce political reforms and in recommending the nomination of Abu Mazin for prime minister. To minimize the risk of Islamists spoiling these efforts, Hamas should be given assurances that will guarantee its inclusion and due weight in the wider Palestinian political game. Concurrently a creative formula must be devised to persuade the Israeli government to overcome the obstacle of accepting Hamas as an inevitable player in the renewal of the peace process.

The best concrete plan that has been on the agenda, both in terms of solving the incorporation of Hamas into the international table and in terms of prospects for conflict resolution, is the peace plan proposed, in 1981, by the Saudi Crown Prince Fahd and endorsed by the Arab League in its Beirut summit in March 2002. This initiative called both for a full Israeli withdrawal to the 1967 borders, including the Golan Heights, and, though vaguely stated, for a "just" solution to the Palestinian refugee problem in return for recognition of Israel, normalization, and a declaration of an end to the Arab-Israeli conflict. At the Riyadh summit in March 2007 the clause dealing with the refugees' problem was modified to imply that a solution should be negotiated by both parties. This constitutes a softening of the dictate-like nature of the original plan, probably intended to increase its attractiveness to the Israeli public. The Arab League initiative should be considered a diplomatic landmark that provides baseline principles for a comprehensive peace in relatively clear terms and as an offer that, for decades before, lacked public legitimacy in the Arab world. Building on the strong Arab Islamic identity and unity value among Palestinians, and providing all-Arab support and backup, it would legitimize tough compromises, for example, regarding Jerusalem. The Arab League initiative may thus be the best facilitator in bringing Hamas into a conflict resolution framework, and may force it to break away from its initial rigid ideology. We believe it provides the overall framework that can successfully bring about conflict resolution between Israel and Palestine, as well as between Israel and Syria.

NOTES

1. Introduction

1. We elaborate upon the two-level game theoretical framework proposed by Putnam (1988) in chapter 3.

2. Complicating things further, a third game could be envisioned in which each side also played a game with their American hosts. More generally, it is possible to consider three-level games, with additional international, cross-level, and transboundary players such as global human rights and civil society organizations, state associations such as the Arab League, globalizing agents such as the World Bank, or diaspora lobbies. See, for example, Knopf 1993; Patterson 1997; and Shain and Cofman Wittes 2002. In this book, however, we stick to Putnam's classic two-level game metaphor, given our focus on the role of domestic factors, and particularly public opinion, in determining the conduct of the Palestinian-Israeli game since the beginning of the second Intifada.

3. The project is described in the next chapter.

4. We discuss the unique nature of the public imperative compared to other domestic imperatives in chapter 3.

5. See a detailed account of the parameters at http://www.brookings.edu/press/appendix/peaceprocessappen_ab.htm (retrieved February 4, 2007).

6. These figures for 2000–2006 are based on the Palestinian Red Crescent Society, B'Tselem, and the Israeli Ministry of Foreign Affairs. The exact figures vary by sources; available at http://israelipalestinian.procon.org/viewresource.asp?resourceID=639 (accessed August 14, 2008).

7. Details are available at http://www.al-bab.com/arab/docs/league/peace02.htm (retrieved February 4, 2007).

8. Details are provided at http://www.state.gov/r/pa/prs/ps/2003/20062.htm (retrieved February 4, 2007).

9. The Geneva Accord was officially launched on December 1, 2003, at a ceremony in Geneva. It was signed by its initiators on October 13 and sent as a letter to the Swiss

foreign minister. In the interim, the Accord was publicized and disseminated to the Israeli and Palestinian publics.

10. For further details, go to http://www.jmcc.org/documents/prisoners.htm (retrieved September 18, 2007).

2. The Joint Israeli-Palestinian Poll

1. Primary credit for the initiation of the project belongs to Professor Amnon Cohen, Director of the Truman Institute at the time, who strongly believed that a joint public opinion research project could furnish both conflict resolution efforts and academic research on the conflict with a reliable, systematic, and comparable knowledge base.

2. Other such projects, for example, the one conducted by Collin Irwin in Northern Ireland (Irwin 2001, 2002) and the one initiated by Alexandros Lordos in Cyprus (Lordos 2005, 2006), were primarily policy-oriented and more concentrated in time.

3. The Palestinian site presents the results of the Palestinian polls. The Truman site provides the results of the Israeli polls as well as Palestinian results of the joint questions side by side to allow easy comparison. When we quote JIPP data throughout the book, we therefore specify the date of the poll, but we do not provide a specific reference each time. Readers interested in detailed frequencies and question wording are encouraged to refer to the sites.

4. These were conducted in July 2001, December 2001, September 2005, and September 2006. The Israeli data were collected by the Dahaf Research Institute, and the Palestinian data by the Palestinian Center for Policy and Survey Research (PSR).

5. For example: social projection (Allport 1924), egocentric attribution (Heider 1958), looking-glass perception (Fields and Schuman 1976), illusory correlation (Spears, van der Pligt, and Eiser 1985), and false consensus (Ross, Green, and House 1977).

6. At first glance, these attributions seem inconsistent with the vast research on social projection. However, Vallone, Ross, and Lepper (1985) suggest that the hostile media phenomenon is, in fact, an outcome of the very processes it appears to contradict. Specifically, group members' habitual tendency to assimilate supportive information and reject information that is incongruent with their preconceptions ultimately establishes strong beliefs in the validity of their own point of view. Media coverage that seems inconsistent with these established convictions is regarded as biased. Giner-Sorolla and Chaiken (1994) provide a somewhat different explanation, suggesting that hostile information could attract greater attention and activate more intensive processing, thus becoming more accessible in memory.

7. Data for the Israeli survey were collected between November 30 and December 16, 2001, by the Dahaf Research Institute, which interviewed by phone representative samples of the Israeli Jewish (n = 506) and Israeli Arab (n = 499) adult population. The Palestinian poll was carried out between December 19 and December 23, 2001, by PSR, using face-to-face interviews of a representative sample of the adult Palestinian population in the West Bank, the Gaza Strip, and East Jerusalem (n = 1,357).

8. This "suspected to be" version was presented in the Palestinian sample, because the common belief among Palestinians is that the 9/11 attack was not committed by Bin Laden. In a question asked in our survey, only 16 percent of the Palestinian sample viewed Bin Laden as the perpetrator.

9. Gilo is a civilian neighborhood in Jerusalem. It became the target of heavy shooting by Palestinians at the beginning of the Intifada.

10. Designated "A" areas are under full military and civilian Palestinian control according to the Oslo agreements.

11. The finding that three-quarters of Israeli Jews define the Goldstein incident as terrorism was quite surprising, particularly since it was never coined as such in the mainstream Israeli media.

12. While back translation usually enhances survey questions equivalence, it obviously does not solve all the equivalence issues raised in the literature.

13. Palestinian Central Bureau of Statistics Mass Media Survey 2000—Current Main Indicators. Retrieved February 4, 2007, from http://www.pcbs.gov.ps/DesktopModules /Articles/ArticlesView.aspx?tabID=0&lang=en&ItemID=275&mid=10982.

14. Personal communication with the researchers, December 2006.

3. The Public Imperative

1. Audience costs and policy costs are obviously not independent, as the former enter into leaders' calculations of the overall costs and payoffs in negotiations.

4. The Israeli and Palestinian Publics

1. Figures refer to the year 2002 and are based on the United Nations Development Programme's "Human Development Report" 2004. Retrieved February 4, 2007, from http://hdr.undp.org/reports/global/2004/pdf/hdr04_HDI.pdf.

2. The gross enrollment ratio is defined as the number of pupils enrolled in a given level of education, regardless of age, expressed as a percentage of the population in the theoretical age group for the same educational level. The population used for the tertiary level is the five-year age group following from the end of secondary school education. Tertiary education is defined as the International Standard Classification of Education (ISCED) levels 5–7, which refers to education at, for example, universities, teachers' colleges, and higher-level professional schools where the minimal requirement for admission is the successful completion of secondary-level education or evidence that one has attained an equivalent level of knowledge. Figures are based on the "Global Education Digest 2005" produced by the United Nations Economic, Scientific and Cultural Organization (UNESCO). Retrieved September 6, 2007, from http:// www.uis.unesco.org/template/pdf/ged/2005/ged2005_en.pdf.

3. Figures are based on the December 2006 poll.

4. Retrieved September 6, 2007, from http://www.niis.tau.ac.il/page.aspx?pid=128 &cid=0&menu=27.

5. Retrieved February 4, 2007, from http://www.freedomhouse.org/template.cfm ?page=251&year=2006; and http://www.freedomhouse.org/template.cfm?page=204& year=2006.

6. See Alia Siksik, *Media in Palestine: Between the PNA's Hammer and the Anvil of Self-Censorship*, Palestinian Human Rights Monitoring Group, 1999. Retrieved December 10, 2007, from http://spirit.tau.ac.il/socant/peace/psp/downloads/10%20-%20 Siksik%20Alia.htm.

7. For the 2005 report, see http://www.pcpsr.org/arabic/domestic/books/2005/di05.

pdf; for the 2006 report, see http://www.pcpsr.org/arabic/domestic/books/2007/di7
.pdf (both retrieved August 10, 2008).

8. A good example is Israelis' and Palestinians' knowledge of details of the Geneva document. Sixty percent of Israelis but only 21 percent of Palestinians said in our December 2003 survey that they have either full or general knowledge of the Geneva document formulated by a group of Israeli and Palestinian doves as a model for a final status framework, and widely publicized in both societies. This difference probably reflects Palestinians' lower newspaper readership habits combined with the different methods employed to disseminate the document (direct mail in Israel and newspaper inserts in the PA).

9. Retrieved February 2, 2007, from http://www.bitterlemons.org/docs/sharon1
.html.

10. Retrieved February 2, 2007, from http://www.pmo.gov.il/PMO/Communica
tion/PMSpeaks/speechele290306.htm.

11. Retrieved September 6, 2007, from http://www.un.int/palestine/PLO/PNAchar
ter.html.

12. Retrieved August 10, 2008, from http://www.mideastweb.org/hamas.htm.

13. Retrieved September 6, 2007, from http://www.mideastweb.org/plc1988.htm.

14. Retrieved September 6, 2007, from http://www.pcpsr.org/domestic/2003/nbro
wne.pdf.

15. Retrieved August 10, 2008, from http://www.pcpsr.org/survey/polls/2003/refu
geesjune03.html.

16. Shlomo Ben-Ami, a former foreign minister of Israel and a chief negotiator in the Camp David summit, saw in the all-Arab unity tenet one of the greatest obstacles in the negotiations. For example, within the context of Jerusalem, he describes a discussion with King Abdullah of Jordan telling him that "Arafat is not eligible and not capable of reaching a decision on Jerusalem without an all-Arab support and backup" (Ben-Ami 2004, p. 149). More generally he commented on the negotiation process: "This negotiation did not take place in a regional and international vacuum, and the Palestinians led by Arafat could not detach themselves from the Arab escort to make difficult decisions . . . the 'Arab world' constituted Arafat's strategic depth and it also served as an alibi to his inability or unwillingness to compromise" (Ben-Ami 2004, p. 56).

17. In our first joint survey, in July 2000, Palestinians and Israelis were asked to rank the most important Palestinian national interest. "Unity of the Palestinian people" received the second-highest rank among Palestinians, with 27 percent considering it most important, surpassed only by the "establishment of an independent and secure Palestinian state" which obtained 34 percent. Other interests listed in the question were "economic prosperity" (17%), "peace" (12%), and "democracy" (7%). In June 2005, however, deep into the Intifada, the value priorities seemed to have changed to reflect actual policy considerations rather that abstract values. When asked about the most important factors determining their vote for parliament, the party's ability to protect national unity came in only fourth after the fight against corruption, reaching peace with Israel, and improving economic conditions.

18. Brown (2003a) comments that many senior Palestinian leaders believe that "the nationalist issue must remain paramount for all Palestinians. To concentrate on domestic issues is to risk dividing the nation at the time when it faces its most fateful choices. The demands of national unity are such that issues of governance, democracy, and corruption should not be raised too forcefully" (p. 14).

19. They were more reserved in these efforts, however, when this could constitute a serious threat to their leadership.

20. National unity became one of the main discourse frames following Arafat's death in November 2004, when fears of violent clashes between Palestinian factions were high and references to it by PLO and opposition leaders appeared abundantly in the Palestinian press. For example, Ramadan Shallah, the Islamic Jihad leader, was quoted by *al-Hayat* as saying "we are concerned with not allowing any side to take advantage of this event [Arafat's death] to fabricate confusion and chaos in the Palestinian situation. All forces have to act with a sense of patriotism and responsibility. We should be united to get over any ordeal in this national turning point" (*al-Hayat*, November 11, 2004). Similarly, Muhammad Dahlan said in an interview on al-Arabiya TV that "whoever thought there would be infighting and clash over power is not aware of the Palestinian people's political and social culture. I have always been one of those who announced that there will be no political vacuum or internal strife over power . . . we, leadership and people, all proved that we deserve life and the respect of those who showed respect for us to confront those who were preparing for a post-Arafat era in a negative manner or expected the Palestinian people to face a difficult situation" (al-Arabiya, November 12, 2004).

21. See the data for Israel (2006). Retrieved February 4, 2007, from http://www.freedomhouse.org/template.cfm?page=22&year=2006&country=6985.

22. See the data for Palestinian Authority–Israeli Administered Territories for 2005 at http://www.freedomhouse.org/template.cfm?page=22&year=2005&country=6884 (retrieved February 4, 2007).

23. See 2006 report at http://www.freedomhouse.org/template.cfm?page=22&year=2006&country=7104 (retrieved February 4, 2007). The 2006 report refers to the year 2005 and thus does not yet cover the PA under the Hamas government.

24. For the 2005 report, see http://www.pcpsr.org/arabic/domestic/books/2005/di05.pdf; and for the 2006 report, see http://www.pcpsr.org/arabic/domestic/books/2007/di7.pdf (accessed September 6, 2007).

25. The Israeli turnout figures are calculated out of all eligible voters following common practice. Palestinians, however, suspected that the list of eligible voters used in the 2005 presidential election was inflated and quoted a more liberal figure of 72.9 percent, based on a smaller list of registered voters. No single turnout figure has been announced by the Palestinian Central Elections Commission.

26. This figure is based on the Palestinian Central Elections Commission. See http://www.elections.ps/template.aspx?id=290 (retrieved February 4, 2007).

27. These include seventeen Knesset elections and one special election for the office of prime minister in 2001.

28. Retrieved February 4, 2007, from http://www.knesset.gov.il/elections17/heb/history/PercentVotes.htm.

29. The use of economic resources to secure loyalty is not exclusive to autocratic regimes. In democracies, too, leaders must maintain the support of some type of "winning coalition" to remain in power. In autocracies this coalition is usually a subset of the "selectorate"—all individuals who have a potential role in choosing the leader (Bueno De Mesquita et al. 1999, 2003). In democracies, where such winning coalitions are rather large, leaders resort to the production of public goods to secure their loyalty. In autocracies, however, this winning coalition is relatively small and leaders can

maintain their loyalty more efficiently by committing resources to private goods. Nevertheless, although autocracies are found to produce fewer public goods than democracies, they still commit resources for this purpose as public goods produce legitimacy.

30. A liberalized autocracy is depicted by a weak party system and parliament with a paradoxically sizable civil society, largely divided and controlled by the government.

5. Camp David 2000

1. Reservation price is the maximum price a buyer is willing to pay in purchasing goods.

2. Israel was committed to this step in the Oslo II agreement and the Wye River memorandum, signed on October 23, 1998, by Israeli Prime Minister Benjamin Netanyahu and PLO Chairman Yasser Arafat. The Wye River memorandum listed a series of steps designed to facilitate the implementation of the Interim Agreement on the West Bank and the Gaza Strip so that the Israeli and Palestinian sides could more effectively carry out their reciprocal responsibilities relative to further redeployments and security.

3. In the survey the Palestinians were asked: "Generally how would you evaluate the performance of the institution of the presidency? Very good, good, fair, bad, very bad, don't know, no answer." Included in Figure 5.1 are the "very good" and "good" categories.

4. See the Peace Index site at http://www.tau.ac.il/peace/ (accessed December 9, 2005).

5. Specifically, for each of the components in dispute such as refugees, Jerusalem, a Palestinian State and borders, settlements, and security arrangements, respondents were asked to assess whether their delegation's position was just right, not enough of a compromise, or too much of a compromise.

6. Retrieved December 9, 2005, from http://www.pcpsr.org/survey/cprspolls/2000/pol148b.html.

7. Jerusalem Media and Communication Center (JMCC) public opinion poll no. 37, June 2000, http://www.jmcc.org/publicpoll/results/2000/no37.htm (accessed December 9, 2005).

8. The Tami Steinmetz Center for Peace Research, Peace Index, June 2000, http://www.bicohen.tau.ac.il/temp1001/download.asp?did=peaceindex2000_6_3 (accessed December 9, 2005).

9. Nevertheless, as Ross points out, there was a logical inconsistency to Barak's calculations, as he leaned toward postponing an agreement on Jerusalem to the future and therefore could not hope for a promise from the Palestinians to end the conflict. The version offered by Ben-Ami (2004, p. 186) is somewhat different, suggesting instead that it was the Americans who were tempted to postpone an agreement on Jerusalem.

10. The interview was held on April 30, 2006.

11. See the *New York Review of Books,* http://www.nybooks.com/articles/14380.

6. The Eruption of the Intifada

1. "We have accepted 22 percent of historic Palestine while UN resolution 181 gives us 46 percent" (Qurei 2007, p. 350); and "Palestinians have accepted Israeli sovereignty over 78 percent of historic Palestine—which is 23 percent more than what Israel was

given under UN partition resolution of 1947—on the assumption that they would be able to gain sovereignty over the remaining 22 percent" (p. 340). This territorial reference point the Palestinians set for themselves, as being deprived of 78 percent of historic Palestine, contrasts with that of the Israelis, whose reference point is the status quo established following the 1967 Six Day War. In terms of prospect theory (Kahneman and Tversky 1979), this is bound to burden any attempt to reach an agreement, considering the big gap in the two publics' expectations. Given these different reference points, Palestinians may see any future concession as a further loss, while Israelis will perceive Palestinians' concessions as non-consequential.

2. Qurei said in his assessment of that event: "We did not find in that summit an initiative to discuss, nor did we find a viable negotiating approach, or a clear and specific work agenda. Meetings at Camp David looked more like a campaign to build social relations rather than make decisions on the issues that were put at the table" (Qurei 2007, p. 330).

3. In his interview with Barak, historian Benny Morris writes: "Barak believes that Arafat sees the Palestinian refugees of 1948 and their descendents, numbering close to four million, as the main demographic-political tool for subverting the Jewish state. Arafat, says Barak, believes that Israel 'has no right to exist, and he seeks its demise.' Barak buttresses this by arguing that Arafat 'does not recognize the existence of a Jewish people or nation, only a Jewish religion.'" Barak is further quoted by Morris as seeing the refugee issue as existential, saying that "we cannot allow even one refugee back on the basis of the 'right of return,' . . . and we cannot accept historical responsibility for the creation of the problem" (Morris 2002). Available at http://www.nybooks.com/articles/15501 (accessed October 16, 2007).

4. The Israeli narrative regarding the "PLO stages plan" is rooted in the political program adopted at the Twelfth Session of the Palestine National Council in June 1974 in Cairo. The program details three stages to achieve the PLO goals: first, "liberate Palestinian territory and establish an independent national authority over every part of Palestinian territory that is liberated. [Second], . . . any step taken towards liberation is a step towards the realization of the Liberation Organization's strategy of establishing the democratic Palestinian State specified in the resolutions of the previous Palestinian National Councils. [Third], . . . once it is established, the Palestinian national authority will strive to achieve a union of the confrontation countries, with the aim of completing the liberation of all Palestinian territory, and as a step along the road to comprehensive Arab unity." The second statement is the one Israelis interpret as a plot to destroy the Jewish state in stages, exploiting any interim achievement on the way. Available at http://www.mideastweb.org/plo1974.htm (accessed April 14, 2007).

5. It is commonly accepted that terrorism, in contrast to most other criminal activities, is politically motivated (e.g., Wilkinson 2000; Hoffman 1998; Jenkins 1975). Terrorism is often seen as a premeditated effort to spread fear and anxiety in order to achieve political goals.

6. JMCC poll no. 39—part 1, December 2000, question 3. Available at http://www.jmcc.org/publicpoll/results/2000/n039.htm#results (accessed February 2, 2008). Similar results were obtained in several later polls conducted by the same organization.

Whereas Palestinians overwhelmingly support the use of both instruments, Israelis are split between these options. For example, when asked in November 2000, "Which way will bring better results in coping with the Intifada, the political way or the military way, 44 percent chose the political way, 37 percent the military way, and 16 percent a combination of the two; in November 2003, 40 percent believed in the political way, a similar percent suggested the military way, and 17 percent suggested that a combination of both ways is best" (Tami Steinmetz Center for Peace Research, Tel Aviv University, November 2000 poll, question 14; November 2003 poll, question 29. Available at the Center's Web site: http://www.tau.ac.il/peace/ (accessed July 7, 2008). All further references to the Tami Steinmetz Center are available at this Web site.

7. Tami Steinmetz Center for Peace Research, Tel Aviv University, May 2005 poll, question 26.

8. See Figure 8.1. It is based on the question, "What do you think Israel should emphasize in order to avoid war with Arab countries—concentrate on peace talks or increase its military power?" These data are from the "Public Opinion and National Security" project of the Jaffee Center for Strategic Studies at Tel Aviv University, 1987–2003. Available at http://www.tau.ac.il/jcss/publications.html#memoranda (accessed April 9, 2008).

9. Available at http://www.pcpsr.org/survey/cprspolls/index.html (accessed August 2, 2008).

10. Ibid.

11. The levels of threat among Israelis, measured by a similar question, resembled those of Palestinians, with an average of 72 percent (ranging between 81 and 60 percent) expressing insecurity in polls taken between March 2003 and September 2006.

12. Berrebi and Klor's 2006 study is based on public opinion polls for the period of 1990–2003; their 2008 study is based on ecological data on Israeli localities between 1988 and 2003.

13. Tami Steinmetz Center for Peace Research, Tel Aviv University, October 2000 poll, question 17; February 2003 poll, question 22; September 2004 poll, question 28.

14. The Tami Steinmetz Center for Peace Research, Tel Aviv University, has been asking these two questions monthly since July 2001. The series fluctuates between 60 and 80 percent support, dropping only once below 60 percent (53% in August 2001). The trend line for support of negotiations between 2001 and 2008 is basically flat, with an average 70 percent level of support. Between July 2001 and December 2003 the trend line indicates an increase of about 10 points from 60 to over 70 percent support. The belief in negotiations series fluctuates around 40 percent, between 54 and 28 percent, but the overall trend line of belief indicates a slight decline throughout 2001–2008 from slightly more than 40 percent to slightly less than 40 percent. Between July 2001 and December 2003 the trend line is almost flat, at around 40 percent.

15. Ibid., December 2000 poll, question 25.

16. Ibid., February 2001 poll, question 12.

17. In August 2001 Israelis were split between applying more military force (37%) and using political means (38%); 15 percent thought "there was no solution today and the current situation will continue until one of the sides breaks down." In November of that year, in response to the same question, 43 percent chose military force and 33 percent chose diplomatic options; 18 percent thought nothing could work. In February 2002 only 24 percent supported the military force option, and almost half, 49 percent, backed diplomatic means; 21 percent said there was no solution. See Tami Steinmetz Center for Peace Research, Tel Aviv University, August 2001 poll, question 26; November 2001 poll, question 15; February 2002 poll, question 25.

18. Ibid., March 2001 poll, questions 15 and 11. Among Jews, the level of support for closures and for more military force was 71 percent.

19. Ibid., October 2001 poll, question 28; June 2002, questions 23 and 24. Among Jews, the level of support was 68 percent.

20. Ibid., April 2002 poll, question 25.

21. Ibid., July 2001, question 14; October 2001, question 27; January 2002, question 27; February 2004, question 34; March 2004, question 19. The figures ranged between 61 percent and 68 percent; among Jews, the level of support for targeted assassinations ranged between 69 percent and 77 percent.

22. Thirty-six percent said it should avoid such an operation if there is a reasonable chance that civilians may be hurt, and 9 percent thought that no targeted killings should be carried out altogether (ibid., July 2002 poll, question 29).

23. This question should be understood in the context of the ongoing discourse in Israel which assumes that certain settlement blocks, agreed upon with the Palestinians, will remain under Israeli control.

24. "Public Opinion and National Security" project of the Jaffee Center for Strategic Studies at Tel Aviv University. Available at http://www.tau.ac.il/jcss/publications.html#memoranda (accessed April 9, 2008).

25. Our data on threat perceptions among Israelis and Palestinians reveal very high levels of threat, even though they were measured after the peak of the Intifada, when violence began to subside. The average percentage of Israelis who worried that they or their family might be hurt was 72 percent in polls between March 2003 and September 2006. Among Palestinians, the average percentage feeling insecure was 77 percent over the period charted in Figure 6.4 (June 2004–September 2006).

26. Matt Rees, "Streets Red with Blood," *Time* magazine, March 18, 2002. Available at http://www.time.com/time/magazine/article/0,9171,1002012,00.html (accessed July 20, 2008).

27. See, for example, the specification of James March (1982) of the necessary elements of a theory of intentional choice, among them a clear distinction between means (actions) and ends (outcomes); see also Mas-Colell, Whinston, and Green 1995.

7. From Geneva to Disengagement

1. Ari Shavit, "The Big Freeze," *Haaretz*, Friday Magazine section, October 8, 2004. Available at http://www.haaretz.com/hasen/spages/485929.html.

2. This question should be understood in the context of the ongoing discourse in Israel which assumes that certain settlement blocks agreed upon with the Palestinians will remain under Israeli control. Percentages in this question refer to the overall Israeli sample; in July 2001 the support question was only asked of Jews (54% supported dismantling settlements for peace). The 58 percent figure in the chart is extrapolated based on a consistent difference between Jews and Israelis in other surveys (about 4% difference). Also, the question in July 2000 was different and referred to the Camp David terms on settlements.

3. Obtaining respondents' perceptions of the majority opinion has long been a standard way of assessing the prevailing norm among public opinion scholars (e.g., Noelle-Neumann 1993; Lazarsfeld 1972; O'Gorman 1988; Shamir and Shamir 2000). This, in fact, grasps the essence of the aggregate shared nature of public opinion, distinct from the sum of private opinions that is detached from the notion of public opinion as a social phenomenon.

4. Immediately after the implementation of the disengagement, in our September

2005 poll, there is a drop both in the level of support and in the perceived level of support for dismantling settlements, but thereafter both series rise again, although they do not reach the same levels observed during the disengagement period.

5. The figure shows some drop in support from 65 percent in March 2005 to 53 percent (with 39% opposing) in our June poll. This drop in support for the disengagement might be attributed to Sharon's decision to postpone it, coupled with renewed shelling from the Gaza Strip on communities within Israel and with the apocalyptic visions of Israel's retiring chief of staff, who predicted the escalation of the conflict after the disengagement. To counterbalance this trend, Israel's recently retired head of the Secret Service (the Shabak) appeared in a well-orchestrated media campaign in which he expressed support for the disengagement. The role played by the retired heads of the Secret Service and the IDF in the public debate over the disengagement provides just a glimpse of the central role that Israel's security establishment has played in the domestic game over the disengagement and the conflict more generally. Thereafter, support for the disengagement bounced back to over 60 percent, according to surveys published in the media in July and August (the Dahaf Survey from June 29 and published in *Yediot Ahronoth,* July 1, 2005; and the Peace Index Survey from August 2–4, published in *Haaretz,* August 8, 2005).

6. The Israeli side of the June 2005 survey included two samples: a representative sample of the general Israeli public with 526 Israelis, and a representative sample of 501 Israeli settlers in the West Bank and the Gaza Strip.

7. In the first incident, an Israeli soldier who deserted his army unit opened fire in a bus in the northern Israeli town of Shfar'am, killing four Israeli Arab civilians and wounding twenty-two others. In the second incident, four Palestinians were killed in a shooting spree by a driver who used to bring Palestinian laborers to work.

8. In the Israel National Election Study conducted in March 2006, 63 percent of the Jewish sample supported the establishment of a Palestinian state (http://www.ines.tau .ac.il/2006.html [accessed August 10, 2008]).

9. The November 2002 data point seems to be an outlier in respondents' self-identification as right-wing. The poll took place November 17–27, 2002. On November 15, a Palestinian ambush killed nine soldiers in Hebron. On the 21st, a suicide bombing in Jerusalem killed eleven and injured forty-four. These circumstances might explain this outlying observation.

10. Available at http://www.pcpsr.org/survey/polls/2005/exitlocaledec05.html (accessed April 2, 2008).

11. PSR's exit poll showed that most voters in the four cities (56%) believed that their former local councils were corrupt, and 93 percent believed that the newly elected councils would fight corruption. When selecting their preferred lists in the local elections, 99 percent of the voters said that the integrity of the candidates in those lists and their incorruptibility was the most important consideration (http://www.pcpsr.org/ survey/polls/2005/exitlocaledec05.html; and see PSR analysis of the 2006 elections exit poll at http://www.pcpsr.org/survey/polls/2006/exitplcfulljan06e.html (both accessed April 2, 2008).

12. Some minor differences exist between the Israeli and Palestinian wording and the order of the questions. These were called for by the contradicting narratives, diverging daily realities, and self-serving discourses of the two sides. Nevertheless, we were assiduous in assuring functional equivalence of the questions to the two publics.

13. The references to the multinational force in this and in the next component appeared in a separate question in December 2003. In December 2004 and in the subsequent polls this issue was split between the demilitarized state and the sovereignty/security components, and the separate question was removed.

14. Here we emphasize that the mutual support for the Clinton/Geneva framework does not preclude other possible conflict resolution packages from consideration, as long as they are at least similarly attractive to both publics.

8. Political Turnabouts

1. The INES preelection surveys are based on representative samples of the electorate, and they are available at http://www.ines.tau.ac.il/ (accessed April 9, 2008). The surveys are directed by Asher Arian and Michal Shamir. Table 8.1 is based on Jewish respondents only for two major reasons: first, only since 1996 have the INES surveys included Arab respondents; and, second, Israeli election studies commonly analyze Arab and Jewish voters separately, assuming causal heterogeneity. The sample size of these surveys was 873 in 1988; 1,192 in 1992; 1,168 in 1996; 1,075 in 1999; 1, 249 in 2001; and 1,083 in 2003.

2. In 1988 this figure is relatively low (29%), but it is still more than double the percentage of respondents who say that economic policy will have a great effect on their vote.

3. During this period Israel changed its electoral system twice. In 1992 the Knesset legislated the direct election of the prime minister and produced a double ballot system, whereby the prime minister was directly elected by popular majoritarian ballot, and the Knesset was elected, as before, under proportional representation (PR) with the whole country constituting one constituency, and a 1.5 percent threshold of representation. This system was in effect in 1996, 1999, and 2001. In 2001 only a special election of the prime minister was held. Following its deleterious effects on the larger parties, it was repealed shortly after the 2001 special election, and the previous strictly parliamentary PR system was reintroduced.

4. These data are from the "Public Opinion and National Security" project of the Jaffee Center for Strategic Studies at Tel Aviv University, directed by Asher Arian. It comprises a yearly survey of the Jewish adult population since 1985 (http://www.tau.ac.il/jcss/publications.html#memoranda [accessed April 9, 2008]).

5. This is the case in all reversals with the exception of the 2001 election, held shortly after the second Intifada erupted. Feniger (2003) similarly analyzes the trends in the support for the Oslo Accord as measured by the Tami Steinmetz Center since 1994 in terms of the thermostat model.

6. The 1991 Madrid Conference is also worth noting, especially in terms of its symbolic meaning, but it was not followed up in any meaningful way.

7. Haim Ramon is an astute observer and practitioner of politics and a long-time Labor Knesset member (and minister). Following the establishment of Kadima, he joined the party and was elected on its ticket to the 17th Knesset.

8. Available at http://www.ramon.co.il/news_item.asp?id=57 (accessed April 9, 2008).

9. Mazal Moalem, "Netanyahu: The Elections Are a Referendum over the Second Disengagement Plan," *Haaretz,* March 12, 2006, p. 2.

10. For example, following the weekend interviews of Olmert, Yossi Verter, the political correspondent of *Haaretz*, wrote:

> One can say many things about Ehud Olmert. One thing is certain: he is not Sharon, for better or for worse. Sharon was the champion of ambiguity, in particular before elections. When Sharon spoke about painful concessions, no one knew what he meant. Who will concede, who will hurt? When Sharon spoke about a Palestinian state, everybody said that in any case it will not happen during his term, so he doesn't mind saying it. After the weekend interviews of Olmert in which he detailed his political program, no one can say that he or Kadima, his party, does not have a platform or a program. Things are clear. Everything is on the table. Even the timetable. By 2010, he promised, this country will look different. Olmert uncovered his cards for all to see. For the voter to decide. The elections on the 28th have become a referendum on his plan. No doubt Olmert acted bravely. Whether he acted wisely, from a political point of view, we will see. ("The End of the Age of Ambiguity," *Haaretz*, March 12, 2006, pp. 1–2)

11. "Indeed a Referendum," *Haaretz*, March 24, 2006, editorial.

12. According to personal interviews with a close campaign adviser (April 26, 2006) and two prominent political commentators (March 13, 2006; May 10, 2006), Olmert's move was clearly taken against the recommendations of most of his campaign advisers, who feared it would hurt his chances in the election. Electoral calculations were not immaterial, but Olmert was willing to lose a few seats. There was no majority support for his plan in the general public, as we discuss in the chapter, but, according to Olmert's campaign adviser, within Kadima's target electorate a majority supported further disengagement from the West Bank. Additional interpretations for Olmert's move were to boost his image, at that time on the decline because of unfavorable media coverage of unethical and corrupt practices by him and other Kadima figures. His move could also be construed as a declaration of independence from Sharon by demonstrating leadership and the courage to make bold decisions on his own.

13. In October 1995 a survey conducted by the Center for Palestinian Research and Studies (CPRS) found that 51 percent of the Palestinians supported a proportional representation system, and 40 percent supported a majority system. More details are available at http://www.pcpsr.org/survey/cprspolls/95/pol120b.html#system (accessed April 9, 2008).

14. Support for Islamists stood at 23 percent in March 1996 and at 20 percent four years later in April 2000. The 1996 data are available at http://www.pcpsr.org/survey/cprspolls/96/pol122d.html#polaff, and the 2000 data at http://www.pcpsr.org/survey/cprspolls/2000/pol148c.html (both accessed April 9, 2008).

15. For example, the percentage of those not affiliated with any faction stood at 41 percent in April 2000. See http://www.pcpsr.org/survey/cprspolls/2000/pol148c.html (accessed April 9, 2008).

16. For details on voters' behavior in local elections, see the PSR findings and analysis at http://www.pcpsr.org/survey/polls/2005/exit05.html (accessed April 9, 2008).

17. Available at http://www.pcpsr.org/survey/polls/2005/exit05.html (accessed April 9, 2008).

18. Ibid.

19. See findings of PSR preelection poll at http://www.pcpsr.org/survey/polls/2006/preelectionsjan06.html (accessed April 9, 2008).

20. Exit poll results, January 25, 2006, available at http://www.pcpsr.org/survey/polls/2006/exitplcfulljan06e.html (accessed April 9, 2008).

21. Available at http://www.pcpsr.org/survey/polls/2006/exitplcfulljan06e.html (accessed April 9, 2008).

9. Conclusion

1. Available at http://www.ynet.co.il/articles/1,7340,L-2414534,00.html (accessed July 26, 2008). Published February 3, 2003.

2. For a summary of framing effects in international relations, see Mintz and Redd 2003; for applications to the Israeli-Arab conflict, see Astorino-Courtois 1996 and Maoz, Yaniv, and Ivri 2007.

3. The notion that strategic framing is an effective persuasive device for leaders to secure public opinion support for international agreements supposedly produces tension with the conception of a rational public and, more generally, with the rational choice paradigm and the premises of expected utility theory. One approach to accommodate this tension suggests that deeming a decision irrational requires a deep understanding of what people desire and how they go about achieving it, a level of understanding that is often lacking and incomplete. For example, when people make choices and take decisions, their expectations regarding how they will feel after taking a decision enters into their reasoning and might affect the very nature of the choice. If submitting to framing is expected to reduce people's regret or disappointment, then it does not necessarily challenge rationality per se. In fact, regret minimization is at the core of minimax regret rational choice models (Bueno de Mesquita and McDermott 2004, p. 281). In the context of international agreements, submission to framing can provide publics a convenient way to climb down from a tall ladder that otherwise might frustrate a highly desired agreement and produce considerable expectations of regret.

4. Indeed, international mediators often cater to this value in their public statements. See, for example, President Bush's reference to the refugee issue in his letter to Prime Minister Sharon from April 2004 (http://www.whitehouse.gov/news/releases/2004/04/20040414-3.html [accessed October 16, 2007]).

5. Aga and Malley (2001) highlight this reference point in their response to Barak's frame of the Camp David negotiations, saying that "Oslo, as they [Palestinians] saw it, was not about negotiating peace terms but terms of surrender. Bearing this perspective in mind explains the Palestinians' view that Oslo itself is the historic compromise—an agreement to concede 78 percent of mandatory Palestine to Israel" (p. 5).

6. Barak's "percentaging game" at Camp David, describing Israel's territorial concessions in terms of percentages, was itself a clever framing device allowing him to conceal contiguity problems that his proposals caused for Palestinians.

7. In our June 2006 poll, 46 percent of Israelis supported, and 50 percent opposed this plan.

BIBLIOGRAPHY

Agha, Hussein, and Robert Malley. 2001. "Camp David: The Tragedy of Errors." *New York Review of Books* 48(13): 59–64.

Aldrich, John H., Christopher Gelpi, Peter Feaver, Janson Reifler, and Kristin T. Sharp. 2006. "Foreign Policy and the Electoral Connection." *Annual Review of Political Science* 9: 477–502.

Allport, Floyd H. 1924. *Social Psychology*. Boston: Houghton Mifflin.

Aneshensel, Carol S., Ralph R. Frerichs, Virginia A. Clark, and Patricia A Yokopenic. 1982a. "Measuring Depression in the Community: A Comparison of Telephone and Personal Interviews." *Public Opinion Quarterly* 46: 110–121.

———. 1982b. "Telephone versus In-Person Surveys of Community Health Status." *American Journal of Public Health* 72(9): 1017–1021.

Arian, Asher. 1989. "A People Apart: Coping with National Security in Problems in Israel." *Journal of Conflict Resolution* 34(4): 605–631.

———. 1995. *Security Threatened: Surveying Israeli Opinion on Peace and War*. New York: Cambridge University Press.

———. 2001. *Israeli Public Opinion on National Security 2001—Memorandum No. 60*. Tel Aviv: Jaffee Center for Strategic Studies at Tel Aviv University.

Arian, Asher, and Michal Shamir. 2005. *The Elections in Israel—2003*. New Brunswick, N.J.: Transaction.

Arian, Asher, Nir Atmor, and Yael Hadar. 2007. *Auditing Israeli Democracy 2007—Cohesion in a Divided Society* (in Hebrew). Jerusalem: Israel Democracy Institute.

Astorino-Courtois, Allison. 1996. "Transforming International Agreements into National Realities: Marketing Arab-Israeli Peace in Jordan." *Journal of Politics* 58(4): 1035–1054.

Bailer, Stephanie, and Gerald Schneider. 2006. "Nash or Schelling: Legislative Bargaining with and without Domestic Constraints." In Robert Thomson, Frans Stokman, Christopher Achen, and Thomas König, eds., *The European Union Decides*, 153–177. Cambridge: Cambridge University Press.

Barak, Ehud. 2005. "The Myths Spread about Camp David Are Baseless." In Shamir

Shimon and Bruce Maddy-Weitzman, eds., *The Camp David Summit—What Went Wrong?* 117–147. Brighton: Sussex Academic Press.

Bar-Siman-Tov, Yaacov. 2007a. "Dialectic between Conflict Management and Conflict Resolution." In Yaacov Bar-Siman-Tov, ed., *The Israeli Palestinian Conflict: From Conflict Resolution to Conflict Management,* 9–40. New York: Palgrave Macmillan.

———, ed. 2007b. *The Israeli Palestinian Conflict: From Conflict Resolution to Conflict Management.* New York: Palgrave Macmillan.

Bar-Tal, Daniel. 2007. *Living with the Conflict: Socio-Psychological Analysis of the Jewish Society in Israel* (in Hebrew). Jerusalem: Carmel.

Bar-Tal, Daniel, and Eran Halperin. 2008. "Fall of the Peace Camp in Israel: The Influence of Prime Minister Ehud Barak on Israeli Public Opinion, July 2000–February 2001." *Megamot* 45(3): 435–463 (in Hebrew).

Beetham, David. 1991. *The Legitimation of Power.* London: Macmillan.

Ben-Ami, Shlomo. 2004. *A Front without a Rearguard: A Voyage to the Boundaries of the Peace Process* (in Hebrew). Tel-Aviv: Yedioth Ahronot.

Berrebi, Claude, and Esteban F. Klor. 2006. "On Terrorism and Electoral Outcomes: Theory and Evidence from the Israeli-Palestinian Conflict." *Journal of Conflict Resolution* 50(6): 899–925.

Berrebi, Claude, and Esteban F. Klor. 2008. "Are Voters Sensitive to Terrorism? Direct Evidence from the Israeli Electorate." *American Political Science Review* 102(3): 279–301.

Berry, John W. 1979. "Research in Multicultural Societies: Implications of Cross Cultural Methods." *Journal of Cross-Cultural Psychology* 10(4): 415–434.

Blount, Sally, and Richard P. Larrick. 2000. "Framing the Game: Examining Frame Choice in Bargaining." *Organizational Behavior and Human Decision Processes* 81(1): 43–71.

Brown, Nathan J. 2003a. *Palestinian Politics after the Oslo Accords: Resuming Arab Palestine.* Berkeley: University of California Press.

———. 2003b. *The Third Draft Constitution for a Palestinian State: Translation and Commentary.* Ramallah: Palestinian Center for Policy and Survey Research. Retrieved January 22, 2007, from http://www.pcpsr.org/domestic/2003/nbrowne.pdf.

Brumberg, Daniel. 2003. "Liberalization versus Democracy: Understanding Arab Political Reform." *Democracy and Rule of Law Project Working Paper, no. 37.* Washington, D.C.: Carnegie Endowment for International Peace.

———. 2004. "Beyond Liberalization?" *Wilson Quarterly* 28(2): 47–55.

Bueno de Mesquita, Bruce, Alastair Smith, Randolph M. Siverson, and James D. Morrow. 2003. *The Logic of Political Survival.* Cambridge, Mass.: MIT Press.

Bueno de Mesquita, Bruce, and Rose McDermott. 2004. "Crossing No Man's Land: Cooperation on the Trenches." *Political Psychology* 25(2): 271–287.

Bueno de Mesquita, Bruce, and Randolph M. Siverson. 1995. "War and the Survival of Political Leaders: A Comparative Study of Regime Types and Political Accountability." *American Political Science Review* 89(4): 841–855.

Bueno de Mesquita, Bruce, James D. Morrow, Randolph M. Siverson, and Alastair Smith. 1999. "An Institutional Explanation of the Democratic Peace." *American Political Science Review* 93(4): 791–807.

Calleja, James. 1994. "Education for Peace in the Mediterranean: A Strategy for Peace Building." In Elise Boulding, ed., *Peace in the Middle East: Challenges for States and Civil Society,* 279–285. Boulder, Colo.: Lynne Rienner.

Clausewitz, Carl von. 1976 [1832]. *On War.* Edited and translated by Michael Howard and Peter Paret. Princeton, N.J.: Princeton University Press.

Coser, Lewis A. 1956. *The Functions of Social Conflict.* New York: Free Press.

Crenshaw, Martha. 1986. "The Psychology of Political Terrorism." In Margart G. Hermann, ed., *Political Psychology,* 379–413. New York: Jossey-Bass.

Crockett, Lisa J., Brandy A. Randall, Yuh-Ling Shen, Stephen T. Russell, and Anne K. Driscoll. 2005. "Measurement Equivalence of the Center for Epidemiological Studies Depression Scale for Latino and Anglo Adolescents: A National Study." *Journal of Consulting and Clinical Psychology* 73(1): 47–58.

Dajani, Omar M. 2005. "Surviving Opportunities: Palestinian Negotiating Patterns in Peace Talks with Israel." In Tamara C. Wittes, ed., *How Israelis and Palestinians Negotiate: A Cross-Cultural Analysis of the Oslo Peace Process,* 39–80. Washington, D.C.: United States Institute of Peace.

Dorussen, Han, and Kyriaki Nanou. 2006. "European Integration, Intergovernmental Bargaining, and Convergence of Party Programmes." *European Union Politics* 7(2): 235–256.

Drucker, Raviv. 2002. *Harakiri* (in Hebrew). Tel Aviv: Yedioth Ahronoth.

Duck, Juli M., Ddbrah J. Terry, and Michael A. Hogg. 1998. "Perceptions of a Media Campaign: The Role of Social Identity and the Changing Intergroup Context." *Personality and Social Psychology Bulletin* 24(1): 3–16.

Enderlin, Charles. 2003. *Shattered Dreams: The Failure of the Peace Process in the Middle East 1995-2002.* New York: Other Press.

Eisenstadt, Shmuel N. 1967. *Israeli Society.* New York: Basic Books.

Erikson, Robert. S., Michael B. MacKuen, and James A. Stimson. 2002. *The Macro Polity.* Cambridge: Cambridge University Press.

Esposito, Vincent J. 1954. "War as a Continuation of Politics." *Military Affairs* 18(1): 19–26.

Etzioni, Amitai. 1959. "Alternative Ways to Democracy: The Example of Israel." *Political Science Quarterly* 74(2): 196–214.

Evans, Peter B. 1993. "Building an Integrative Approach to International and Domestic Politics: Reflections and Projections." In Peter B. Evans, Harold K. Jacobson, and Robert D. Putnam, eds., *Double-edged Diplomacy: International Bargaining and Domestic Politics,* 397–430. Berkeley: University of California Press.

Evans, Peter B., Harold K. Jacobson, and Robert D. Putnam, eds., 1993. *Double-Edged Diplomacy: International Bargaining and Domestic Politics.* Berkeley: University of California Press.

Fearon, James D. 1994. "Domestic Political Audience Costs and the Escalation of International Disputes." *American Political Science Review* 88(3): 577–592.

———. 1997. "Signaling Foreign Policy Interests: Tying Hands versus Sinking Costs." *Journal of Conflict Resolution* 41(1): 68–90.

Feniger, Yariv. 2003. "Analysis of the Change in Israeli Jewish Public Opinion with Respect to the Oslo Agreement under the Netanyahu and Barak Governments" (in Hebrew). Unpublished paper. Tel-Aviv: Tel Aviv University.

Fields, James M., and Howard Schuman. 1976. "Public Beliefs about Beliefs of the Public." *Public Opinion Quarterly* 40: 427–448.

Fiske, Susan T., and Shelley E. Taylor. 1991. *Social Cognition.* New York: McGraw Hill.

Foyle, Douglas C. 1997. "Public Opinion and Foreign Policy: Elite Beliefs as a Mediating Variable." *International Studies Quarterly* 41(1): 68–90.

Frank, Thomas M. 1995. *Fairness in International Law and Institutions.* Oxford: Clarendon.

Frisch, Hillel. 1998. *Countdown to Statehood: Palestinian State Formation in the West Bank and Gaza.* Albany: State University of New York Press.

Friedland, Nehemia, and Ariel Merari. 1985. "The Psychological Impact of Terrorism: A Double-Edged Sword." *Political Psychology* 6(4): 591–604.

Gamson, William A. 1992. *Talking Politics.* Cambridge: Cambridge University Press.

Giner-Sorolla, Roger, and Shelly Chaiken. 1994. "The Causes of Hostile Media Judgments." *Journal of Experimental Social Psychology* 30(2): 165–180.

Ginossar, Yossi. 2005. "Factors That Impeded the Negotiations." In Shamir Shimon and Bruce Maddy-Weitzman, eds., *The Camp David Summit—What Went Wrong?* 51–60. Brighton: Sussex Academic Press.

Gordon, Carol, and Asher Arian. 2001. "Threat and Decision Making." *Journal of Conflict Resolution* 45:196–215.

Gordon, Haim. 1994. "Working for Peace in the Middle East: The Educational Task." In Elise Boulding, ed., *Peace in the Middle East: Challenges for States and Civil Society,* 311–318. Boulder, Colo.: Lynne Rienner.

Groves, Robert M. 1990. "Theories and Methods of Telephone Surveys." *Annual Review of Sociology* 16: 221–240.

Groves, Robert M., and Robert L. Khan. 1979. *Surveys by Telephone: A National Comparison with Personal Interviews.* New York: Academic Press.

Gunther, Albert C. 1992. "Biased Press or Biased Public? Attitudes towards Media Coverage of Social Groups." *Public Opinion Quarterly* 56(1): 147–167.

Harkness, Janet A. 2003. "Questionnaire Translation." In Janet A. Harkness, Fons J. R. van de Vijver, and Peter Ph. Mohler, eds., *Cross-Cultural Survey Methods,* 35–57. Hoboken, N.J.: Wiley.

Hampson, Fen Osler. 1995. *Multilateral Negotiations: Lessons from Arms Control, Trade and the Environment.* Baltimore, Md.: Johns Hopkins University Press.

Hanieh, Akram. 2001. "The Camp David Papers." *Journal of Palestine Studies* 30(2): 75–97.

Heider, Fritz. 1958. *The Psychology of Interpersonal Relations.* New York: Wiley.

Hermann, Richard K., Philip E. Tetlock, and Enny S. Visser. 1999. "Mass Public Decisions to Go to War: A Cognitive-Integrationist Framework." *American Political Science Review* 93(3): 553–573.

Hermann, Tamar. "Changes in Israel's Official Security Policy and in the Attitudes of the Jewish Israeli Public toward the Management of the Israeli-Palestinian Conflict (2000–2004)." In Yaacov Bar-Siman-Tov, ed., *The Israeli Palestinian Conflict: From Conflict Resolution to Conflict Management,* 133–168. New York: Palgrave Macmillan.

Hermann, Tamar, and Ephraim Yuchtman-Yaar. 2002. "Divided yet United: Israeli-Jewish Attitudes toward the Oslo Process." *Journal of Peace Research* 39(5): 597–613.

Hinckley, Ronald. 1992. *People, Polls, and Policymakers: American Public Opinion and National Security.* New York: Lexington.

Hoffman, Bruce. 1998. *Inside Terrorism.* New York: Columbia University Press.

Hogg, Michael A., and Dominic Abrams. 1988. *Social Identification: A Social Psychology of Intergroup Relations and Group Processes.* London: Routledge.

Holsti, Ole R. 1992. "Public Opinion and Foreign Policy: Challenges to the Almond-Lippmann Consensus Mershon Series: Research Programs and Debates." *International Studies Quarterly* 36(4): 439–466.

————. 2004. *Public Opinion and American Foreign Policy.* Ann Arbor: University of Michigan Press.

Horowitz, Dan, and Moshe Lissak. 1989. *Trouble in Utopia: The Overburdened Polity of Israel.* Albany: State University of New York Press.

Hug, Simon, and Thomas König. 2002. "In View of Ratification: Governmental Preferences and Domestic Constraints at the Amsterdam Intergovernmental Conference." *International Organization* 56(2): 447–476.

Huddy, Leonie, Stanley Feldman, Charles Taber, and Gallya Lahav. 2005. "Threat, Anxiety, and Support of Antiterrorism Policies." *American Journal of Political Science* 49(3): 593–608.

Huddy, Leonie, Stanley Feldman, and Erin Cassese. 2007. "On the Distinct Political Effects of Anxiety and Anger." In Russell W. Neuman, George E. Marcus, Ann N. Crigler, and Michael MacKuen, eds., *The Affect Effect—Dynamics of Emotion in Political Thinking and Behavior,* 202–230. Chicago: University of Chicago Press.

Iida, Keisuke. 1993. "When and How Do Domestic Constraints Matter? Two-Level Games with Uncertainty." *Journal of Conflict Resolution* 37(3): 403–426.

Indyk, Martin. 2005. "Camp David in the Context of US Mideast Peace Strategy." In Shamir Shimon and Bruce Maddy-Weitzman, eds., *The Camp David Summit— What Went Wrong?* 22–29. Brighton: Sussex Academic Press.

Irwin, Colin J. 2001. "How Public Opinion Polls Were Used in Support of the Northern Ireland Peace Process." *Global Review of Ethnopolitics* 1(1): 62–73.

————. 2002. *The People's Peace Process in Northern Ireland.* Basingstoke, England: Palgrave MacMillan.

Jaeger, David A., Esteban F. Klor, Sami H. Miaari, and Daniele M. Paserman. 2008. "The Struggle for Palestinian Hearts and Minds: Violence and Public Opinion in the Second Intifada." *NBER Working Paper* 13956. Retrieved August 6, 2008, from http://www.nber.org/papers/w13956.pdf.

Jenkins, Brian Michael. 1975. *International Terrorism: A New Mode of Conflict.* Los Angeles: Crescent.

Jentleson, Bruce W. 1992. "The Pretty Prudent Public: Post-Post-Vietnam American Military Force." *International Studies Quarterly* 36(1): 49–74.

Kahneman, Daniel, and Amos Tversky. 1979. "Prospect Theory: An Analysis of Decision under Risk." *Econometrica* 47(2): 263–291.

Katz, Daniel, and Floyd H. Allport. 1931. *Student Attitudes.* Syracuse, N.Y.: Craftsmen.

Kelman, Herbert. 1997. "Social-Psychological Dimensions of International Conflict." In Zartman I. William and J. Lewis Rasmussen, eds., *Peacemaking in International Conflict: Methods and Techniques,* 191–237. Washington, D.C.: United States Institute of Peace Press.

————. 1999. "Transforming the Relationship between Former Enemies: A Social-Psychological Analysis." In L. Robert Rothstein, ed., *After the Peace: Resistance and Reconciliation,* 193–206. Boulder, Colo.: Lynne Rienner.

Key, Valdimer O. 1961. *Public Opinion and American Democracy.* New York: Knopf.

Khalidi, Rashid. 1997. *Palestinian Identity: The Construction of Modern Consciousness.* New York: Columbia University Press.

Kimmerling, Baruch, and Joel S. Migdal. 2003. *The Palestinian People: A History.* Cambridge, Mass.: Harvard University Press.

Klecka, William R., and Alfred J. Tuchfarber. 1978. "Random Digit Dialing: A Comparison to Personal Surveys." *Public Opinion Quarterly* 42(1): 105–114.

Knopf, Jeffrey W. 1993. "Beyond Two-Level Games: Domestic-International Interaction in the Intermediate-Range Nuclear Forces Negotiations." *International Organization* 47(4): 599–628.

———. 1998a. *Domestic Society and International Cooperation: The Impact of Protest on U.S. Arms Control Policy.* Cambridge: Cambridge University Press.

———. 1998b."How Rational Is 'The Rational Public'? Evidence from U.S. Public Opinion on Military Spending." *Journal of Conflict Resolution* 42(5): 544–571.

König, Thomas, and Hug Simon. 2000. "Ratifying Maastricht: Parliamentary Votes on International Treaties and Theoretical Solution Concepts." *European Union Politics* 1(1): 93–124.

Krepon, Michael, Dominique M. McCoy, and Matthew C. J. Rudolph, eds. 1993. *A Handbook of Confidence-Building Measures for Regional Security.* Washington, D.C.: Henry L. Stimson Center.

Krueger, Joachim. 1998. "On the Perception of Social Consensus." In Mark P. Zanna, ed., *Advances in Experimental Social Psychology* 30: 163–240. New York: Academic Press.

Lazarsfeld, Paul F. 1972. "Public Opinion Research and the Classical Tradition." In Paul F. Lazarsfeld, ed., *Qualitative Analysis,* 300–317. Boston: Allyn and Bacon.

Lederach, John Paul. 1997. *Building Peace: Sustainable Reconciliation in Divided Societies.* Washington, D.C.: United States Institute of Peace Press.

Lehman, Howard P., and Jennifer L. McCoy. 1992. "The Dynamics of the Two-Level Bargaining Game: The 1988 Brazilian Debt Negotiations." *World Politics* 44(4): 600–644

Leventoğlu, Bahar, and Ahmer Tarar. 2005. "Pre-Negotiation Public Commitment in Domestic and International Bargaining." *American Political Science Review* 99(3): 419–433.

Levine, Irwin P., Sandra L. Schneider, and Gary J. Gaeth. 1998. "All Frames Are Not Created Equal: A Typology and Critical Analysis of Framing Effects." *Organizational Behavior and Human Decision Processes* 76(2): 149–188.

Levy, Jack S. 1996. "Loss Aversion, Framing, and Bargaining: The Implications of Prospect Theory for International Conflict." *International Political Science Review* 17(2): 179–195.

Lida, Keisuke. 1993. "When and How Do Domestic Constraints Matter? Two-Level Games with Uncertainty." *Journal of Conflict Resolution* 37(3): 403–426.

Long, David E. 1990. *The Anatomy of Terrorism.* New York: Free Press.

Lordos, Alexandros. 2005. "Civil Society Diplomacy: A New Approach for Cyprus?" Retrieved January 22, 2007, from http://www.dzforum.de/downloads/0501013.pdf.

———. 2006. "Building Trust: An Inter-Communal Analysis of Public Opinion in Cyprus." Retrieved January 22, 2007, from http://www.dzforum.de/en/0501017.pdf.

Malley, Robert. 2005. "American Mistakes and Israeli Misconceptions." In Shamir Shimon and Bruce Maddy-Weitzman, eds., *The Camp David Summit—What Went Wrong?* 108–116. Brighton: Sussex Academic Press.

Maoz, Ifat, and Clark McCauley. 2005. "Psychological Correlates of Support for Compromise: A Polling Study of Jewish-Israeli Attitudes towards Solutions to the Israeli-Palestinian Conflict." *Political Psychology* 26: 791–807.

Maoz, Ifat, Ilan Yaniv, and Naama Ivri. 2007. "Decision Framing and Support for Concessions in the Israeli-Palestinian Conflict." *Journal of Peace Research* 44(1): 81–91.

March, James. 1982. "Theories of Choice and Making Decisions." *Society* 20(1): 29–39.

Marks, Gary, and Norman Miller. 1987. "Ten Years of Research on the False Consensus Effect: An Empirical and Theoretical Review." *Psychological Bulletin* 102(1): 72–90.

Mas-Colell, Andreu, Michael Whinston, and Jerry R. Green. 1995. *Microeconomic Theory.* Oxford: Oxford University Press.

Matheson, Kimberly, and Sanela Dursun. 2001. "Social Identity Precursors to the Hostile Media Phenomenon: Partisan Perceptions of Coverage of the Bosnian Conflict." *Group Processes and Intergroup Relations* 4(2): 116–125.

Mayer, Fredrick W. 1992. "Managing Domestic Differences in International Negotiations: The Strategic Use of Internal Side-Payments." *International Organization* 46(4): 793–818.

McDonald, Michael D., and Ian Budge. 2005. *Elections, Parties, Democracy—Conferring the Median Mandate.* Oxford: Oxford University Press.

Miller, David. 2005. "The Effects of the 'Syria First' Strategy." In Shamir Shimon and Bruce Maddy-Weitzman, eds., *The Camp David Summit—What Went Wrong?* 93–99. Brighton: Sussex Academic Press.

Miller, Peter V., and Charles F. Cannell. 1982. "A Study of Experimental Techniques for Telephone Interviewing." *Public Opinion Quarterly* 46(2): 250–269.

Milner, Helen V. 1997. *Interests, Institutions, and Information: Domestic Politics and International Relations.* Princeton, N.J.: Princeton University Press.

Milner, Helen V., and Peter B. Rosendorff. 1997a. "A Model of the Two-Level Game." In Helen V. Milner, ed., *Interests, Institutions, and Information: Domestic Politics and International Relations,* 67–98. Princeton, N.J.: Princeton University Press.

———. 1997b. "Democratic Politics and International Trade Negotiations." *Journal of Conflict Resolution* 41(1): 117–146.

Mintz, Alex, and Steven B. Redd. 2003. "Framing Effects in International Relations." *Synthese* 135(2): 193–213.

Mo, Jongryn. 1994. "The Logic of Two-Level Games with Endogenous Domestic Coalitions." *Journal of Conflict Resolution* 38(3): 402–422.

———. 1995. "Domestic Institutions and International Bargaining: The Role of Agent Veto in Two-Level Games." *American Political Science Review* 89(4): 914–924.

Moravcsik, Andrew. 1993. "Introduction: Integrating International and Domestic Theories of International Bargaining." In Peter B. Evans, Harold K. Jacobson, and Robert D. Putnam, eds., *Double-Edged Diplomacy: International Bargaining and Domestic Politics,* 1–42. Berkeley: University of California Press.

Morris, Benny. 2002. "Camp David and After: An Exchange (1. An Interview with Ehud Barak)." *New York Review of Books* 49(10): 42–45.

Noelle-Neumann, Elisabeth. 1993. *The Spiral of Silence: Public Opinion—Our Social Skin.* Chicago: University of Chicago Press.

Muller, Harald M. 2004. "Arguing, Bargaining and All That: Communicative Action, Rationalist Theory and the Logic of Appropriateness in International Relations." *European Journal of International Relations* 10(3): 395–435.

O'Gorman, Hubert J. 1988. "Pluralistic Ignorance and Reference Groups: The Case of Ingroup Ignorance." In Hubert J. O'Gorman, ed., *Surveying Social Life: Papers in Honor of Herbert H. Hyman,* 145–173. Middletown, Conn.: Wesleyan University Press.

Oren, Neta. 2005. "The Impact of Critical Events in the Arab-Israeli Conflict on the Ethos of the Arab-Israeli Conflict (1967–2000)." Ph.D. diss., Tel-Aviv University, Israel.

Page, Benjamin I., and Robert Y. Shapiro. 1992. *The Rational Public: Fifty Years of Trends in Americans' Policy Preferences*. American Politics and Political Economy series. Chicago: University of Chicago Press.

Pahre, Robert. 1997. "Endogenous Domestic Institutions in Two-Level Games and Parliamentary Oversight of the European Union." *Journal of Conflict Resolution* 41(1): 147–174.

————. 1999. *Leading Questions: How Hegemony Affects the International Political Economy*. Ann Arbor: University of Michigan Press.

————. 2006. *Democratic Foreign Policy Making: Problems of Divided Government and International Cooperation*. New York: Palgrave MacMillan.

Patterson, Lee A. 1997. "Agricultural Policy Reform in the European Community: A Three-Level Game Analysis." *International Organization* 51(1): 135–165.

Peng, T. K., Mark F. Peterson, and Shyi Yuh-Ping. 1991. "Quantitative Methods in Cross-National Management Research: Trends and Equivalence Issues." *Journal of Organizational Behavior* 12(2): 87–107.

Peri, Yoram. 2006. *Generals in the Cabinet Room: How the Military Shapes Israeli Policy*. Washington, D.C.: United States Institute of Peace Press.

Powell, Bingham G. 2000. *Elections as Instruments of Democracy*. New Haven, Conn.: Yale University Press.

Powlick, Philip J. 1995. "The Sources of Public Opinion for American Foreign Policy Officials." *International Studies Quarterly* 39(4): 427–451.

Price, Vincent. 1989. "Social Identification and Public Opinion: Effects of Communicating Group Conflict." *Public Opinion Quarterly* 53(2): 197–224.

Putnam, Robert D. 1988. "Diplomacy and Domestic Politics: The Logic of Two-Level Games." *International Organization* 42(3): 427–460.

Qurei, Ahmad. 2007. *The Complete Palestinian Narrative of the Negotiations: From Oslo to the Road Map* (in Arabic). Beirut: Institute for Palestine Studies.

Rachamim, Yehezkiel. 2005. *"No One to Talk To": A Critical View of the Politics-Media Connection*. Symposium held at the Chaim Herzog Institute for Media Politics and Society, Tel Aviv University, January 12, 2005 (in Hebrew). Retrieved April 14, 2008, from http://www.tau.ac.il/institutes/herzog/talking.pdf.

Rasmussen, J. Lewis. 1997. "Peacemaking in the Twenty-first Century: New Rules, New Roles, New Actors." In Zartman I. William and J. Lewis Rasmussen, eds., *Peacemaking in International Conflict: Methods and Techniques*, 23–49. Washington, D.C.: United States Institute of Peace Press.

Riker, William H. 1986. *The Art of Political Manipulation*. New Haven, Conn.: Yale University Press.

Risse-Kappen, Thomas. 1991. "Public Opinion, Domestic Structure, and Foreign Policy in Liberal Democracies." *World Politics* 43(4): 479–512.

Ross, Dennis. 2004. *The Missing Peace: The Inside Story of the Fight for Middle East Peace*. New York: Farrar, Straus and Giroux.

Ross, Lee, David Green, and Pamela House. 1977. "The False Consensus Effect: An Egocentric Bias in Social Perception and Attribution Processes." *Journal of Experimental Social Psychology* 13(3): 279–301.

Rubinstein, Danny. 2001. *Arafat: A Portrait* (in Hebrew). Lod: Zmora-Bitan Publishers.

Rubinstein, Danny, Robert Malley, Hussein Agha, Ehud Barak, and Benny Morris. 2003. *Rashomon Camp David*. Tel-Aviv: Yedioth Ahronoth.

Russett, Bruce M. 1990. *Controlling the Sword: The Democratic Governance of National Security*. Cambridge, Mass.: Harvard University Press.

Sabet, Amr G. E. 1998. "The Peace Process and the Politics of Conflict Resolution." *Journal of Palestine Studies* 27(4): 5–19.

Said, Edward W. 2000. *The End of the Peace Process, Oslo and After*. New York: Pantheon.

Sayigh, Yezid. 2000. *Armed Struggle and the Search for State: The Palestinian Nationalist Movement, 1949–1993*. New York: Oxford University Press.

———. 2001. "Arafat and the Anatomy of Revolt." *Survival* 43(3): 47–60.

Schelling, Thomas C. 1960. *The Strategy of Conflict*. Cambridge, Mass.: Harvard University Press.

Schoppa, Lenoard J. 1993. "Two-Level Games and Bargaining Outcomes: Why Gaiatsu Succeeds in Japan in Some Cases but Not Others." *International Organization* 47(3): 353–386.

Schultz, Kenneth A. 1998. "Domestic Opposition and Signaling in International Crises." *American Political Science Review* 92(4): 829–844.

Sechrest, Lee, Todd L. Fay, and Hafeez M. H. Zaidi. 1972. "Problems of Translation in Cross-Cultural Research." *Journal of Cross-Cultural Psychology* 3(1): 41–56.

Sekaran, Uma. 1983. "Methodological and Theoretical Issues and Advancements in Cross-Cultural Research." *Journal of International Business Studies* 14(2): 61–73.

Shafir, Gershon, and Yoav Peled. 2000. *The New Israel: Peacemaking and Liberalization*. Boulder, Colo.: Westview.

———. 2002. *Being Israeli: The Dynamics of Multiple Citizenship*. Cambridge: Cambridge University Press.

Shain, Yossi, and Tamara C. Wittes. 2002. "Peace as a Three-Level Game: The Role of Diasporas in Conflict Resolution." In Thomas Ambrosio, ed., *Ethnic Identity Groups and U.S. Foreign Policy*, 169–197. Westport: Praeger.

Shamir, Jacob, 2007. *Public Opinion in the Israeli-Palestinian Conflict: From Geneva to Disengagement to Kadima and Hamas*. Research monograph No. 60 in PEACEWORKS series. Washington, D.C.: United States Institute of Peace.

Shamir, Jacob, and Khalil Shikaki. 2002a. "Determinants of Reconciliation and Compromise among Israelis and Palestinians." *Journal of Peace Research* 39(2): 185–202.

———. 2002b."Self-Serving Perceptions of Terrorism among Israelis and Palestinians." *Political Psychology* 23(3): 537–558.

Shamir, Jacob, and Michal Shamir. 1997. "Pluralistic Ignorance across Issues and over Time: Information Cues and Biases." *Public Opinion Quarterly* 61(2): 227–260.

———. 2000. *The Anatomy of Public Opinion*. Ann Arbor: University of Michigan Press.

Shamir, Michal, and Asher Arian. 1999. "Collective Identity and Electoral Competition in Israel." *American Political Science Review* 93(2): 265–277.

———. 2002. "Abstaining and Voting in 2001." In Asher Arian and Michal Shamir, eds., *The Elections in Israel—2001*, 29–54. Jerusalem: Israel Democracy Institute.

———. 2005. "Introduction." In Asher Arian and Michal Shamir, eds., *The Elections in Israel—2003*, 1–12. New Brunswick, N.J.: Transaction.

Shamir, Michal, and Jacob Shamir. 2007. "The Israeli-Palestinian Conflict in Israeli Elections." *International Political Science Review* 28(4): 469–491.

Sheleg, Yair. 2004. "The Political Ramification of Evacuating Settlements in Judea, Samaria, and the Gaza Strip." *Position Paper 5E*. Jerusalem: Israel Democracy Institute.

Sher, Gilad. 2001. *Within Reach: The Israeli-Palestinian Peace Negotiations, 1999, 2001, Testimony* (in Hebrew). Tel-Aviv: Miskal.

———. 2005. "Lessons from the Camp David Experience." In Shimon Shamir and Bruce Maddy-Weitzman, eds., *The Camp David Summit—What Went Wrong?* 60–67. Brighton: Sussex Academic Press.

Shikaki, Khalil. 2002. "Palestinians Divided." *Foreign Affairs* 81(1): 89–105.

———. 2004. "The Future of Palestine." *Foreign Affairs* 83(6): 45–60.

———. 2006a. "Palestinian Elections: Sweeping Victory, Uncertain Mandate." *Journal of Democracy* 17(3): 116–130.

———. 2006b. *Willing to Compromise: Palestinian Public Opinion and the Peace Process.* United States Institute of Peace, Special Report 158.

Shomali, Walid. 2006. "Landslide Victory of Hamas and Prospective Scenarios." Paper presented at the Twenty-second Annual Meeting of the Association for Israel Studies, Banff, Alberta, Canada.

Siksik, Alia. 1999. "Media in Palestine: Between the PNA's Hammer and the Anvil of Self-Censorship." *A Human Rights Report,* retrieved January 22, 2007, from http://spirit.tau.ac.il/socant/peace/psp/downloads/10%20-%20Siksik%20Alia.htm.

Smooha, Sammy. 2005. *Index of Arab-Jewish Relations in Israel 2004.* Haifa: University of Haifa.

Sobel, Richard. 2001. *The Impact of Public Opinion on U.S. Foreign Policy since Vietnam: Constraining the Colossus.* New York: Oxford University Press.

Spears, Russell, Joop Van der Pligt, and Richard J. Eiser. 1985. "Illusory Correlation in the Perception of Group Attitudes." *Journal of Personality and Social Psychology* 48(4): 863–875.

Sprinzak, Ehud. 1991. *The Ascendance of Israel's Radical Right.* New York: Oxford University Press.

Stimson, James. 1991. *Public Opinion in America: Moods, Cycles, and Swings.* Boulder, Colo.: Westview.

Stimson, James A., Michael B. MacKuen, and Robert S. Erikson. 1995. "Dynamic Representation." *American Political Science Review* 89(3): 543–654.

Susskind, Lawrence, Hillel Levine, Gideon Aran, Shlomo Kaniel, Yair Sheleg, and Moshe Halbertal. 2005. "Religious and Ideological Dimensions of the Israeli Settlements Issue: Reframing the Narrative?" *Negotiation Journal* 21(2): 177–191.

Swisher, Clayton E. 2004. *The Truth about Camp David: The Untold Story about Arafat, Barak, Clinton, and the Collapse of the Middle East Peace Process.* New York: Nation Books.

Tajfel, Henry, and John C. Turner. 1979. "An Integrative Theory of Intergroup Conflict." In William G. Austin and Stephen Worchel, eds., *The Social Psychology of Intergroup Relations,* 33–47. Monterey, Calif.: Brooks-Cole.

Tarar, Ahmer. 2001. "International Bargaining with Two-Sided Domestic Constraints." *Journal of Conflict Resolution* 45(3): 320–340.

Telhami, Shibley. 2001. "Camp David II: Assumptions and Consequences." *Current History* 100: 10–15.

Tessler, Mark A. 1994. *A History of the Israeli-Palestinian Conflict.* Bloomington: Indiana University Press.

Trumbore, Peter F. 1998. "Public Opinion as a Domestic Constraint in International Negotiations: Two-Level Games in the Anglo-Irish Peace Process." *International Studies Quarterly* 42(3): 545–565.

Turner, John C. 1982. "Towards a Cognitive Redefinition of the Social Group." In Henry Tajfel, ed., *Social Identity and Intergroup Relations*, 15–40. Cambridge: Cambridge University Press.

Ulbert, Cornelia, Thomas Risse, and Harald Muller. 2004. *Arguing and Bargaining in Multilateral Negotiations*. Berlin: Center for Transnational Relations, Foreign and Security Policy (ATASP).

Vallone, Robert P., Lee Ross, and Mark R. Lepper. 1985. "The Hostile Media Phenomenon: Biased Perception and Perceptions of Media Bias in Coverage of the Beirut Massacre." *Journal of Personality and Social Psychology* 49(3): 577–585.

Weber, Max. 1968. *Economy and Society*. Berkeley: University of California Press.

Wilkinson, Paul. 2000. "The Strategic Implications of Terrorism." In M. L. Sondhi, ed., *Terrorism and Political Violence: A Sourcebook*, 19–49. Indian Council of Social Science Research, India: Har-anand.

Wittcopf, Eugene R. 1990. *Faces of Internationalism: Public Opinion and American Foreign Policy*. Durham, N.C.: Duke University Press.

Wlezien, Christopher. 1995. "The Public as Thermostat: Dynamics of Preferences for Spending." *American Journal of Political Science* 39(4): 981–1,000.

Wolfsfeld, Gadi. 1988. *The Politics of Provocation: Participation and Protest in Israel*. Albany: State University of New York Press.

———. 2004. *Media and the Path to Peace*. Cambridge: Cambridge University Press.

Yishai, Yael. 2003. *Civil Society in Israel* (in Hebrew). Jerusalem: Carmel.

Zertal, Idit, and Akiva Eldar. 2004. *Lords of the Land: The Settlers and the State of Israel, 1967–2004* (in Hebrew). Or Yehuda: Kinneret, Zmora-Bitan Dvir.

INDEX

Page numbers with a t *or an* f *represent a table or figure, respectively.*

Beirut summit in 2002, 5, 167–168

Ben-Ami, Shlomo, 1–2, 51, 63, 161, 172n16, 174n9

Berrebi, Claude, 77, 176n12

"Big Bang" realignment of parties in Israel, 77, 98, 100, 124–128, 126f, 126t, 127t, 128t, 179n7

Bloc of the Faithful (Gush Emunim), 27. *See also* settlers, in territories

Blount, Sally, 161

borders issue: Camp David and, 57, 58t; framing failure of Camp David and, 181n5; Gaza Disengagement Plan and, 122, 155–156; Gaza Strip and, 156; Netanyahu and, 122; normalization and reconciliation and, 111; Olmert on, 41; permanent status framework and, 107, 108t, 162; unity tenet and, 167; West Bank and, 156

Brown, Nathan J., 172n18

Bush, George W., 5

Camp David summit in 2000: about, 1, 4, 9, 50–52, 174n1; Arab Islamic identity and, 172n16; Arafat and, 1, 2, 51, 52, 63; Barak and, 1, 4, 51, 52–53, 62–63, 174n9; borders issue and, 57, 58t; "closed lips syndrome" during, 2, 3, 50–51, 52, 56–60, 58t, 59–60, 152; domestic constraints, and information about, 1–2, 52, 54f, 60–62, 86, 155; domestic political environment surrounding, 1–2; framing failure of, 4, 5, 64–68, 174n1, 175nn2–4, 181n5; international table and, 169n2; Israeli domestic table, and domestic constraints surrounding, 52, 54f, 60–62, 86, 155; Israeli domestic table and, 1–2; Jerusalem and, 57, 58t; justice tenet and, 161; miscalculations analysis for, 62–63; Palestinian state tenet and, 57, 58t; permanent status framework and, 53; preparedness and expectations of publics, and leaders' bargaining at, 2, 51, 52–59, 54f, 55f, 58t, 59, 174n5; prospect theory and, 162, 181n5; public opinion constraints during, 2, 3, 50–51, 52, 56–60, 58t, 59–60, 152; refugees

issue and, 57, 58t; reservation price calculations and, 50, 52, 59, 62, 152, 174n1; right of return and, 57, 175n3; security tenet and, 58t; settlers in territories and, 58t; three-level games and, 169n2; "tied hands" conjecture and, 9, 50, 60, 152–153; two-level games and, 1, 50, 51, 60; unity tenet and, 172n16; win-set and, 51, 57, 59, 92, 152, 155

Chaiken, Shelly, 170n6

Clausewitz, Carl von, 64, 68

Clinton, Bill: Camp David and, 1, 2, 53

"Clinton Parameters" (Clinton's Permanent Settlement Framework), 4–5, 106–109, 108t, 158–160, 179n14

Clinton-Assad summit in Geneva, 53, 158–160

"closed lips syndrome," and Camp David, 2, 3, 50–51, 52, 56–60, 58t, 59–60, 152

compromise and violence: Arafat's death, and public's beliefs about, 75, 133, 139–140, 141t; Geneva Initiative, and simultaneous support from Palestinian public for, 80, 81f; political psychology perspectives, and simultaneous support during second Intifada for, 82–83, 177n25; rational choice perspective, and simultaneous support during second Intifada for, 84, 156; second Intifada, and simultaneous support for, 79–85, 81f, 154, 177n25

conflict management recommendations, 10, 157, 162–168, 163t

conflict resolution recommendations, 10, 91, 157–162, 181nn3–6

Convergence Plan, 7–8, 10, 41, 97, 117, 129–131, 149, 165

corruption: Fatah and, 103, 134–136, 139, 142, 156; Hamas and, 139, 141–145; Israeli public and, 119t; Kadima Party and, 180n12; Olmert and, 180n12; in PA, 29, 47, 103, 133, 134–136, 136t, 172n18; Palestinian public and, 49, 134–136, 136f, 138, 139, 140–145, 172n17, 178n11; PLO and, 4, 54; Sharon and, 6

Dahaf Research Institute, 170nn4,7, 178n5

or weaken other side's leader's status, 103, 155

leaders' policy opportunities supported by force of public opinion: about, 2–3, 30–34, 69, 91, 152–157, 171n1; Abu Mazin and, 7–8, 148; Gaza Disengagement Plan and, 6–7, 10, 91, 93–94, 93f, 105–106, 106f, 153, 155; Geneva Initiative and, 92; Hamas and, 7–8, 148; Olmert and, 8; Oslo Accord and, 94; PA and, 9, 48–49, 106; PLO and, 106; two-level games and, 153

Lebanon, second war in, 8, 12–13, 68, 72, 87, 101–102, 131, 165

the Left, 28, 41, 99–100, 100f, 118. *See also* Labor Party

Legislative Council. *See* Palestinian electoral politics in 2006

legitimacy issues, 3, 34, 48, 94, 151, 173n29

Lepper, Mark R., 170n6

Likud Party: about disintegration of, 7, 28, 98, 99; on Convergence Plan, 129; dynamic representation since first Intifada and, 100, 118, 119t, 121–124; Gaza Disengagement Plan, and opposition from, 94; party platforms, and adaptations of, 122, 123–124; political "Big Bang" realignment of parties and, 124–128, 126f, 126t, 127t, 128t; Sharon as prime minister and, 5, 73, 77; Temple Mount, and provocative visit by, 4, 66. *See also* the Right

MacKuen, Michael B., 117

Madrid Conference in 1991, 121f, 122, 179n6

Mahmoud Abbas. *See* Abu Mazin (Mahmoud Abbas)

Malley, Robert, 61, 63, 181n5

Mecca Agreement of February 2007, 148

media environment, 15, 19, 20, 35–36, 170n6

Miller, David, 53

Miqias al Dimokratiyya fi filisteen (Palestine Democracy Index), 37, 45

Morris, Benny, 62, 65, 175n3

Muller, Harald, 161

Nanou, Kyriak, 69

National Conciliation Document of the Prisoners, 7–8, 44, 104, 148, 156, 166

"National Security and Public Opinion" project, Jaffee Center for Strategic Studies, 23, 121f

National Unity Party, 121–122

negotiations and violence preferences as instruments, 69–72, 71f, 78, 79, 145–146, 175n6, 176n14, 179n17

Netanyahu, Benjamin, 28, 54–55, 71, 72, 84, 121, 122, 129

NGOs (nongovernmental organizations), 6, 46, 47, 92, 160

normalization and reconciliation, 111–115, 112f, 113f, 114f

old guard, Palestinian, 4, 29, 54, 67, 86, 87, 88

Olmert, Ehud: on borders issue, 41; Convergence Plan approach by, 7–8, 10, 41, 97, 117, 129–131, 149, 165; in Israeli election in 2006, 128–131, 180nn10,12; Kadima Party and, 98; leaders' policy opportunities supported by force of public opinion and, 8; legitimacy and, 131, 149; on State of Israel, 41

"Operation Defensive Shield," 79, 84, 91

Oslo Accord in 1993: balance of power since first Intifada and, 132; borders issue and, 155; Israeli electoral politics in 2006 and, 122–123, 131, 179n5; Israeli public and, 54, 55–56, 59; leaders' policy opportunities supported by force of public opinion and, 94; PA and, 132, 148; Palestinian public and, 53–54, 59; Palestinian state tenet and, 155; prospect theory and, 162, 181n5

Oslo II/Taba agreement in 2001, 5, 70, 91, 106, 160, 174n2

PA (Palestinian Authority): about establishment of, 3, 4, 54, 132; Arafat, as chair of, 1, 174n2; as autocracy, 46, 133, 174n30; balance of power since first Intifada in, 28–29, 132–137, 134t, 136f, 148, 166, 180nn13–15; corruption in, 29, 47, 103, 133, 134–136, 136t, 172n18;

democratization reforms in, 36, 37, 45–46, 132–135, 134t, 180nn13–15; electoral politics in 2006 and, 46–47, 117, 144t, 147t, 156, 166; framing failure of Camp David and, 64–65, 174n1; Hamas and, 28, 29, 43, 97–98; law and order enforcement issues in, 49, 103, 137, 141; leaders' policy opportunities supported by force of public opinion and, 9, 48–49, 106; legitimacy and, 32–33, 48–49, 54, 54f, 87, 132–133, 135–136, 136f; old guard, 86, 87; Oslo Accord and, 132, 148; party affiliation determinants and, 139; peace tenet and, 7, 132, 142, 144t, 145, 146, 147, 147t; presidency of, 54–55, 54f, 139, 174n3; prime minister and, 5, 91; Prisoners' Document of 2006 and, 104, 148, 156, 166; public behavior characteristics under, 45–48; public imperative, and connection with, 10, 116, 123, 131, 146, 149; security forces, 29, 44; two-level games and, 10, 116; unilateral disengagement and, 167; unity tenet and, 43–44; young guard, 86–88. *See also* Fatah; Hamas; Palestinian electoral politics in 2006

Palestine Democracy Index (Miqias al Dimokratiyya fi filisteen), 37, 45

Palestinian Authority (PA). *See* PA (Palestinian Authority)

Palestinian Center for Policy and Survey Research (PSR), 11

Palestinian constitution (Draft Constitution), 41, 42, 44, 156

Palestinian Declaration of Independence of 1988, 41, 42–43, 44

Palestinian democratization reforms, 36, 37, 45–46

Palestinian domestic table: Gaza Disengagement Plan and, 97–98, 155–156; during second Intifada, 27, 28–29, 86–89, 166; two-level games and, 1, 2, 27, 28–30, 150, 152–153

Palestinian electoral politics in 2004–2005, 141–142

Palestinian electoral politics in 2006: about, 10, 32, 116–117, 148–150, 156–157; Abu Mazin and, 134, 135, 140, 141–142,

148; democratization since first Intifada and, 132–135, 134t, 180nn13–15; Fatah in parliamentary, 7, 142–148, 144t, 147t; Gaza Strip and, 132, 141–142; Hamas and, 135–137, 136f, 141–148, 144t, 147t, 156–157; international table and, 150, 165; PA and, 46–47, 117, 144t, 147t, 156, 166; party affiliation determinants, and turnabout in, 138–139; presidency of PA and, 54–55, 54f, 139, 174n3; third parties in, 134, 137, 138, 143, 144t, 147, 147t; West Bank, and parliamentary, 132. *See also* Israeli electoral politics in 2006

Palestinian Liberation Organization (PLO). *See* PLO (Palestinian Liberation Organization)

Palestinian National Authority (PNA), 3. *See also* PA (Palestinian Authority)

Palestinian National Charter of 1968, 41

Palestinian public: about fundamental dimensions of, 9, 35; Arafat's death, and compromise and reconciliation beliefs of, 75, 133, 139–140, 141t; behavioral participatory characteristics and, 45–48, 173nn25,27; Camp David, and constraints on, 2, 3, 50–51, 52, 56–60, 58t, 59–60, 152; on Camp David, and preparedness and expectations for leaders' bargaining, 2, 51, 52–59, 54f, 55f, 58t, 59, 174n5; channels for, 48–49; compromise and violence, and simultaneous support from, 80, 81f, 82–83, 177n25; on corruption, 49, 134–136, 136f, 138, 139, 140–145, 178n11; economics and, 33, 46–47, 54, 138–143, 172n17; Gaza Disengagement Plan and, 6, 84, 101–102, 102f, 104, 106; Geneva Initiative and, 80, 81f; Hamas, and perceptions by, 145–147; information and knowledge about daily affairs and, 35–39, 38f, 68–69, 171n2, 172n8; international rights for, 65; media environment and, 35–36; normalization and reconciliation prospects and, 111–115, 112f, 113f, 114f; Palestinian state tenet and, 42; peace tenet and, 44, 118, 140–141, 143–145; permanent status framework and, 108–111, 108t, 155, 158–160, 179n14; religious tenet, and effect on, 41; right of return and, 42, 44; on second Intifada, 3, 162–164, 163t; on settlers in territories, 95–96; Sharon and, 7, 141; on State of Israel, 41, 105, 147, 147t; two-level games, and role of, 30, 33–34, 35, 85; two-state solution, 80; unilateral disengagement and, 8, 165; unity tenet and, 42–44, 172nn16–18, 173nn19,20; value dimensions and dilemmas for, 21, 25, 41–45; on violence and negotiations preferences as instruments, 69, 70–71, 71f, 72, 79, 145–146, 175n6; "violence pays" belief and, 8, 73, 74f, 101–102, 102f, 137, 145, 164, 165; on violence preferences after second Intifada, 3, 73–76, 74f, 75f, 76f, 77, 146, 176n11

Palestinian state tenet: Camp David and, 57, 58t; Gaza Disengagement Plan and, 122, 155–156; Gaza Strip and, 156; Israeli public and, 98, 121f, 178n8; Netanyahu and, 122; Oslo Accord and, 155; Palestinian public and, 42; permanent status framework and, 107, 108t, 159, 160; two-state solution and, 80, 132, 141, 143, 146, 147, 147t, 159; West Bank and, 156

Palestinian-Israeli conflict, overview, 3–5

peace tenet: Israeli public and, 98, 99, 99f, 118; PA and, 7, 132, 142, 144t, 145, 146–148, 147t; Palestinian public and, 44, 118, 140–141, 143–145

Peres, Shimon, 32, 73

Permanent Settlement Framework, Clinton's, 4–5, 106–109, 108t, 158–160, 179n14

permanent status framework: borders issue and, 107, 108t, 162; Camp David and, 53; conflict resolution and, 157–160; Gaza Disengagement Plan and, 106–111, 108t, 178n12, 179nn13,14; Geneva Initiative and, 106–109, 108t, 179n14; Jerusalem and, 107, 108t, 162; Palestinian state tenet and, 107, 108t, 159, 160; publics and, 108–111, 108t, 155,

158–160, 179n14; refugees issue and, 107, 108t; right of return and, 33, 107, 159, 160; second Intifada and, 158; security tenet and, 107, 108t; win-set and, 13, 106, 158

PFLP (Popular Front for the Liberation of Palestine), 13, 134

PLO (Palestinian Liberation Organization): corruption and, 4, 54; leaders' policy opportunities supported by force of public opinion and, 106; legitimacy of, 53; old guard in, 4, 29, 54, 67, 88; political life of, 46; the "stages plan," 66, 67, 175n4; unilateral disengagement and, 167; unity tenet and, 43, 173nn19,20; value dimensions and dilemmas, and role of, 41–43. See also Arafat, Yassir

PNA (Palestinian National Authority), 3. See also PA (Palestinian Authority)

policy implications and recommendations: conflict management, 10, 157, 162–168, 163t; conflict resolution, 10, 91, 157–162, 181nn3–6; diplomacy, 164; justice, 167; unilateral disengagement, 164–165, 181n7; violence, 164

political psychology perspectives, and simultaneous support for compromise and violence by publics, 82–83, 177n25

politics, and economics, 28, 173n29, 179n2. See also Israeli electoral politics in 2006; Palestinian electoral politics in 2006

Popular Front for the Liberation of Palestine (PFLP), 13, 134

Powell, Bingham G., 116

Powlick, Philip J., 30

Prisoners' Document of 2006, 7–8, 44, 104, 148, 156, 166

prospect theory, 162, 181n5

PSR (Palestinian Center for Policy and Survey Research), 11

public imperative: about, 2–3, 8–9; electoral politics, and connection with, 9, 10, 116, 123, 131, 146, 149; normative nature of, 21–22, 34; perceptions versus actual policy preference and, 14–15, 34; right of return and, 28; during second

Vallone, Robert P., 170n6
value conflicts, 21, 25, 41–45
violence: Gaza Disengagement Plan, and support for, 84; Hamas and, 132, 133; Hezbollah model of methods of, 8, 68, 72, 73, 87, 101–102, 165; negotiations and, 69–72, 71f, 78, 79, 145–146, 175n6, 176n14, 179n17; policy on rewards for, 164; preferences after second Intifada for, 73–79, 74f, 75f, 76f, 77f, 176nn11,14,17,18, 177nn19–22; preferences before second Intifada for, 70–72, 71f; second Intifada and, 68–70, 175n5; Sharon on use of, 69, 77–78, 90; two-level games, and role of, 68–70, 175n5; "violence pays" belief of Palestinians, 8, 73, 74f, 101–102, 102f, 137, 145, 164, 165. *See also* compromise and violence

wall policy, separation, 100, 165, 181n7
Weisglass, Dov, 92

West Bank: borders issue and, 156; Convergence Plan and, 129, 165; electoral politics and, 132, 141–142; Palestinian state tenet and, 156; permanent status framework and, 160; reverberation strategies and, 155; separation wall policy and, 100, 165, 181n7; settlers' evacuations from, 6, 97, 145, 165
win-set: about, 8, 12, 26, 32–33, 57; "closed lips syndrome," and Camp David, 51, 57, 59, 92, 152, 155; Gaza Disengagement Plan and, 92, 106, 155; permanent status framework and, 13, 106, 158; public imperative and, 26, 34, 51; "tied hands conjecture" and, 50
Wye River Plantation memorandum of October 1998, 55, 72, 122, 174n2

young guard, Palestinian, 29, 86–88

Zaidi, Hafeez M. H., 21–22

JACOB SHAMIR is Associate Professor, Department of Communication and Journalism, and Senior Research Fellow, Harry S. Truman Institute for the Advancement of Peace at the Hebrew University of Jerusalem. He is author (with Michal Shamir) of *The Anatomy of Public Opinion* and numerous articles and reports on public opinion in the Israeli-Palestinian conflict.

KHALIL SHIKAKI has taught political science at several universities, and is currently the director of the Palestinian Center for Policy and Survey Research in Ramallah and a senior fellow at the Crown Center for Middle East Studies at Brandeis University. Author or co-author of many books and research reports, he has conducted more than one hundred opinion polls among Palestinians in the West Bank and the Gaza Strip, Jordan, and Lebanon.